Tales of the Mississippi

1995

DATE DUE

GAYLORD			PRINTED IN U.S.A.

Tales of the Mississippi

by

Ray Samuel

Leonard V. Huber

Warren C. Ogden

PELICAN PUBLISHING COMPANY
GRETNA 1981

First printing, 1955
Second printing, 1966
First Pelican edition, 1981

Library of Congress Cataloging in Publication Data

Samuel, Ray.
  Tales of the Mississippi.

  Reprint. Originally published: New York:
Hastings House, c1955.
  Bibliography: p.
  Includes index.
  1. Mississippi River—History.   2. Mississippi
River—Description and travel.   3. Mississippi
Valley—History.   4. Mississippi Valley—Description
and travel.   I. Huber, Leonard Victor, 1903-
II. Ogden, Warren C.   III. Title.
F351.S3   1981   977   81-5937
ISBN 0-88289-291-6   AACR2

Manufactured in the United States of America

Published by Pelican Publishing Company, Inc.
1101 Monroe Street, Gretna, Louisiana 70053

AAS-8678

TO THE THREE MOST PATIENT WIVES ON
THE MISSISSIPPI'S BANKS; MARTHA ANN,
AUDREY, AND FRANCES.
THE AUTHORS

ACKNOWLEDGMENTS

To Dr. Garland F. Taylor, Director of Libraries, Tulane University, for unselfish aid, suggestions and advice.

To Albert L. Lieutaud, authority on pictures of the American scene, for his help and encouragement.

To the following institutions:

Howard-Tilton Memorial Library of
 Tulane University
New Orleans Public Library
Louisiana State Museum (The Cabildo)
New York Public Library
The Library of Congress
City Art Museum of St. Louis
The River Museum, Marietta, Ohio

University of Cincinnati Library
New York Historical Society
Missouri Historical Society
Ohio Historical Society
Marine Museum of the City of New York
Yale University Press
Historical and Philosophical Society of Ohio

To the following who graciously gave us permission to reproduce pictures that they own:

Capt. Frederick Way, Jr.
Samuel Wilson, Jr.
Mrs. Ferdinand Claiborne Latrobe
Mrs. Cecile Duke Levy
Ike D. Scharff, Jr.
M. Vance Higbee
Boyd Cruise

Mrs. E. C. Chadbourne
Allan Douglass
Mrs. P. L. Winchester
City Art Museum of St. Louis
Mariners' Museum, Newport News, Va.
Tulane University of Louisiana
Lee F. Conrey and *The American Weekly*

To the following for the permission to quote from published works:

Dr. N. Philip Norman
Dr. Philip Graham and the University of Texas
 Press
Dr. Jim Dan Hill and the University of Chicago
 Press
Leland D. Baldwin and the University of Pittsburgh Press

Miss Mary Wheeler, the late Dr. Pierce Butler and
 the Louisiana State University Press
William Edwards Clement
Dewey A. Somdal
Dr. R. A. Steinmeyer

To Capt. Donald T. Wright and to Capt. Frederick Way, Jr., our special thanks for critical reading of several chapters, suggestions for their improvement and for the use of material from "The Waterways Journal", and from the works of Capt. Way.

To George W. Healy, Jr., Vice-President, Times-Picayune Publishing Co. and Editor of the Times-Picayune, for permission to use the *Tales of the Great River* series which appeared in the newspaper's *"Dixie" Roto Magazine*.

To Glen Stinnett, photographer, whose photographic assistance was invaluable.

To:

Jo Hallman Aldrige
Dr. Virgil Bedsole
M. D. Brett
Lester Bridaham
Josie Cerf
The late Louis E. Cormier
Maurice Crain
Essae M. Culver
Henry J. Davis
Capt. Jesse P. Hughes
Mrs. William V. Huye
John Hall Jacobs
Felix H. Kuntz
Dorothy Lawton

Margie Ledoux
Harold Leisure
Lee Lorio
Betty Mailhes
Dr. Wm. D. McCain
Mrs. W. P. ("Frenchie") McNair
The late J. Mack Moore
Rosa M. Oliver
Martha Ann Peters
Edith Reiter
Marguerite Renshaw
Evangeline Thurber
Margaret Ruckert
U. S. Corps of Engineers, New Orleans District

WITH THE demise of the "floating palace", the good old days of the Mississippi River have gone forever. Or so many have claimed, sounding the funeral bell.

Not so. Those good old days have merely become the good new days, as anybody who stands on the levee at New Orleans, Baton Rouge, or Memphis, can plainly see. The Great River never had it so good. Why, then, lament about the days gone by, when, with all its glitter and romance, livin' was comparatively primitive? Oil lamps, cinders, floods, snags — you can have 'em!

Never-the-less, that doesn't lessen interest in reading about the good old days, in looking at pictures of what went on in bygone eras on the mighty Mississippi. There will always be room for nostalgia, and maybe for a slight tear it brings to the eye of an old-timer who knew it "when".

There's many a lesson to be learned from the early days of the river; there's many an hour of delightful entertainment in reading about the background of the river.

That's why I am delighted to see the dream of Ray Samuel, Leonard Huber, and Warren Ogden come to reality in this book. I followed the series, "Tales of the Great River" from its start in *The Times Picayune's DIXIE Magazine*. With Mr. Samuel's ability to make the old times live again; under Mr. Ogden's careful and intelligent editing; and illustrated by Mr. Huber's collection of river material (which is a source of continual amazement to me, a collector myself for over forty-five years) — this book can't miss filling a gap in the literature of the Mississippi Valley.

This is a happy combination of word and picture. The authors have done a superlative job in research, and in colorfully recording between the covers of a single volume the high lights of the Great River's past from De Soto down to the United States Engineers.

CAPT. DONALD T. WRIGHT

PREFACE TO THE SECOND EDITION

A LOT OF WATER has flowed under the many bridges of the river since the first edition of *Tales of the Mississippi* in 1955. Over 25,000 copies were sold, in several printings by the initial publisher and others. It seemed like the book had about run its course; but the demand continued. The original publisher, long gone on to other projects, offered to sell the plates to the authors. Happily, Dr. Milburn Calhoun of Pelican Publishing Company, Gretna, Louisiana, agreed to work with the authors to bring *Tales* to light again. So, like Ol' Man Ribber, it keeps rollin' along. We appreciate the assistance of Pelican's staff in bringing this reissue to fruition, and express the hope that a whole new generation of river buffs will find pleasure in its pages. As the expression goes, "It's nice to be able to smell the flowers—standing up."

RAY SAMUEL
LEONARD V. HUBER
WARREN C. OGDEN

New Orleans
August, 1981

THE AUTHORS hope that this volume may be found to be, like the criteria of a patent, "new and useful". To which they also hopefully add, "interesting and enlightening."

New? Something *new* about "Ol' Man River"? Well, like the Ol' Man himself, it is inconceivable that stories about him will ever cease rollin' along. Be they entirely new, as some of these "Tales" are to the present generation, having been unearthed from old records, newspaper files, and long forgotten books; or, be they little known, due to the romance of the river having passed by two generations; or, be they fresh approaches to familiar stories — "Tales of the Mississippi", with its hundreds of illustrations is at any rate, somewhat of a new departure in books about America's great river.

We definitely want to avoid the use of the word "history", even though our underlying purpose is to reveal the magnificent scope of development of the river. We hope that by highlighting the river's big moments in word and picture, its history will tell itself.

Useful? In our research, we have yet to come upon a book which covers this subject — from hapless Hernando DeSoto to the brilliant U. S. Corps of Engineers — illustrating as it goes along the annals of the river's fabulous past and present. We cherish the modest hope that this book will stimulate renewed interest in the Mike Finks, the Capt. Shreves, the Nicholas Roosevelts and other mighty men who made the Mississippi what it has become. And in disinterring the records of their accomplishments, we trust that this book will serve as a point of departure for countless novels, plays, movies, TV dramas, and short stories.

The big names are all here. DeSoto, for instance. Any schoolchild knows that DeSoto "discovered" the Mississippi; but where, when, how, and why?

Then, there is Mike Fink, the prodigy of the pre-paddle-wheel-propelled steamboat period, the giant who claimed to be half-man and half-alligator, whose aim with the long rifle could split an apple on a man's head at an unbelievable distance. Yet, Mike Fink was no legend.

The race between the *Rob't E. Lee* and the *Natchez,* one of the great sports events of all times, comes into focus as a grudge match of gigantic proportions. What made two river titans stake their reputations on the fastest trip from New Orleans to St. Louis?

River gamblers helped make dime novels novel; but here is the story of a real one who was not only fast with his fingers, but also handy with his head. George Devol, who had "the hardest head on the Mississippi", literally butts his way into immortality.

No period in the history of modern peacetime transportation has witnessed such carnage as the exploding of packets. The lowly shrimp could also sink a steamboat, and the muddy crawfish could flood a plantation. Thereby hang a couple of "Tales" of incredible crustaceans!

Did you know that the Mississippi once flowed upstream? That it did, and the man who told about it bore a famous name, Roosevelt. He earned more claim to river fame as the first man to negotiate the Mississippi in a steamboat.

Ever hear of Ab Grimes? Not likely, but he had more lives than a cat while smuggling mail through the Yankee lines. A man so marvelous was Grimes, that movie-makers might hesitate at telling his true story. It simply couldn't happen; but it did.

It all is told in the following pages. What's more, you can see "what it looked like" when it happened, thanks to the illustrations, painstakingly gathered from many sources, some inaccessible to the average seeker. On-the-spot artists and early photographers contribute rare items to this kaleidescope.

Before someone asks it, we want to answer the question: "It took THREE of you to write this?"

Yes, three individuals put their energies into the production of "Tales of the Mississippi", and here's how it came about:

Warren C. Ogden, Editor of *The Times-Picayune's DIXIE Roto Magazine,* is a man steeped in the lore of the Deep South. That lore he often imparted to his young son, Warren, Jr., in the form of tales of imaginary "coureurs de bois" whose adventures he wove into factual stories of Louisiana and New Orleans history. He soon realized that such stories might have appeal in book form, and he began to think of them in terms of a collection which might be called "Tales of the Great River". He also realized that many of the "Tales" had never appeared even in *DIXIE Magazine.* One day he summoned the Assistant Editor of *DIXIE,* Ray Samuel, another Orleanian long enraptured with the area's historic charms, and said:

"You know, here we are on the banks of the greatest river in

North America, and most of our readers don't know the fabulous stories about it. How about you writing a series called, 'Tales of the Great River'?"

The idea of languishing in air-conditioned libraries, far from the rattle of typewriters and the rush of deadlines while writing stories about the old days of the river, fascinated Ray Samuel. He and Ogden began to stake out some of the "musts" — the packet era, the Civil War, the pirates, the gamblers, the explorers, the builders, and the first steamboat on the Mississippi, the story which had begun the whole idea in Ogden's mind.

Samuel took off, occasionally returning to the office to deliver stories, to pick up his mail and pay envelope, or to argue with Ogden over the deletion of deathless prose.

Naturally, the subject of adequate illustrations arose. The newspaper's morgue provided some; the libraries and archives turned up many. It was realized, however, that to keep the series above the ordinary, new material would have to be found for illustrations, such as the author was striving to find for copy.

At this point, Samuel found himself the innocent victim of a new hobby, collecting old volumes and prints. Primarily, he began to seek material which could be used to illustrate the "Tales", and secondarily, he knew that any writer on the subject of the Mississippi should have a personal library. This, of course, proved fatal to Samuel's pocketbook. He found that the French Quarter is as fertile a field for rare books and prints as it is for antiques and belly dancers.

All of these Vieux Carré attractions seemed to be much in demand. Nearly always, after tracking down a print, an old newspaper or magazine, maybe an ancient long-out-of-print book with eyewitness accounts, he would be told: "Mr. Huber just bought it. You should go see Mr. Huber."

Enter the third member of the triumvirate. Leonard Victor Huber, possessor of a fine collection of packet-carried mail as well as illustrative material on the Mississippi River, was a recognized authority on just about everything Samuel sought — and probably owned it! Graciously, Huber began to lend items from his collection to illustrate Samuel's "Tales". At this point both of them stopped chasing the same game. With his formidable collection, Huber was already toying with the prospect of publication. Upon learning of the Ogden and Samuel ultimate aim in this direction, it was only logical that the three interests should merge.

In the process from individual "Tales" to book form, eighteen of the stories published in *DIXIE Roto Magazine* were used, and ten more were developed to round out this volume. Huber has come up with a grand total of more than 600 illustrations over and above those he originally lent for use in *DIXIE Roto,* including the discovery of hitherto unknown drawings of the earliest steamboats which he found in the Bibleothèque Nationale while on a trip to Paris.

Some of the original "Tales" have been bobbed and consolidated, until 19 chapters remain. The original title "Tales of the Great River" has been changed to the present one to avoid confusion with a volume about the Rio Grande since published. Out of Huber's vast collection some 300 pictures have been selected to illustrate this book.

Leonard Huber authored several chapters and did valuable research on others. Ray Samuel, in turn, provided some of the illustrations.

Generally speaking, however, we may paraphrase the quip about the Gershwin brothers and say that Ray Samuel has been "Mr. Words"; Leonard Huber, "Mr. Pictures"; and Warren Ogden, "Mr. Idea and Editor".

RAY SAMUEL
LEONARD V. HUBER
WARREN C. OGDEN

NEW ORLEANS, JUNE 28, 1955

CONTENTS

Tales of the

Mississippi

DeSoto on the Shores of the White River.
Drawing by Alfred Russell.

HE SAW IT FIRST

THE MYSTERY OF DESOTO

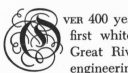VER 400 years have passed since the first white man gazed across the Great River, and today, the best engineering brains of the nation are still trying to fathom its problems.

The Mississippi starts humbly as a creek in the lake region of Minnesota, where one can easily step across it. Gathering momentum and substance from the rich topsoil of Wisconsin, Illinois and Iowa, it courses southward until it merges with the mighty Missouri and then, further along, it is augmented by the Ohio and Tennessee. Down where its furious onrush begins to seek release from confinement, it takes in the Arkansas and the Red. Thereafter, surging past New Orleans in grandeur, the Great River finally empties itself through finger-like passes into the Gulf of Mexico, carrying its fresh currents far out into the salty waters as if resisting the inevitable to the last.

This is the river today. Its bed is comparatively stable now. Oh, it still floods occasionally in its uplands. A new cut threatens now and then downstream. The river still takes a notion to up and leave a port high and dry. A channel here and there may need dredging, or a caved-in bank may need mending.

Why, then, is the river an enigma? Well, where was its original channel located? Some of its prehistoric meanderings across many states can be charted by geologists and have been. But its first bed is buried beneath eons of deposits. Its mouth was at one period as far inland as Cairo, Illinois.

Who was the white man to see it first? Again, that man will never be known exactly. It is probable that some of the early Spanish, Portuguese or Italian explorers and navigators sailed past the unusual mouth of the Mississippi in the 15th century.

Columbus, on his fourth and last voyage, in which he sailed past Cuba and came to Central America, must have sighted the mouth; or, Amerigo Vespucci did when he is said to have "explored the Gulf of Mexico" in 1497. Another Spaniard, Alvarez Pineda, also explored the gulf from Florida to Vera Cruz in 1519.

Certainly reports of the existence of some

great stream to the west of Florida must have come to the ears of the intrepid gentleman who today is celebrated as its discoverer. He saw it first hundreds of miles from its mouth, or, at least, some members of his expedition did. No record of their names has survived, those members of the bedraggled band of Conquistadores who first spied the Great River with white men's eyes. So to the leader of the expedition goes the credit.

His name was Hernando DeSoto, and his origin is wrapped up in as much mystery as that of the river he discovered. His birthday and birthplace are in doubt: "Somewhere between 1496 and 1501", with the accent on 1500; the Spanish town of Jerez de los Caballeros, with two other serious contenders.

Records of his early days are equally hazy. The first reliable gleanings come to light when DeSoto emerges as a prodigy in the art of warfare, a Captain in his early 20's.

Hernando DeSoto served his apprenticeship in the New World in the armies which overran Panama and Peru. He fought in Mexico, sometimes against other soldiers of fortune like himself, for the choice prize of native treasuries. By 1536, he had accumulated a vast hoard in the New World. It was time, he opined, to go back home to Spain and give the king his share, perhaps obtain a new concession for himself, or organize a new expedition.

Charles the Fifth smiled bountifully on his doughty cavalier, and DeSoto received Florida as a reward. Florida in those days meant all of the country lying south of Virginia, and west to Spanish possessions in Mexico. The understanding was that DeSoto had to subjugate it and govern it, paying his royal benefactor the customary share of the profits, of course.

DeSoto was granted the title of "Adelantado," or President, named Governor of Cuba and Florida, and given as added honor the title of "Marquis de. . . ." the blank to be filled in with the names of islands he would conquer.

His Imperial Majesty, Charles the Melancholy, already owned "La Florida", thanks to an earlier expedition of DeSoto's friend, Ponce de León. The story of that knight's quest in search of eternal youth, together with the tales of another court raconteur, Cabeza de Vaca, were enough to whet DeSoto's appetite for the gold and pearls reported to abound in the region, and for the glory of bringing Christianity to the native population.

Cabeza had survived the Navarez expedition which had set sail in crude boats from the shores of Florida. A storm hit them at what seems to have been the mouth of the Mississippi. All the boats were swamped, and only Cabeza managed to save himself from drowning. He finally made his way by land to Mexico, and perhaps it was he who told DeSoto of the mighty stream.

Cabeza de Vaca came back to Spain with a wild story of what he had seen in Florida. He spread beguiling rumors: "It is the richest country in the world", but hastily added, "the rest of which here I saw, I leave to confer of between His Majesty and myself. . . ."

DeSoto appears to have been beside himself with curiosity. He offered Cabeza an important post with his expedition. Cabeza accepted, then withdrew because of disputes over financial arrangements. He apparently was angling for his own expedition, or his own "government" in New Spain. Meanwhile, a mighty fleet was being outfitted. The noblest sons of Spain and Portugal were assembling and begging posts in the army of DeSoto.

The flotilla finally got under way on April 7, 1538. DeSoto remained a year in Cuba, exploring and subjugating the natives.

There is extant only one letter of DeSoto telling of those uninspiring first few days of the assault on Florida. It is dated July 9, 1539, and is addressed to the Municipal Authorities back in Santiago de Cuba. He had written them three previous letters, he says, "without being honored with a reply to either." He had set sail from Havana on Sunday, May 18, and no sooner had the flotilla entered the gulf than it was becalmed!

For eight whole days, nearly, the 620 knights and soldiers, the 223 horses, hundreds of hogs, and impedimenta of conquest, bobbed up and down on the gulf swells. The coast of Florida was reached on "Whitsunday the 25th."

He had directed the expedition toward the previous landing place of Navarez, Espiritu Santo, now called Tampa Bay. They missed this by five or six leagues "through the carelessness of the pilots," one of whom had been there before. "Another cause of the delay," DeSoto admitted, "was my ignorance of the channel from which I found it difficult to extricate myself."

DeSoto described the landing, made after some stumbling about, of "all the troops and horses at a village at the foot of the bay." The exact spot is still in dispute.

The Expedition Landing at Tampa Bay. 620 knights and soldiers, 223 horses, hundreds of hogs, as well as considerable equipment, landed at Tampa Bay (Espiritu Santo), May, 1539. Drawing by Capt. Seth Eastman (c. 1854).

The Grand Expedition's Route that Ended for DeSoto on the banks of the Mississippi, Opposite Present-day Natchez.

After this inauspicious start, things began to improve. The first Indians encountered were friendly, or rather, non-belligerent. They quickly informed him of a Christian among them, who turned out to be a "gentleman of Seville" named Juan Ortiz, one of Navarez' left-behinds. Having given up hope of rescue, Ortiz had gone native, so much so, indeed, that he had nearly "forgotten Spanish." He was appointed staff interpreter, and directed DeSoto to a neighboring chief named Hurripacuxi.

"I negotiated with him a treaty of peace which he broke very soon afterwards," DeSoto reported.

"Several old men related to me so many improbable things about it's [the country's] magnificence, that I dare not repeat it all to you, all kinds of poultry, deer, fish, trade in gold and pearls in great quantities." He added: "I trust in God it may be so, for I have threatened to punish them if they attempt to deceive me."

Although we have only this one letter from DeSoto's own hand, describing his adventures, three eye-witness accounts of the expedition have come down the centuries to us almost intact, written by three men who accompanied the Adelantado. The three eye-witnesses were Luis Hernandez de Biedma, "facteur de sa Majesté," or the man watching the royal purse; Rodrigo

Ranjel, the Governor's official secretary; and a soldier who remains anonymous as "the Gentleman of Elvas" (Portugal).

Moreover, years later, a half-Inca, half-Spanish nobleman, Garcilaso de la Vega, wrote a fabulous account of the expedition as told him by one of its members, and embellished by written notes of two others. The three on-the-spot reporters, plus the de la Vega narrative, *The*

Battle Between Spaniards and Indians. Drawing by Capt. Seth Eastman, U.S.A. (1854)

Rescue of Juan Ortiz, Captured by Indians and Saved from the Stake by a Florida Pocahantas. Drawing by Alfred Russell.

Execution of an Indian Captive. Artist Unknown. Pub. 1853.

Florida of the Inca, add up to as carefully documented an expedition of that early period as has yet been found.

Except for one quaint fact: None of these accounts agrees in important details. Such as, exactly where the army landed; or how many men comprised the army; or — that most important bit of information — where DeSoto discovered the Mississippi.

We should also stop a moment and examine Juan Ortiz, a remarkable character. He had been to Florida with Navarez, had returned to Cuba, but was drawn back to the wilds a second time. It was on this trip that he and his companions had been captured by a chief named Ucita. Those who resisted were killed. Oriz, taken prisoner, was ordered burned by Ucita.

"But a daughter of his," according to the Gentleman of Elvas, "desired him that he [Ucita] would not put him to death, alleging that only one Christian could do him [Ucita] neither hurt nor good." Ortiz was spared, and historians may some day settle which came first, this story or the Pocahontas-Smith tale.

Ortiz was given the job of keeping wolves from stealing corpses out of the temple at night. But one night a wolf sneaked in and made off with the corpse of a royal infant. Ortiz tracked the wolf in the dark and killed it, but failed to recover the royal corpse and restore it to the temple before Ucita found out that it was missing, and so he was placed on a pyre once more. But just before the torch was applied, an Indian guard found the baby's body and the dead wolf, and Ortiz, aided by another plea of the "damsel," regained favor just in the nick of time. When found by DeSoto, he had been the guest of various Indian tribes some twelve years.

Ortiz was a sorry sight when first spotted by the Spaniards. They were about to slay him along with the helpful Indians bringing him to DeSoto, when he cried out, approximately: "Sirs, I am a Christian, slay me not, nor these Indians, for they have saved my life." Another account says he merely shouted "Virgin Mary" and crossed himself, having just about completely forgotten his native tongue. He told DeSoto some strange tales, including a beauty about an Indian village where, when the inhabitants shouted aloud, "the birds flying in the air would fall dead to the ground."

But the most disquieting news Ortiz had for DeSoto was: "No gold." He knew the countryside, the crops DeSoto could expect to find for the army, but was reluctant to enthuse over prospects for treasure.

The great, clumsy European war machine, complete with knights in armor, cannon, hogs on the hoof, and innumerable vans, resumed its march, sloshed into the swamps of Florida, swatting mosquitoes, dodging hostile arrows, fighting hunger and disease.

The Indians didn't take to the Governor's plans to bring them civilization and religion accompanied by the roar of cannon and the whine of crossbows. The heavy warriors on horseback were no match for the elusive red men; nor were their wits in warfare any sharper.

They fought their way across Florida, into Georgia, and Alabama. Always the same. Treachery; ambush; no food; no pearls; no gold. The devastating battle at the Indian town of Mauville, a little north of the head of what is now known as Mobile Bay, inflicted serious losses in men, horses, equipment and morale, from which they never fully recovered.

Biedma tells the story in one sentence: "We were not upon our guard." The strongly palisaded town, surrounded by a plain, on the north side of the Alabama River, turned out to be a dismal trap. The army had dismounted inside the town, had stacked all its baggage — lances, shields, saddles, medicines, food, and clothing. When the attack came, the Spaniards retreated outside the walls, leaving everything for the Indians to pillage and burn. In the battle which followed, about twenty men were killed, some 250 wounded, but the Spaniards accounted for several thousand Indians.

The battered Conquistadores retreated toward Mississippi and took a breather for several months, but not without losses in sustained attacks in which thirteen or fourteen men were killed, fifty-seven precious horses slain, and over 300 of the hogs. But the flower of Spanish knighthood acquitted itself bravely. Accounts of individual acts of heroism and self-sacrifice are everywhere reported by the three scribes, and in de La Vega's story.

In April, 1541, the fort of Alibamo, in the central part of Mississippi, was carried by the Spanish arms, but not without many wounded. And by this time, another hardship was plaguing the men — the lack of salt. What was more, the interpreting problem was getting out of hand. At each new Indian nation, Ortiz would find Indians who could speak only the last nation's language, and so on, until by this time he had

Indian Encampment West of the Mississippi.
Artist Unknown. Pub. 1858.

to relay messages through twelve or fourteen interpreters before he could get a reply back for the Adelantado's ears. De La Vega slyly relates that this cumbersome language barrier didn't hold in the case of "women whom our soldiers had seized for their services . . . when they talked of things necessary and common to all."

So nearly two years after their arrival in Florida, the remnant of DeSoto's mighty army arrived at an Indian town near the banks of the great river reported by savages to lie toward the setting sun. The three eye-witnesses called the village Quizquiz. De La Vega's old-timer remembered it as Chisca. Of the river, the latter says:

"Now since this was the largest of all the rivers that our Spaniards discovered in Florida, they called it the Great River (Rio Grande) and never gave it any other name; but in his record Juan Coles says that in the language of the Indians this river is called the Chucagua. Later we shall speak more at length of its immensity, which is amazing. . . ."

But the Indians had a variety of names for it. In one place is was known as Tamalisen, in another Tapata, and where it entered the gulf, Ri. The Spaniards, de la Vega to the contrary notwithstanding, also called it La Palizada, and The Lost River (Rio Escondido). It is also reported to have been called Sassagoula, Malabanchia, Iser, Mamese-Sipou (river of fishes) and later by the French, it was called Colbert, St. Louis, and the river of the Immaculate Conception.

But the name which stuck was made up of two Indian words: Mecha (great); and Ceba (River). This corresponds to the Spanish Rio Grande, and so Mechacebe, or Mississippi, it is. One thing it definitely wasn't called in those days: Father of Waters, a popular romantic name, possibly also of Indian origin.

Legend has DeSoto tramping to the river bank with pomp and ceremony, surrounded by knights in armor on prancing chargers, and gaily bedecked natives. One later writer says:

"He seemed to feel the influence of an important culminating era in his history," as he gazed out over the broad expanse. It is reported, but not by any of our correspondents on the scene, that he fired cannon, had a high mass said, and planted a cross on the spot.

However, the Gentleman of Elvas, one of the three official reporters, merely says of this historic moment that: "He [DeSoto] went to see the river, and found that near unto it was a great store of timber to make barges, and a good situation of ground to encamp in."

Now the order still was: "Forward march!" — up the river bank four days, looking for a likely crossing place. Dense forests and steep cliffs had prevented a crossing until a pass was sighted. Camp was made in the pass, and immediately DeSoto set his men to building "piraguas" or barges, "all working equally and no distinction being made between Captains and soldiers, since he who was most diligent was regarded as the leader."

The reporters do not agree on how long it took to build the four boats — somewhere between twenty and thirty days probably. They must have been well built, for they could hold "150 footsoldiers and 30 cavalrymen."

Meanwhile, thousands of Indians appeared on the west bank, ready to repel any landing attempt. On the east side, the camp and its workers were constantly harassed by arrows. Indians in full war regalia would sail past the camp in bright war canoes, shooting volleys at the Spaniards.

"In order that their enemies might see these vessels well and in consequence despair of doing them harm, they took them up and down the river both by sail and oar." This bravado apparently worked. The Indians disappeared from the banks.

DeSoto planned the crossing carefully. He wanted to move under cover of darkness, before the savages could return. He divided the boatloads into cavalry, infantry, crossbowmen, and oarsmen, loading them for easy mobility if they had to fight their way ashore, like beach landings of World War II.

At three hours before daybreak, June 18, 1541, the first piragua slid into the water. They figured the swift current accurately, it seems, for by heading one-quarter mile upstream first, they landed on the west bank exactly opposite their camp. The horsemen rode out from the boats "twice a stone's throw from the banks," reaching high ground without incident. No Indians.

"When the sun was two hours high, the whole army was across safely." Looking back across the river, they judged the distance was "nearly half a league." "A man couldn't be distinguished on the other bank." "The stream was swift and very deep." "The water always flowed turbidly, bringing along from above many trees and much timber." "There were many fish of several sorts, unlike anything in Spain."

Such were the remarks of the men on the spot. But where was that spot? They write of the crossing place being near an Indian village, that marshes had to be crossed to get to the pass. The river has changed since, and perhaps even a more definite description of the site, save for latitude and longitude, would no longer suffice.

Historians have narrowed the field to three sites: Memphis, Tunica, Miss., and a small place later called Sunflower Landing near Clarksdale, Miss. Each has its champions. Two different sites in Memphis have markers!

Studies have been made from the scant clues given by the three scribes, and by others years later. In 1941, in recognition of the 400th anniversary of the DeSoto Expedition, Congress authorized a definitive study of the expedition. Scholars examined all the evidence, and although admitting that the exact spot will perhaps never be known agreed that Sunflower Landing seemed the most likely. Ironically, the river has long ago left Sunflower Landing far from the Great River's banks, on a small lake named DeSoto.

For nearly a year the dwindling army pushed on through present-day Arkansas. By this time DeSoto had resigned himself to the inevitable: "No gold." He realized, however, that far more wealth than mere gold nuggets awaited the nation which first settled on the Great River and built a seaport on its banks. It was with this in mind that he finally turned the weary band back to find the mighty stream.

He was racked with fever, discouraged, haunted by fear of his sovereign's wrath and the souls of the noble fighters he had led to their death. Biedma wrote of the Adelantado's demise:

"At length the Governor, finding his situation becoming every day more embarrassing and his affairs going wrong, fell sick and died." The date was recorded as May 21, 1542.

DeSoto Sees It First. Mural in the
Mississippi State Capitol. By A. Alaux.

Discovery of the Mouth of the Mississippi by
La Salle, in 1682. Old engraving by Unknown
Artist. Note the non-existing mountains
in the background.

Fearful lest the Indians rise up at the news of DeSoto's death, his followers took pains to conceal it. The great leader, the mighty warrior, still commanded respect and awe. He had claimed to be a "Child of the Sun," even though one Chief had mocked that claim, saying he would believe DeSoto to be a Child of the Sun when he saw him dry up the Great River.

DeSoto had carried a looking glass with him. Allowing the amazed Indians to see themselves in it, he explained that it enabled him to watch their every move, to know their innermost thoughts.

For good reasons, then, it was advisable to keep them thinking this fearsome man was still alive. But this became increasingly difficult. Word presumably got out, the Indians became restless, and fearing that the grave would be discovered, DeSoto's body was removed, placed in a hollow oak log, taken out to the middle of the Great River at midnight, and consigned to the depths. DeSoto was buried at the age of 42 in the river he had discovered. The site of his burial is said to be near Ferriday, La., now off the river's present course, across from Natchez.

Luis de Moscoso was appointed DeSoto's successor. He, too, realized that abandoning Florida was the expedition's only hope. They decided against voyaging down the Great River; and deemed it best to try the land route to Mexico, still not overlooking the possibility of the pot of gold somewhere beyond the horizon.

More misfortune overtook them. The Indians on the plains of Texas proved even less hospitable than those previously encountered. They turned eastward again in search of the river. The weather bore down with sun, rain, and ice. Finally, "Our Spaniards gazed upon the Great River with the utmost contentment and joy in their hearts, because in their opinion, this river offered an end to all the hardships of their journey."

Not quite yet. More Indians, floods, difficulties in building vessels, and then a harrowing trip down the river. Few sea stories can match that voyage. With but a scant supply of arms left with which to defend themselves, they were set upon by howling savages in war canoes nearly the entire length of the journey to the mouth of the Great River.

About one hundred men, and several women, made it to the open gulf. A fifty-two-day trip was ahead, without navigation instruments, low on food and water, buffeted by storms, until they reached the Panuco (Tampico) River and a haven with their fellow countrymen in Mexico.

Nearly a century and a half was to pass before further explorations of the Mississippi. In 1673, the French Governor of Canada, M. Talon, having heard wonderful tales from Indians and traders about the mighty stream and its riches, sent Father Marquette and Joliet to explore the river and secure claims to the lands south of the Great Lakes for France. They descended as far as Arkansas and returned to Canada. Nine years lated, Sieur Robert Cavalier de la Salle set out from Canada and reached the mouth of the Mississippi on April 9, taking possession of all the territory he passed through in the name of France and calling it Louisiana. But on a return trip by sea to find the river's mouth again, he missed it entirely.

From there, the modern age of the Great River begins. Taking over from the Spanish Conquistadores, the French colonialists were to bring the Mississippi to life, and set the stage for the Americans who were to follow.

Burial of DeSoto. They placed his body in a hollow log which they consigned to the waters of the mighty river he had discovered.

Raftsmen Playing Cards (1849-50).
By George Caleb Bingham (1811-79).

I'M ALL MAN,

SAVE WHAT IS WILDCAT...

Mike Fink.

OR Mike Fink, a joke was a joke, and no opportunity should be missed for a laugh. It was the crude but accepted code of his calling.

"So yer th' best gunshot on the river, Mike Fink," a fellow keelboatman had taunted him, as the group frolicked on a sandbar at nightfall, somewhere along the tortuous way up the Mississippi.

"Well, then, prove yer my friend fer life," continued Mike Fink's taunter. The strenuous, inch-by-inch poling of the heavy craft against the current developed mighty muscles on these men of iron, and it also developed the will to play hard when evening came. But friendship was something stronger than muscle among them, and friendships, by a strange quirk of reasoning, had to be proved.

"I'll prove it, and these hands that can t'ar a hide off a buffalo, can shoot an apple off yer head." Marksmanship was Mike Fink's long suit.

Now, Mike Fink really existed, although the stories about him are legend. He died in 1822, and the tales about his exploits were told, retold,

embroidered, and told again for generations. Therefore, there are two versions of this particular tale.

One story goes like this:

As the smoke from the smudge fire rose lazily into the twilight, Mike placed a red-ripe apple on his taunter's noggin. The "victim" of this curious show of amity is not named, nor is his brother, a shy young chap who stands at the edge of the crowd of boatmen, fingering his pistol.

They had fought like beasts, these two had, but that was past. Now they were fast friends, and Mike was going to prove it. He backed away, turned, and smiled. Then he paced off forty giant strides.

He lifted his rifle, aimed, smiled again — and fired. All eyes saw the man pitch forward to the moist sand. The apple fell unharmed to his side.

"Bang!"

The pistol of the man's younger brother cracked the stillness again, and Mike Fink staggered slowly, trying to support himself on his gun until he, too, sank to the sand.

11

But nobody was looking at Mike. They were looking at the man who had the apple shot off his head, Mike's pal, who had suddenly gained his feet, as if risen from the dead, and was stumbling toward Mike in astonishment.

The young man, believing that Mike had killed from pure wantonness, had avenged his brother. What Mike had done was merely to displace the apple by shooting between it and his friend's skull. Not even blood had been drawn.

That took marksmanship. It also took Mike's life — if we are to believe this version which appeared substantially as related in the December, 1855, edition of *Harper's Weekly*.

Now here's the other version. It is told by Leland D. Baldwin in his book, *The Keelboat Age on Western Waters*:

Mike and his two closest friends, Carpenter and Talbot, had joined the Henry and Ashley expedition to the Yellowstone in 1822, and Mike and Carpenter had quarreled. Later they were amusing each other by shooting tin cups off each other's heads, and Mike "elevated a little too low." Carpenter was killed.

Later, while drunk, Mike is said to have boasted that he'd purposely shot Carpenter. So Talbot shot him.

Who were such people as Mike Fink? Where did they come from? What does the Mississippi owe to them?

It took more than a lot of muddy water coursing down the twisting channel of the Mississippi to make it great. It did that for millenniums before the white man took over, and it was only a canoe route for Indians.

What it took was enterprising people, fearless people, immune to hardships. These hearty souls made the river a great thoroughfare. The valley prospered.

The lower extremities of the river, as everyone knows, were populated by a succession of French and Spanish colonies which built, fought, suffered, and survived against great odds, only to be traded back and forth over the council tables of Europe.

But further up the banks, along the broad reaches of the Upper Mississippi, the people who were to supply the products to be sold downriver came from two distinct classes.

The uplands, including the mighty streams which feed into the Mississippi, saw a new people crowding into the virgin fields of the West — away from the battle-scarred country on which the life-and-death struggle for independence was fought.

One class of them comprised the famous names of Revolutionary War days, the officers and soldiers who returned from Yorktown's glories to find their homes gone, their fortunes dissipated, their profitable occupations non-existent.

Many of these went West to seek new homes. They laid out new cities, and farmlands. These were the builders whose names still echo through the years.

But there was a second group. These men were the working class of colonial America who had found a new excitement in battle, to whom settling down anywhere was now impossible. They were tough, rude, crude — but they developed unexpectedly a definite and valuable place for themselves in the Mississippi's broad plan.

Spawned on the "war path," they needed extreme outlets for their surplus energy. The budding farms of the Ohio, Missouri, and Mississippi valleys needed men to take their produce to market at St. Louis, and lower down, to Natchez, and New Orleans, and from that magic seaport, to bring upriver the treasures and manufactured goods of industrialized Europe and Eastern seaboard states.

Thus the keelboat developed, to navigate the swift currents. It was long and narrow, sharp at bow and stern, shallow of draft. It took fifteen to twenty strong hands to propel it along. The crew was divided equally on each side, taking their places along the "walking boards" extending the length of the craft. One end of each long pole was set into the river's bottom. The other was brought to the shoulder. With steel-hard bodies bent forward, they literally walked the boat upstream, against the formidable current.

A traveler in November 1819, described an alternate method for getting a keelboat upstream:

"The only method of ascending this rapid river by keel-boats was 'cordelling', and this process was by putting out on shore a long, stout rope, which six or eight men would take on their shoulders, and by main strength pull the boat up against the current; opposed to this pulling, the captain of the boat would steer his craft so as to keep her from running into the river bank. It was very hard work, and very slow proceeding, seldom accomplishing more than twenty or twenty-five miles a day. . . . The young men were well satisfied, for it was a source of sport and pleasure to them; they had shot-guns along and

(Right) Fink Doing the William Tell
Apple Trick-Shot.
But Fink never lived to boast about it.

(Below) Life on a Keelboat. Going
downstream was easier than pushing
upstream, but had its dangers too,
treacherous currents, falling river
banks and trees, snags and lawless gangs.

ammunition; could go ashore when the boat started, keep ahead of the 'cordellers', and shoot whatever game came in their way, of which there was no lack in those days in the woods bordering on the river."

To a novice starting down the river in a keelboat, this advice was given: "Keep the boat as much as possible in the swiftest part of the current; never venture upon apparent cut-offs, unless the current is strongest in that direction; whenever wishing to tie up at night, never do so alongside a falling bank, or near tall timber, lest the bank should cave in as it does frequently on the Mississippi River, and the falling trees crush the boat; watch for snags and sawyers, and once past these, beware of gangs of river thieves. Don't pass their well-known lairs alone. Wait a few miles above until you find other boats passing, and go on with them. . . ."

A race of gigantic, sinewy supermen, the keelboat developed. They thrived on overcoming obstacles. Snags and sawyers, floating trees, shoals, bars, other boats — they took them in prideful stride. Many a keelboatman boasted that "his boat never swung in the swift current, and never backed from a 'shute'!"

They were famous for feats of incredible strength, and for fights that would shame a Turk. "Rough frolics" were their chief amusement, and like a pressing hunger, their thirst for the fray had to be appeased whenever the men made camp at night, or encountered other crews at such popular meeting places as Natchez-Under-the-Hill.

An early traveler on the river jotted down this boast which he overheard, presumably at a distance, from a keelboatman:

"I'm from the Lightning Forks of Roaring River. I'm ALL man, save what is wildcat and extra lightning. I'm as hard to run against as a cypress snag — I never back water . . . Cock-a-doodle-do! I did hold down a bufferlo bull, and t'ar his scalp with my teeth . . . I'm the man that single-handed towed the broadhorn [flatboat] over a sandbar — the identical infant who girdled a hickory by smiling at the bark, and if any one denies it, let him make his will . . . I can out-swim, out-sw'ar, out-jump, out-drink and keep soberer, than any man at Catfish Bend. I'm painfully feroshus — I'm spiling for someone to whip me — if there's a creeter in this diggin' that wants to be disappointed in tryin' to do it, let him yell — whoop-hurra!"

It is of record that the peaceable inhabitants of the Natchez bluff looked down with horror upon the wild bands of powerful "rowdies" who occasionally broke through the accepted boundaries of their own district "under the hill" and carried the beautiful city by storm.

But withal, these physically perfect specimens had their own code of honor which included the unique rule of proving friendship which perhaps cost Mike Fink his life.

For years, old-timers recalled the story of Bill McCoy. Bill was a veteran of every scrap on almost every sand bar visible at low water on the Mississippi. He was, they said, the champion. After one particularly vicious row, "where blood had been spilled and a dark crime committed," Bill was involved, and "momentarily off his guard" he fell into the clutches of the law.

Brought before a court sitting at Natchez, Bill became the victim of mass hysteria — the demand to make him the example and to punish him for the "oft-insulted majesty of justice." This happened just before the court was to conclude its spring session.

Bill was charged, committed under $10,000 bail.

At the last moment, a wealthy Natchez planter whom we shall call Col. Williams came to his rescue and agreed to go his bail. McCoy went free.

Months passed. When the morning of the trial came, McCoy failed to appear. As the evening wore on, everybody but Col. Williams was resigned to the inevitable.

The court was on the point of adjourning, when a cry went up in the street. A few moments later, a strange figure stumbled into the courtroom. McCoy, his beard long and matted, his hands torn to pieces, his eyes haggard, and sunburned to a degree "that was painful to behold," fell prostrate on the floor from sheer exhaustion.

Starting from Louisville as a "hand on a boat," McCoy found that owing to the river's low stage, and other delays, it would be impossible for him to reach Natchez that way on time.

So he abandoned the "flat," and with his hands, shaped a canoe out of a fallen tree. He had rowed and paddled, almost without stop, hundreds of miles — to live up to his promise. The trial was a formality, and Bill McCoy went free.

The flatboat was the real king of river transportation in the early days before steamboats took over, because it could bring such quantities of the valley's products to downriver points. Flatboating was a slow, lazy life, but picturesque too,

(*Above*) Ohio River Boatmen.
By Capt. Basil Hall. 1829.

(*Below*) Keelboat with sail,
on the Mississippi.

as can be seen from the painting of that great artist of the West, Caleb Bingham. This type of boat was often called a "Kentucky flat," or a "broadhorn." It looked like an oblong Noah's ark, with a slightly curved roof to shed rain. Generally, these boats were about fifteen feet in beam, and from fifty to a hundred long. They could carry two to four hundred barrels at a time, many head of cattle, hogs and horses. Some of them had cabins neatly fitted out, showing the feminine touch.

Unlike the keelboats, getting these clumsy affairs back up river was next to impossible. Most were dismantled at New Orleans and sold for lumber. Many houses in certain sections of the city, built entirely from flatboat timbers, are still extant.

Fighting along the river, whether by keel- or flatboatmen, was matter of honor, and let no self-respecting boatman shirk a good fight or mouse over a few wounds. One bruiser was described as "cut up with twenty dirk-knife wounds at least, some of which, according to his own statement, 'reached into the hollow'.

"On sympathizing with his deplorable condition, he cut us short by remarking:

"'Stranger, don't be alarmed about these scratches—I've mighty healing flesh!'"

Brawls were welcome diversions.

"In the course of time," writes one traveler, "the craft on which I was a passenger put into Napoleon in the state of Arkansas, 'for groceries.' At the moment, there was a general fight extending all along the 'front of the town', which at that time consisted of a single house.

"Unhappily fidgeting about and jerking my feet up and down as if walking on hot bricks, I turned to a 'used up' spectator, and observed, "Stranger, is this a free fight?'

"'It ar; and if you wish to go in, don't stand on ceremony'.

"I did 'go in', and in less time than I can relate the circumstance, I was literally 'chewed up'. Groping my way down the flat, my hair gone, my

(*Left*) Keelboat. Only known Contemporary Drawing of a Keelboat. 12 to 20 men had to pole against the current. They took especial pride in running up "rapids." The slightest error of judgment might throw the boat across the current or fling it onto hidden rocks, and end in shipwreck.

Raft on the Upper Mississippi. Capt. Willard Glazier went down-river in 1886. "Every trade is represented on these floating dens." When tied up to shore, "the men trap coons, mink and foxes—They find other game, however, and feast upon the hogs (stolen) of the back-woodsmen and small farmers."

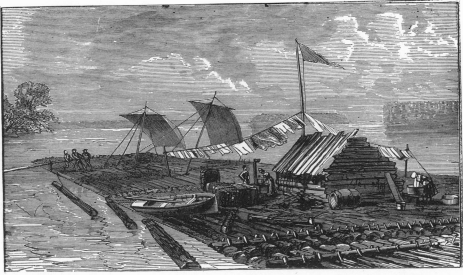

eye closed, my lips swollen, my face generally 'mapped out', I sat down on a chicken coop and thought to myself that Napoleon was indeed a lively place, and the only one in which I have had any fun since I left home."

The river had its wicked spots: Natchez-Under-The-Hill, and little Napoleon, to name two. Perhaps the wickedest, however, was a small island at the very end of the Great River's long journey to the Gulf of Mexico.

The Balize! Its name meant "buoy" or "beacon." A lonely outpost on a small island at the entrance of Southeast Pass; lonely, that is, in its early years, following its establishment by the French engineer, Adrien de Pauger, in 1721. A considerable colonial settlement developed there; but near the end of the French regime, the island began to sink and had to be abandoned. The settlement was reëstablished farther up the Pass, at its junction with Northeast Pass. The old location which became known as Bayou Balize, gradually filled up and has now disappeared.

The second settlement was a worthy successor, or unworthy, depending on the point of view. The French and Spanish colonists had maintained lookouts, garrisons and customhouses there. The Americans built a lighthouse, designed by none other than Benjamin H. B. Latrobe, architect of the Capitol in Washington, and of many other distinguished buildings, in New Orleans and in the East.

By the time Latrobe had been sent to the Balize to look over the site for the lighthouse, it had already become a seedy sight. He reported:

"The Balize (or beacon) is properly a wooden blockhouse calculated to mount 4 cannon on the lower floor, and provided for with loopholes for muskets all around. It is surmounted by a wooden tower not more than 50 feet above the water, in which at present (1819) a light is kept.

"This building gives the name to one of the most wretched villages in the country . . . The regular population consists at present of 90 men and 11 women. The tavern, which is the principal

The Balize at the Mouth of the Mississippi. This was the toughest town, bar none, on the river, from its upper to its lower end. From water color by Benj. H. B. Latrobe.

building, and a few other houses, are built on the United States land. The boarding Officer of the Customs inhabits one of the most miserable of them. His situation here is indeed pitiable. After a high wind his floor is often covered with several inches of water, and after the last hurricane there was 5 feet of water in his house.

". . . There is nowhere a more convenient spot from which smuggling may be carried on and connived at. The present inspector, Capt. Gardner—little encouragement there is for him to do his duty in the comforts of his situation—has, as you have stated to me in detail, broken up the petty smuggling of the pilots, and has thereby excited the hostility of the whole village . . ."

Latrobe's report was just four years after the Battle of New Orleans. For the next eighteen years, the Balize was wide open. It was officially described as "the wickedest spot in Louisiana," which in those frontier days, was saying plenty. No imagination is necessary to picture what went on at this haven for the lonely sailor, after weeks or months at sea. Here thrived a hard-living crew of thieves, murderers, cutthroats, and wild women. There was no law, no closed season on weapons, drinking, or gambling.

Never a night passed, it was said, without a murder at the Balize. "Drunken shouts, maddened screams rose and thinned into silence over the wide marshes by the river mouth. Natchez-Under-The-Hill was tough and wild, but it was the home of innocence compared to the Balize . . ."

It was certain then, as it would be today, under similar circumstances, that a legislative committee would "investigate" the Balize. This investigation resulted in the Pilot Law of 1837, after which the Balize reversed its wicked ways and became a model community. Ten years after that, another committee took a look and compared its "then" and "now":

"From the existence of the state . . . up to the year 1837, the pilot service was negligently performed and more especially were the persons engaged in it, as a body, a desperate, worthless, reckless class of men. The Balize, during that period, was a scene of barbarous strife and drunken debauch.

". . . Anterior to the law, it was a mere mudbank, whose natural loathsomeness was made more intolerable by the beastly scenes enacted there. Riots and brawls were daily exhibitions, and low revelry and debauches the pastime of the night. It was a place dangerous to visit; the savageness of man invested the desolation of

Mississippi Raft (Near Port Gibson), 1856. These were long rafts which of course, were readily sold to saw-mills in New Orleans. Then the rafter, after blowing in his earnings, had to trek wearily back up the long trace to his distant home.

Natchez-Under-the-Hill. By A. R. Waud. Under-the-Hill, as opposed to respectable On-the-Hill, was celebrated as one of the wickedest spots on the river, with a bloody brawl, if not a murder, every night.

Arrival of a Steamer at Natchez. By A. R. Waud.

nature with appalling attributes . . . it is appalling to reflect, that the character of the people who dwelt there, and held appointments from the state was yet more savage than the scene that surrounded them . . ."

Until 1865, the community of 300 to 350 law-abiding souls, which the Balize became, was noted for its homes, their "trim parterres of flowers," the church, and the moral lives of the inhabitants. In that year, a hurricane did extensive damage, and the Balize was abandoned.

New Orleans also had a "wickedest spot," however, which was infinitely more accessible than the Balize. It was the flatboatmen's paradise, whereas the Balize was more of a deepwater sailor's river haunt.

In the 1820's, the area along the levee in the vicinity of St. Mary's market was the "end of the line" for most flatboatmen. This later was to become the starting point for steamboat races. But in the early 20's, the flatboatman ruled supreme

here. It is said that hundreds of these craft were tied up so closely, side by side, that one could walk a mile on their curved decks without going ashore.

Having arrived at his destination, with the hull of his boat crammed with salable goods, the flatboatman waited for his consignee to pay off. Then, his pockets bulging with cash, he looked around for amusement before heading back up-river, along the dangerous Natchez trace for home—and another flatboat.

He didn't have to look far. Just behind the levee, along the front street, was a row of saloons. From the banquette could be heard, "Twenty-eight on the red," or "Eagle bird by chance." The faro and the roulette tables, at the rear of the saloons, were to flatboatmen like the Sirens to Ulysses. And upstairs were boarding houses and what-not for the accommodation of this transient population.

But it was not likely that our flatboatman

Natchez Under-the-Hill. By A. R. Waud.

The Jolly Flatboatmen, by George Caleb Bingham
(1811-1879).

The Man of the Free Fight at Napoleon.

would tarry too long here, either. Another attraction lured him further back from the river. On Girod Street, in a low area, literally and figuratively, was a flatboatmen's rendezvous known as "The Swamp."

You wouldn't find the captain or the owner of a flatboat here, generally; only the hired hands. They seldom saved their money, preferring to spend or gamble it away before heading home. They usually managed to keep a few dollars back, and banding together in threes, would purchase a horse and "whip-saw" back up through Mississippi and Tennessee. This process meant that, after crossing Lake Pontchartrain with the horse, one of the men would ride him for about two hours, and the other two could trudge along on foot. The rider, his time up, would dismount and tie the horse to a tree, and start ahead on foot. When the next man in turn came to the tied-up horse, he would ride for two hours; and so on.

This trip took as much stamina as the trip downriver, especially since murderers lurked along the way, the Murrels, the Masons, the Harpes, and others.

When flatboatmen were discussed, the name of Bill Sedley was mentioned in hushed tones. No Mike Fink, Bill. Not a vague character evolved from a few swatches of fact, Bill Sedley was the genuine article, and well authenticated. His fame derives from his great fight, known as the "Sedley fight of '22," or simply as "The Fight."

"The Fight" made sporting conversation and saloon gossip "uptown," "downtown," and "backatown" for several generations in New Orleans. It occurred in the establishment owned by old Mother Colby, "a dame of about fifty winters and 200 pounds" who ran a "respectable" boarding house and caravansary—comparatively speaking. It was respectable by The Swamp standards, anyway.

The "Sure Enuf Hotel," as Old Mother Colby quaintly called it, had the traditional lower floor, devoted to refreshments in front, and to games of chance in the rear room. The Colby personal management extended only to the rooms upstairs; she leased the downstairs concessions. But Mother Colby's popularity served to attract the lads to both departments.

The barroom and gambling rights were in the hands of two Mexican brothers, Juan and Rafael Contreras. Juan dispensed drinks behind the bar, while Rafe dealt faro.

It was never determined to which brother we are indebted for the start of "The Fight," but either Juan served Bill Sedley too stiff a "fire juice" cocktail, or Rafe too "fast" a card. Regardless, one afternoon, Bill Sedley walked out of the barroom "as savage an individual as could be found in the Swamp."

"I'll be danged," he bellowed, "whether it's the whiskey or I seed it right, but I'm a yellow bantam pullet but I thought I saw Rafe Contreras deal a keerd from his sleeve."

The boys in the saloon nervously hoped they hadn't heard what they knew they had.

Bill Sedley came back into the bar and ordered another drink. Whatever his doubts were before, this last "cocktail stiff, you bet" settled them.

"I'm a chee-yild of the snappin' turtle, and raised with the painters [panthers]," echoed the familiar war-cry of the flatboatmen, and he flung open the door into the gambling room, where Rafe Contreras had just risen from the table to go to dinner.

Customers raced for the exits, some leaping through windows. The rooms were cleared of everybody but Bill Sedley and the Contreras boys, in record time. Juan Contreras closed and barred the door.

The boys crowded around doors and windows. One Aleck Masters, described as a "short, thickset Kentuckian," offered to go in the back way to "see fair play," but was ignored, as sounds of pistol shots were heard, followed by the crash of glasses, the smashing of tables and chairs, punctuated with frequent, "I'm a chee-yild of the snappin' turtle, I am!"

At last the anxious audience outside heard the bar on the door being removed; and the door was flung open. From the dim, smelly haze within, a voice called:

"Gentlemen, walk in; it's free drinks today. The American Eagle has lit on the Alleghenies."

As the boys minced in, they saw Bill Sedley covered with blood, but grinning from ear to ear. His left hand hung powerless at his side, and a stream of blood gushed from a wound in his temple. His clothing was a sieve of bloody knife cuts.

"Gentlemen," continued Bill, "the proprietor of this here place has gone on a journey and left me in charge. Help yourself, and drink hearty."

Juan Contreras was crumpled up under an overturned table, clutching a knife in his lifeless hand. In the backroom, Rafe was pinned to the fatal faro table by a Bowie knife.

Bill Sedley was hurried across Lake Pontchartrain, and started up the trail to Kentucky, and "though he never returned, it is said he lived to a good old age."

But bloody brawls sometimes also broke out among members of the upper class, who usually settled their differences in more dignified fashion: with pistols at so-and-so-many paces.

One of the wildest melees of river fighting, in fact, developed as the aftermath of a gentlemanly duel, fought with all the strict rules of the code——the bloody brawl of September, 1827.

To a sand bar in the Mississippi River, near Vidalia, Miss., across from Natchez, rowed 13 grim men from Alexandria, La. Their purpose: to settled an affair of honor between Dr. Thomas H. Maddox and Col. Samuel L. Wells. The insult which prompted the duel couldn't even be remembered years later by some of the witnesses.

With Dr. Maddox were R. A. Crain, Norris Wright, Alfred and Carey Blanchard, and his surgeon, Dr. Denny. With Wells stood George C. McWhorter, Jefferson Wells, Richard and Samuel Cuney, and his surgeon, Dr. Cox. He also had another man with him whose name was to become associated with the sleek knife of his own devising, James Bowie.

Four of the seconds were sworn enemies. Bowie, even then famous as a knife fighter, had

already exchanged shots with Wright on a previous occasion, and Richard Cuney and Crain detested each other passionately. And yet, the amenities of the code were quietly observed.

From Natchez, thousands of eyes along the bluff were piercing the morning mist for sight of the figures moving on the sand bar.

Then: "You have agreed on the terms," Crain, Maddox' second intones. 'I will repeat them so that there is no misunderstanding. You are to take eight paces, stand left side to left side. At the word 'Prepare', you are to raise your pistols in directions opposite to each other. At the word 'Fire', you are to fire as you choose. Will you take your places?"

Dr. Maddox and Col. Wells silently pace off the distance, turn sideways abruptly.

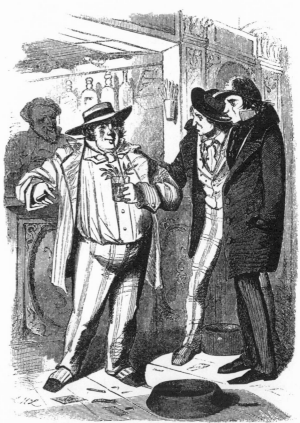

The Unexpected Encounter. Of one character travelling the river, it was said: "He took his place beside the bar when 'somewhere about the mouth of the Ohio', and maintained his postion and his legs, 'though constantly liquoring', all the way down to New Orleans."

Gentlemen grouped around that indispensable of those days — a spittoon.

"Prepare" shouts Crain. Pistols rise.

"Fire!" Two blasts shatter the still morning air.

No hits! A long pause. Then the seconds begin reloading the pistols. The duelists' eyes never meet. Again:

"Prepare!"

"Fire!" No blood this time either. Dr. Maddox, one of the duellists, now ventures:

"It appears to me that we are wasting a good deal of powder. I propose that we consider that our honor has been satisfied."

Col. Wells, his antagonist, and Wells' second hold a brief consultation, and then nod agreement. They rejoin Dr. Maddox and his second, eyes meet for the first time again without pistol sights intervening, and they shake hands.

But suddenly smouldering hatred among the seconds flares up.

"Now would be as good a time as any to settle our differences," Richard Cuney, one of the Wells seconds, shouts as his arch-enemy, Crain, a Maddox second. In a flash two shots are fired—apparently by Crain and Bowie, respectively. Bowie had no grudge against Crain, but was trying to protect his friend, Cuney. But the latter falls, mortally wounded.

The bloody brawl goes on with a sort of aimless fury.

Bowie shoots at Crain and misses, and Crain fires on Bowie and wounds him in the thigh.

Steel glints from Bowie's belt as he lunges for Crain. Crain throws his pistol in Bowie's face and runs. Bowie falls.

Now a really deadly feud takes over. Wright, of the Maddox party, and Bowie's mortal enemy, whips the blade out of his sword cane and aims it at Bowie's heart. But Bowie, with a lightning move, deflects the blade, grabs Wright's coat and pulls him down. Again that glint of steel and Wright collapses.

The brawl might have continued until all the men of both groups had killed each other. Fortunately Wells intervenes and forces Crain at gun point to desist. Doctor Maddox tries to get into the fray with a shotgun which he has hidden for just such an emergency behind a nearby tree, but the two surgeons have had enough of bloodshed, and they hold him back until he has calmed down somewhat.

As Wright's body is rolled off him, Bowie stammers to Crain:

"Colonel, you ought not to have shot me."

"And you ought not to have drawn on me," replies Crain.

"I didn't draw on you," explains Bowie. "I was only trying to protect my friend Cuney."

The toll of this bloody brawl adds up as follows: Cuney dead; Wright dead; Bowie wounded; Alfred Blanchard, another of the Maddox seconds, and an innocent bystander, nicked by a stray bullet, probably one of Bowie's.

But the two principals survive unscratched. They stand chatting in the friendliest fashion under a tree nearby.

The Mississippi at New Orleans. From a sketch made about 1828, by Capt. B. Hall, of the Royal British Navy. In the 1820's you could walk a mile on the curved decks of the flatboats moored along the shore without getting your feet wet.

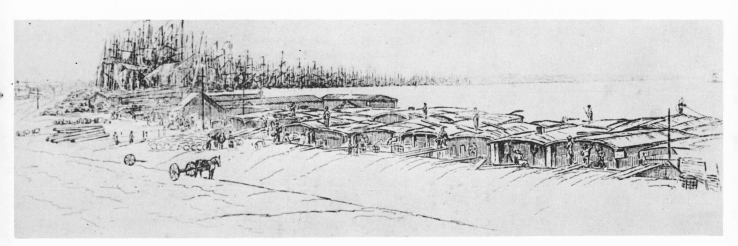

COMMENCEMENT OF STEAM NAVIGATION

ON THE WESTERN RIVERS.

ORLEANS. FIRST BOAT BUILT ON THE WESTERN WATERS, 1812.

This very early wood-cut of the *New Orleans,* first
steamboat on the Mississippi, shows her as a
stern-wheeler, and at least one eye-witness
described her as such, although most
authorities agree that she was a side-wheeler.

mity, and a community of interests, where we had a right to expect a friend of the most unequivocal sincerity, we have met an enemy of the most dangerous capabilities, and we must act accordingly.

Liverpool Courier.

NOTICE.—THE STEAM BOAT, NEW-ORLEANS, will run from this place to the English Turn and back on Friday next, to start precisely at 10 o'clock A. M.—Tickets of admission may be procured at the two Coffee-Houses, at three dollars each. The Boat it is expected will return at 3 o'clock P. M. all passengers therefore who may desire to dine before that hour it is expected will carry with them their own provisions.

January 15.

St. Philip street Theatre.

On Thursday 16th instant,

FIRST STEAMBOAT
TO NEW ORLEANS

ROBERT FULTON, pioneer steamboat builder, was ambitious, aggressively ambitious. He saw that the new mode of transportation had enormous commercial possibilities on the Ohio and Mississippi Rivers. Less than two weeks after the successful voyage of his *Clermont* up the Hudson, in 1807, he was making inquiries about the Mississippi. He and his partner, Robert Livingston, had been successful in obtaining a monopoly of steamboat operation in New York. They now tried to get similar exclusive rights on the western rivers from the legislatures of the riparian states. Turned down by all of the river states, Livingston was fortunate only in selling his idea to Governor Claiborne of the Territory of Orleans, (Louisiana after 1812) and on Claiborne's recommendation the territorial legislature granted the partners an eighteen-year monopoly. The mouth of the Mississippi was closed to all steamboats but those of the Fulton-Livingston combine!

Americans had been experimenting with steamboats for twenty years before Fulton's time. Oliver Evans, John Fitch, James Rumsey, John Stevens and even Livingston, himself, had made and run, with varying success, some types of steamboats. Fulton, though, gets the credit; besides possessing a fertile brain, he was shrewd, he had the right partner with money and political connections and he had vaulting ambition.

About two years after the *Clermont's* epochal voyage, Fulton and Livingston sent Nicholas I. Roosevelt to Pittsburgh with instructions to make a preliminary survey of the rivers. Roosevelt, an engine builder of more than ordinary skill, had worked for Livingston before. In May, 1809, Nicholas Roosevelt and his wife, Lydia, who was a daughter of Benjamin H. B. Latrobe, traveling aboard an especially built flatboat, began floating down the Ohio and then the Mississippi, observing as they went, asking questions, taking soundings and even lining up coal mines along the way for possible future use. The voyage between Natchez and New Orleans was accomplished in a rowboat for better study of the mysterious currents, bars and banks of the lower river.

The party arrived at New Orleans Dec. 1, 1809. The Roosevelts took passage on the first vessel sailing for New York. Then near-tragedy began stalking the opening of western waters to steam navigation. Mrs. Roosevelt later said:

"We had a terrible voyage of a month, with a sick captain. The yellow fever was on board. A passenger, a nephew of Gen. Wilkinson, died with it. Mr. Roosevelt and myself were taken off the ship by a pilot boat and landed at Old Point Comfort. From thence we want to New York by stage . . ."

Roosevelt greatly impressed Fulton and Livingston with his studies and his conviction that a steamboat could lick the rivers. At every stop he had made and told his plans, river folks had laughed at the idea. But Nicholas Roosevelt, like his distinguished descendants, was a man of determination. The boat, he told his backers, should be started at once.

The Roosevelts took up residence at the teeming frontier town of Pittsburgh in the spring of 1811. Beelen's iron foundry, under a lofty bluff called Boyd's Hill, on the Monongahela, was chosen as the historic site for building the steamboat. Plans were furnished by Fulton. The boat was to be 148.5 feet long, 32.5 feet wide with a draft of 12 feet. The engine was to have a 34-inch cylinder.

Cutters were sent into the surrounding forests to hunt tough timbers for ribs, knees, beams and plankings. Saw pits droned constantly. Mechanics brought the machinery from New York.

Then, near-tragedy again. Floods. Repeated risings of the Monongahela floated the contents and equipment of the shipyard hither and yon. Surging waters almost launched the boat before its time. By superhuman perseverance, the work continued. Finally, by Stepember, the boat was christened *New Orleans* and readied for her trial run.

Another storm arose, this time a storm of protest over the widely criticized Roosevelt for announcing plans to take along his pregnant young wife on the hazardous trip. But Mrs. Roosevelt stood by her husband. She would go anyway.

For his wife he furnished the after cabin with all the comforts — plus. Two women servants waited on her, and a giant Newfoundland dog, Tiger, added to the homey atmosphere.

Besides Roosevelt, there was an engineer

Robert Fulton, by S. F. B. Morse.

named Baker, a captain, a pilot named Andrew Jack, six hands, a waiter, and a cook.

After several spins on the river, the departure was scheduled. The banks were lined. Pittsburgh turned out *en masse* to wave God-speed. There were tears and prayers, and there were curses for the "foolhardy" Roosevelt and his "inconsiderate care" of his wife.

Up came the anchor at Roosevelt's signal, and the steam engine urged the paddles around. Cheers doubled as the paddles bit into the water and slowly sent the boat ahead. The *New Orleans* steamed upriver a bit, then made a wide arc and settled on her course.

The crew had been under certain misgivings, and no one can blame them. But as the little vessel steamed along that first day — beautifully puffing down the river, answering her helm — fears soon vanished.

In the morning, the crew answered the cheers from crowds gathered at every village passed. On the second day after leaving Pittsburgh, the *New Orleans* rounded to opposite Cincinnati and cast anchor.

"Well, Roosevelt, you are as good as your word," called the mayor from shore, remembering Nicholas' boasts on his exploratory trip. "You have visited us in a steamboat, but we see you for the last time. Your boat may go down the river, but as to coming up, the very idea is an absurd one."

Similar words of skepticism have reached the ear of every inventor and innovator, and these words went out Roosevelt's other ear.

On the night of Oct. 1, the *New Orleans* reached Louisville. There was a bright moon, and as the steamboat hissed to the landing, the crowds came running. All the excitement was not due to the *New Orleans*. The comet of 1811 had been in the heavens, and the noise of the engines brought many who thought the comet had fallen into the Ohio!

The Roosevelts were complimented by a dinner ashore, and, as usual, regrets were expressed

that this was the first and last time a steamboat would be seen above the Falls of the Ohio. But Roosevelt had a surprise for his hosts.

He set a big spread for his Louisville hosts aboard the *New Orleans*. While this affair was under way, the boat started to groan and move. The diners rushed topside — to find the *New Orleans* blithely sailing upstream! They were dumbfounded.

The conquest of the falls — that was the next real danger facing Roosevelt. It had been hoped to reach Natchez as fast as possible to start realizing income on the heavy investment. But the Falls of the Ohio had other ideas. The water was too low to allow the *New Orleans* to run through. So Roosevelt occupied his time to ad-

To celebrate the centenary of the first steamboat voyage, a replica was built in 1911 which bore little resemblance to the original. No plan of the original *New Orleans* has survived.

vantage. He took the boat back up to Cincinnati to convince the incredulous citizens that upstream trips were possible.

Returning to Louisville, they had more anxious waiting. The weather, instead of bringing rain, brought a dull, misty sky that "weighed heavily upon the spirits." The sun shone dully through the mist like a "globe of red hot iron." The portents were not understood. A citizen of ancient Pompeii might have caught their meaning.

Then two things happened. Rain upstream brought a rise in the river — and Mrs. Roosevelt had her baby, fortunately while the boat was still in port. In the last week of November, Roosevelt assured himself that despite a narrow margin, the attempt should be made to run the falls.

With all hands on deck, the boat steamed towards the falls, Mrs. Roosevelt, who had refused to remain on shore, stood at the stern watching. Two extra, rapids-wise pilots were engaged to stand at the bow. Steerage way and control depended on the *New Orleans'* speed exceeding that of the current, so all the boiler steam possible was poured on.

Every hand was tensed as the boat dipped into the first eddy of the swirling waters, spun around and righted herself, headed downstream. Spray whipped their faces. The engine roared, the vessel pitched to what seemed certain destruction, then bobbed up again.

The pilots waved directions to the helmsmen. The Newfoundland dog crouched at Mrs. Roosevelt's feet. Fortunately the passage soon was over. The *New Orleans* safely rounded to below the falls.

But there was little time for rejoicing, or even relaxing. Hardly had she anchored than the world seemed to rend itself at the seams. The ground heaved and shook. The waters rushed madly from bank to bank. At one point they even flowed upstream. The greatest earthquake ever to strike North America, the New Madrid tragedy of 1811, as it has been labeled, seemed to grasp the little boat as if resenting the intrusion of steam to challenge Father Mississippi's long reign.

This "night of horror" battered the *New Orleans,* and only by great effort was she maintained on even keel. The rumblings and earthquakes continued through the next day, but Roosevelt had gotten up steam and the boat raced down the river.

Scenes of terror and destruction unraveled along the banks. Flocks of birds darkened the air, going anywhere to escape they knew not

The replica—built in 1911—of the *New Orleans* made the Pittsburgh–New Orleans trip to the applause of townspeople along the Ohio and Mississippi rivers.

Interior of a steamboat pilothouse.

Front view of a pilothouse.

Nicholas J. Roosevelt, Mrs. Lydia Roosevelt and I. Montgomery Roosevelt Schuyler, Living (1912) Grandson of Nicholas Roosevelt. Nicholas Roosevelt and his wife made two trips down the Ohio and Mississippi; one trip on a flatboat and the final stage in a rowboat, to explore the river channels; the second in 1811, from Pittsburgh, in the newly launched *New Orleans*. Roosevelt was criticized for taking his wife along in 1811, as she was then in a "delicate" condition.

Some early artists let their imaginations run wild when sketching steamboats. Neither of these drawings of the original *New Orleans* match known details of the steamship's actual design.

what. Wild animals were running aimlessly along the shore, many drowning themselves in the river. Indians in full war paint sped down the river in great war canoes, terrified at the hidden foe.

At stops for fuel, inhabitants pleaded with Roosevelt to take them away. Indians shouting war whoops tried to attack the breathing, sparks-spitting steamboat monster.

In the midst of all this, the *New Orleans* caught fire! A servant in the forward cabin had placed some wood too near the stove. The fire was extinguished after gutting the forward end of the cabin.

The earthquake continued to harass the trip. Whole islands would disappear before their eyes. The bed of the river, carefully studied by Roosevelt, had changed. The boat proceeded cautiously and slowly. At New Madrid, the center of the earthquake, pitiful entreaties by the survivors had to be ignored, painful though this was. There was no room on board, not enough food.

When the men went ashore to cut wood, frightened Indians joined them, asking to be taken along. It was learned that the natives called the *New Orleans* "Penelore," or fire canoe. To them it was an omen of evil.

Mrs. Roosevelt recalled that she "lived in constant fright, unable to sleep, sew or read." The threats continued unabated, with new dangers at every turn. A new channel would develop, passing over the tops of engulfed forests, with topmost branches of trees ready to entangle the *New Orleans.*

Tying up at night was a problem. Trees or river banks might topple over at any time. By using the long oars, the boat was kept in the middle of the strongest current, that having been deemed the safest plan. Slowly the river was descended, and the area of greatest disturbance passed safely.

Thousands awaited the *New Orleans* on the bluff at Natchez and at the foot of the bluff early in January 1812. The boat came downriver, rounded to opposite the landing place, but it was noticed that her paddles, turning more and more slowly, finally stopped. The *New Orleans* was drifting downstream with the current! The engineer had allowed steam pressure to go down too quickly in anticipation of landing. More wood was thrown on the fire and soon enough steam to start moving upstream was generated.

As the "first" steamboat, belching smoke and exhaust steam, neared the Natchez shore, a Negro on the bank is said to have thrown his hat into the air and shouted: "Ole Mississippi done got her marster now!"

The rest of the voyage was accomplished without incident. The "first" steamboat arrived at New Orleans on January 12, 1812. A newspaper "card" a few days later tells of an "excursion" aboard the vessel to English Turn; shortly thereafter the *New Orleans* was placed in the New Orleans-Natchez trade, thus establishing the Fulton-Livingston claim to their monopoly.

The *New Orleans* lasted until July 13, 1814, when she impaled herself on a stump near Baton Rouge, and sank when an attempt was made to free her.

A final note of romance: The captain of the *New Orleans* wooed and married Mrs. Roosevelt's maid en route.

Break in the Levee. The steamboat is actually above
level of flooded plantations.

"CREVASSE!"

THIS was the ominous cry which awoke Pierre Sauvé from his afternoon nap one bright day in May 1849. In the morning of May 3, the Creole planter, whose lands, fifteen miles upstream from New Orleans, stretched back from the river for miles, had ridden the crops and satisfied himself that this was going to be the most beautiful, the most promising sugar cane crop in years. There would be a handsome income, perhaps a trip to France . . . and here this post-dinner reverie ended in slumber.

At 3 P.M., M. Pierre Sauvé was a poor man. He was wiped out. A crevasse had developed in his levee and before he even knew about it, a 20-foot-wide cleft in the dike was disgorging tons of muddy Mississippi into his lap, and shortly, as we shall see, New Orleans would be flooded too, and have to travel about in boats.

But let us double back a bit, for some background explanations of disasters like this one at Sauvé's plantation.

His Majesty's Engineer, Le Blonde de la Tour, assigned to Bienville, founder of New Orleans, threw up his hands in horror at the thought of building a city on the Mississippi's banks at the spot designated by the explorer. Bienville insisted, and he wanted it right here.

De la Tour protested that this site was like a bowl. The river would overflow every year and make a mess of the new city.

De la Tour was quite right, of course. Not only at New Orleans, but from the mouth of the Mississippi almost to the Ohio, keeping the river from overflowing its banks has been a ceaseless, expensive, and until recent times, a heartbreaking task.

The very year when New Orleans was laid out, 1718, orders were issued directing "a dyke or levee to be raised in front, the more effectively to preserve the city from overflow." This seems to have been the earliest effort by man to make the river behave. The colonial government then required the individual landowners to build and maintain levees along their grants. By 1727, Governor Perrier was able to announce that the

33

New Orleans levee was finished, 5,400 feet long, eighteen feet wide at the top, and he added that within a year, the levee would be constructed above and below the city for a distance of eighteen miles.

By the time of the Civil War, the levees were as far North as Memphis; though they could hardly be called levees by later standards. Frail and weak, it is remarkable that they gave any protection at all. Very little action was taken to coördinate levee building and flood control, the effort being entirely in the hands of local interests. As the development of the valley progressed, each flood caused more havoc. In 1882 there were 284 levee breaks with a total length of fifty-six miles!

Oddly enough, Congress did create a Mississippi River Commission in 1879, but it had power to construct a levee only if it could be shown as a benefit to navigation. Flood control was incidental.

Thus the planters and the fast-growing river cities were almost helpless against the spring rises.

From the first, a break in the levee has been called a *crevasse* (French for crevice, crack, chink, cleft — take your pick). The shout "Crevasse!" on the river road by a Creole Paul Revere was enough to start a panic and brought river-fighting Minute Men on the double. The men who had most to lose, the planters, would rush with all hands and the cook to stem the ruinous tide swiftly surging through the crevasse. In ten minutes the work of generations could be lost. The threat of the river bound neighbors, sometimes sworn enemies, into "all for one, one for all" brothers in shovels.

Often the breaks could be localized. Sometimes the Mississippi wandered all over the bordering states, becoming a sprawling sheet of water instead of a stream. Only the most skillful river steamer pilots could pick out the old bed. It might skip across a big bend and never go back to its former route, leaving prosperous river towns high and dry. It might cave in banks, as it skipped about, crumbling fertile plantations into the torrent.

Now to return to the crevasse of 1849.

There is a rise in the land on the outskirts of New Orleans known as Metairie Ridge. This ridge which started at the back of Sauvé's plantation and ran roughly parallel to the levee though some distance from it, served to neatly conduct the torrent, pouring through Sauvé's crevasse,

straight for the heart of the city. As soon as New Orleans saw that efforts to stem the tide were not meeting with immediate success, the city began to take notice of what was going on atop Sauvé's remaining levee.

Sauvé and his neighbors, slaves and whites, pitched in. They called for help from New Orleans, for workers, steam pile-driving barges, bags, shovels — anything that would help. A driving rain made the work more difficult. But it didn't dampen the sense of humor of one fellow who dispatched a message to *The Daily Picayune:*

"I am rigging a boat — have procured a compass and intend next Thursday to start on an errand from the second story of my house, steer through the woods, and land on Canal Street at your office where I hope you will have a lot of mint juleps ready for me.

"The Police Jury" [County Commissioners], continued this rare humorist, "concluded that the notice calling the meeting had not been legally served, and therefore the crevasse could not legally be stopped."

Three days later there was still no help from New Orleans and the rift had widened to 100 feet with more levees threatened. A pile-driving steamboat arrived on the scene just as the men were about to give up. On May 8th, the editor of *The Picayune,* returning from Sauvé's, reported that more than 25,000 acres of cultivated land were ruined and he warned that if the several intervening levees between the crevasse and the city did not hold, that there would be water in Chartres Street by noon the next day.

The next day was gloomy indeed: No help from the city; the crevasse widening; no hope of closing it; more rain; planters ready to give up; water creeping into the outskirts of New Orleans.

"One hundred men were sent yesterday," wrote a correspondent near the scene. "They went to Carrollton and marched up here, nine miles above, wheeling wheelbarrows (for which we have no use) and carrying their tools. After marching four miles, they declined to go further. That is the last we heard of them . . . We have been left, six days, we planters, to contend against the mighty stream of the Mississippi."

But the planters seemed to rise to the occasion, and soon M. Sauvé reassured all that a rumor that work had stopped was unfounded, that they had bravely brought the opening to twenty-five feet and that more piling was going in hourly. Then, at last, the steamboat *Patrick Henry* arrived from the city with men and materials.

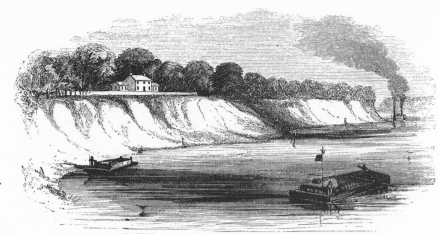

The Mississippi at Low Water.

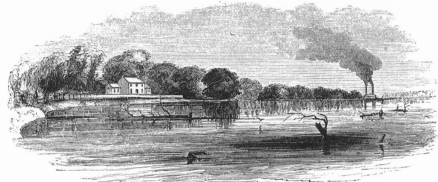

At High Water.

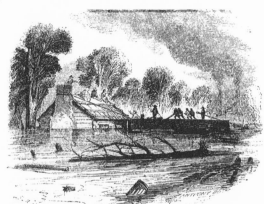

A Freshet.

Steamboat taking on refugees at a crevasse at Bonnet Carre (Louisiana), by Alfred R. Waud.

It was, however, much too early for optimism. Just when things looked good, two barges tore loose and crashed into the piling, drawn in by the vicious current. They tore away pilings and pile driver. Men jumped to safety just in time; the pile driver sank in the breach.

Reports came in that the Mississippi was really on a rampage. Crevasses all up and down the river. Above Vicksburg, from Milliken's Bend to Richmond, all was under water. Then, across the river below New Orleans, the levee gave way and the land was inundated. At Morganza, in Point Coupée Parish up-river, a quarter-mile wide crevasse was "ravaging the countryside", with one witness stating that "the roar of the water is heard many miles distant." A crevasse on Bayou Lafourche, a connection of the Mississippi, was flooding the surrounding country. Nothing like this had been experienced since 1816!

Meanwhile, New Orleans was slowly settling into the water. New Basin Canal, a waterway which was used to transport freight into the heart of town and which had its own levees, loomed as a barrier which might stop the flooding of part of the city. The levees did halt the flood waters but in so doing part of the city above the canal received the back-up. Some wanted to cut the canal levees, while others said, perish the thought. So the lower bank of the canal became an armed camp. Three hundred men with pistols and guns patrolled it to prevent breaches and the police force had to be called out to prevent bloodshed.

Two more crevasses opened: one far below New Orleans at English Turn; the other across from Sauvé's, on Fortier's plantation.

At Sauvé's the men were apparently doing better. The pilings were nearly across the breach and sandbagging was under way. Then two of his neighbors, the Kenner brothers, withdrew their forces; a third, Trudeau, stuck it out. A couple of Negroes came down with cholera and the white men quit to go back to threatened New Orleans and work there for $2.50-$3.00 per hour. Poor Sauvé — it began to look as if he just couldn't win!

On May 13th an old steamboat hulk was dragged to the weakest part of the piling to be scuttled there to relieve the pressure. This didn't work. It weakened the existing piling even more, and made "a crevasse in a crevasse," as one person put it. What made it all more futile, they couldn't get anybody to work at night. So the day's work was often swept away in the dark hours.

New Orleans people began to feel the damp.

Inhabitants on the outer fringes of the city proper were moving out, "leaving their houses to the rats." Men were working frantically to build a protection levee around the gas works, so that the city wouldn't be left in darkness. The man with a skiff was king.

"All sorts of aquatic conveyances are in great demand, and the proprietors of skiffs and yawls are the most independent individuals to be met in the inundated districts. . ."

But gay old New Orleans wasn't to be slowed down by a mere flood. The theatres remained open, the amusement centers went merrily on, and even the crevasse was turned into a good thing. Three steamboats were pulled off their regular runs and turned into excursion boats for the Sauvé crevasse!

> Pleasure excursion for the Crevasse — 50¢ each way.
> Splendid band of music, will give a collation, and every comfort extended to the passengers.
> Steamboat VIOLA

Alas, another section of M. Sauvé's harried levee now gave away. If it was any consolation to him, one of his deserting neighbors, Butler Kenner, had his own crevasse to contend with the same day.

May 19th. More heavy rains, strong winds which whipped the torrent against the pilings being driven into the breach. And the old hulk which had been sunk at the opening was finally pulled through by the current, opening the breach wider again.

Next day, another crevasse ripped loose across from New Orleans. The city began to take things seriously. Benefit concerts were arranged for the refugees. Warnings were issued not to "Taste, touch or handle" fish in the streets, and to beware of deadly "conger snakes." The number of dry streets, if not the flood, was shrinking.

Onto the scene at this point arrived one Capt. Grant from Mobile. Who touted him off to the city fathers is not stated in the newspapers, or even his first name. But he got $15,000 plus all the hopes of the city, and hustled off to Sauvé's crevasse.

That was May 21st, eighteen days after the crevasse first opened up. Capt. Grant appears to have taken on more than he could handle. He worked like a beaver, which is about the best way to stop a crevasse, but ten days later the Captain was back in New Orleans having completely abandoned the job. It was worse than he

(Above) Crevasse on Chim's Plantation, West of
Baton Rouge. By Alfred R. Waud. It's an ill
crevasse does nobody any good. Here it seems
to have improved the fishing.

(Below) The Great Crevasse at Bonnet Carré.
Sketch by Alfred R. Waud.

Bursting of Crevasse at Bonnet Carré.

had anticipated, he admited, and took all the blame for spending the fifteen grand. He refused any pay, and the city gave him a vote of thanks for his efforts.

The breach was now wider than ever. All that had been done heretofore to close it was lost. Things looked desperate in New Orleans. A meeting was called. Almost everybody in town had a "plan to close the crevasse." Even Bernard de Marigny de Mandeville, the Creole City's elder statesman, came up with one.

"The truant waters of the Mississippi continue to encroach upon our city," began an editorial, "and the song of the gondolier rather than the shout of the municipal boatmen, is fast nearing St. Charles Street. There is much to amuse, novel and exciting scenes."

The wooden bridges and walks across the city's deep gutters at street intersections were washed away. "Gentlemen were seen to disappear for a time beneath the dirty flood when they stepped off the banquettes."

Recorder Baldwin had a field day. May 29th he fined "four interesting young ladies and one nice young man" $50.00 for "floating about in a gondola, making the night hideous with their uproarious jollity." Suits for flood damage ap-

peared in the courts and the legal question arose as to whether a lease for the rental of a house terminated when the tenants waded out with their belongings.

Paraphrasing a Latin expression about the durability of Rome, New Orleaneans gritted their teeth and said: "While the Mississippi flows, New Orleans will flourish." But they didn't say where.

The outcome of the meeting was the appointment of two of the city's own surveyors, jacks-of-all-trades, to go up the river and close the crevasse. The Messrs. Surgi and Dunbar went on the first day of June.

By mid-June encouraging reports, the first in many long weeks, began to arrive at the city from Sauvé's. Besides, the weather improved, the river crest passed, and the waters in the city slowly receded. The newspapers began talk about spreading lime everywhere and hauling off the dirt when the water departed. Success was in the air.

Then on June 18th, a steamboat working at the crevasse was suddenly thrown against the piling. The hard-pressed laborers gasped. The pilings swayed — and held!

When this tense moment occurred, Surgi and

Dunbar were ready with the *coup de maitre* for dat ol' debbil crevasse. They had worked up the piling into a V shape, narrowing inside the breach and had prepared a twenty-six-foot flood gate to drop into the neck of the V. Shortly after, while all hands held their breath, the flood gate was dropped into place.

"After a few ineffectual surges on the part of the Father of Waters to overcome the barrier, the current resumed its accustomed flow within its ancient bed, and the Sauvé crevasse emphatically became a thing that was."

When New Orleans took on the aspect of Venice.
Sketches by Alfred R. Waud.

Flooded Interior on Bienville Street.
Sketch by Alfred R. Waud.

(*Above*) Flood in the Mississippi.

(*Below*) View of Canal Street. Sketch by Alfred R. Waud. Ducks, dogs and boys had a lot of fun, but poisonous snakes, conger eels and even alligators made bare legs risky.

This Navigator Remarked: "I'm taking my **folks** on a little excursion to see the flood." Sketch by Alfred R. Waud.

Flooded Plantation House.

Feeding Stock Along the Levee.

Coming From the Woodpile.

Grabbing For Craw-fish Holes. A single crawfish hole can cause a crevasse.

"CRAYFISH" HOLE TO CREVASSE

The cane crops of Louisiana in the Spring of 1912 were extremely good. Just coming up, the shoots promised one of the finest yields in many a year. Then, the river began to rise to unprecedented heights, and levees started to break.

From Vicksburg on down, there was devastation. Thousands were homeless, many people drowned, whole towns and plantations ruined. By May, the worst appeared over. The U. S. Engineers were starting to predict "levees holding" further down; "no higher crest predicted." Reports in the newspapers said the river was falling at Cairo. Refugees had been evacuated to higher ground. Relief agencies and fund drives were responding admirably, as they always had in the flood country.

Closest to New Orleans, the levee at Bonnet Carré Plantation, about thirty-two miles above the city, had gone out and the waters were flooding a wide area. But much of the flood was spilling over into Lake Ponchartrain, again illustrating the advisability of a man-made spillway there to relieve the city in such disasters.

Suddenly, when least expected, "a crawfish hole" appeared, at 6:30 p.m. May 14, inside the levee at Hymelia Plantation, directly across the Mississippi from Bonnet Carré. Emile Burch, owner of Hymelia, J. B. Murphy, manager of Milliken and Farwell's Waterford Plantation, and others in the neighborhood rushed to the spot when the alarm was given. They went to work, quickly building a "crib" around the hole in the base of the levee, alongside the common road. They were making progress, but all at once the hole began to spurt like a geyser. A terrific suction developed, and then all hell broke loose.

"Water spurted all over the public road," said an eye-witness, "with waterspouts shooting seventy-five feet from the base of the levee." Some logs in the road were picked up and strewn about, so strong was the hydraulic head of the pressure. "We knew all was lost," continued the account, "and in one half hour, the hole was fifty feet wide and we had a first-class crevasse on our hands. The levee was small and sandy. We had ten feet of water outside the levee on the batture, and although we thought we had a fighting chance to close the break ourselves, we decided to wait for expert advice."

From the almost forgotten pages of a snapshot album belonging to the Lorio family of New Orleans, formerly of Star Plantation, four and a

During the Civil War, Levees in New Orleans had to be kept in repair, just the same. The U. S. Government was paying the bill.

half miles below Hymelia, a series of pictures show the initial steps taken to stem the flow.

The *Daily Picayune* says that the "first aid, came from the Cummings & Moberly sawmill" which was a tenant of George Lorio, the patriarch of the family, at the rear of Star Plantation. Mr. Lorio was a member of the Levee Board for that area and a popular worker in parish affairs. Promptly alerted, he got the sawmill to rush its logging train to the scene with laborers, emergency supplies, and equipment.

By 9 p.m. the next evening, the crevasse was already nine hundred feet wide and "caving badly." But the seriousness of the flood was overshadowed by the arguments over who was going to pay for the work of closing. The Army engineers estimated it would take $150,000. Already exhausted from the previous crevasses upriver, state and Federal funds were non-existent. It would be up to the local planters to raise the necessary sum. Governor J. Y. Sanders couldn't even promise convict labor right away, so many calls did he have from other areas.

Meanwhile, Dr. Emile Burch, son of Hymelia's owner, had fled his lovely home. Some of his laborers, marooned in an old sugar house, were "rescued with difficulty." The water was pouring through at the rate of three million gallons per minute!

Then the anguished crowd at the levee got a telegram which must have further jangled already shaky nerves. It was from the President of the Mississippi River Commission: "Hold ends of crevasse, but do not attempt to close it until Commission meets Thursday." One can almost hear a Creole oath, and the remark, "Hol' it wit' what?"

This area claimed 362 people per square mile, the newspaper related, the highest rural population in the world except Holland. And the rain was falling hard.

Slowly, preparations began to consolidate. Men and materials were being rushed up from New Orleans and down from Baton Rouge to fight the "serious calamity." The levee at Hymelia had always been thought to be in first class condition, said the mourners, and they admitted that none of the precautions taken at Bonnet Carré right across the river had been taken at Hymelia. Emile Burch said he thought the foundation of the levee was entirely safe.

Ten thousand small sand sacks were en route downriver; the quarter-boat *New Orleans* was coming down with more. W. L. Knobloch, assistant engineer, went to Hymelia aboard the steamboat *Newton* to take command. Things were finally happening!

Jules Godchaux, another large plantation-owner in that section whose family holdings still produce "Godchaux Sugar," said that a crevasse had occurred at the same spot in the great flood of 1903; and two miles away, in the years 1894 and 1891, the levee had broken. So this land, "some of the very richest production soil in Louisiana," had "had it" already.

But with all the preparations, there was still no money. The U. S. Engineers advised the planters that they would have to dig down and come up with the expenses. Then the La Fourche Levee Board met and voted to share the costs. Pile drivers were moved to each end of the crevasse. The plan was to start driving "cribbing" out from the levee, across the batture, from each end, arching them out in the river until they came close enough together so that steel nets and sand bags could be dropped into the remaining breach.

This pile-driving began, but the work of the swift and unrelenting water ate it way as fast as it was put down. Over one thousand laborers including convicts were at work. By May 20, at 10 a.m. the crevasse was 1171 feet wide. The two batteries of pile drivers, working eight-hour shifts around the clock, were trying to make 350 feet per day. It was estimated that seven days would be needed to close the gap, and that one million sand sacks would be required. On the 21st, the engineers were using "reinforced canvas sheets," and a new pile driver arrived on the scene to help.

On May 25, the width of the opening was 2100 feet; the depth in the hole was forty feet, and the flow was 5,037,600 gallons per minute. The cost to date — $60,000. And the hand of man was losing the fight.

The high hopes of several days previous were dashed. No headway could be made against the torrent. "There is no spirit in the work now," said a bystander, "as there was when prospects were good." All private labor was withdrawn. "It was a magnificent struggle, but everything was swept over," was another comment.

By May 27, the crevasse was a "mecca for sightseers." A motorcycle club made a pilgrimage. Five thousand people visited the place in one day, now that the Army had lifted restrictions, and all work had stopped.

Six hundred and fifty feet of cribbing had been driven at one end, 300 feet at the other, before the work was abandoned. The only bright spot was an announcement that "not a building has been washed away on the plantations." The crevasse was now 2500 feet wide.

"The soil was too sandy and loose," was the Engineers' verdict.

The Great River had won by a knockout. Months later, with low water, a cofferdam was easily built, and the Mississippi once more returned to its narrow confines.

It took floods like this and the one that followed in 1913 to awaken the national conscience. The first Flood Control Act, in 1917, started the ball rolling, but still another calamity, the great flood of 1927, ranking among the great national disasters, had to happen before the Federal Goverment would commit itself to a real flood control program. The Act of 1928 marked the beginning of the end of serious flooding in the Lower Mississippi Valley.

The endless task continues to this day. The Corps of Engineers slides giant asphalt mattresses down the levee to the river bed to prevent erosion from eating away the modern "dykes," but Ol' Man River can still thumb his nose at the Army and bust loose if he feels like it. In 1950, at Mulatto Bend, across the river from Baton Rouge, Louisiana's capital city, a sudden crevasse flooded a large area. With spillways, floodways and well-constructed levee systems, however, widespread disaster is a thing of the past in this ancient stamping ground of the Mississippi.

Story of the Great 1912 "Crawfish" Crevasse at Hymelia Plantation, Opposite Bonnet Carré.

Pile Drivers Set Up.

A. Water Rushing Through the Crevasse.

B. Convict Labor Filling Sandbags,
Estimated one million would
be needed.

C. Months Later. Come Low Water,
Levee Is Rebuilt.

A.

B.

C.

Government Snagboat. Direct descendant of Shreve's *Heliopolis,* first and most famous of the snagboats.

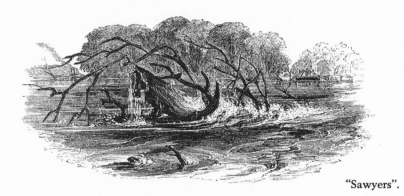

"Sawyers".

THREE great developments, in the early days of Mississippi steamboating, contributed very greatly to the upsurge of the great waterway: vastly improved steamboat engine design, one of which corrected the earlier defects of the Fulton boats and actually ushered in the rapid growth of the steamboat age; the breaking of the strangling monopoly on river steamboating held by the Fulton-Livingston group, thus fostering unlimited trade; and finally the monumental task of clearing the river and its tributaries of dangerous snags which made navigation a hazardous and uncertain risk.

All three were accomplished by one incredible man, Henry Miller Shreve, a Pennsylvania Dutchman. And besides this, he played an important part in the Battle of New Orleans.

Courage, inventiveness, resolution, these qualities were wrapped up in a slight, nearly six-foot build, with muscles of steel. This was Henry Miller Shreve, captain of his own homemade flatboat at 21. In addition, he had a shrewd sense for turning a dollar. In 1810 he made a killing by going up the Mississippi to the lead mines at Galena, Illinois, where he took on seventy tons of lead and floated it down the Mississippi to New Orleans. There he loaded it aboard a sailing vessel for Philadelphia, where he cleared $11,000.00 profit on the deal. Not bad for a lad of 23!

Swift current downstream; the toil of human hands upstream. Shreve instinctively knew there was something wrong with this arrangement in river transportation and, on a subsequent trip to New Orleans, he carefully examined Nicholas Roosevelt's *New Orleans,* the first steamboat on the Western Waters (*see* Chapter 3). Later, he followed the troubled career of the second boat to be built by the Fulton-Livingston combine, after the *New Orleans.* This was the *Vesuvius.* Meanwhile, rival group of builders headed by Daniel French of Pennsylvania built two tiny steamboats, the *Comet* and *Despatch.*

When French built the larger *Enterprise,* Shreve was ready to get into the new steamboat act. In December, 1814, he applied for and was appointed Captain of the *Enterprise,* his first

47

destination being New Orleans. Upon his arrival, Captain Shreve ran into two things which might have turned back another: the Fulton-Livingston monopoly, which gave them exclusive right to run steamboats on the Mississippi; the preparations for the Battle of New Orleans.

Although Edward Livingston took immediate steps to seize the intruding *Enterprise,* he had to wait his turn. General Andrew Jackson already had designs on the new steamboat and her capable master. He ordered Shreve to go upriver in search of three keelboats, carrying small arms, which had not arrived. After getting these down, the *Enterprise* was used to ferry refugees from the city and to take supplies downstream to Fort St. Philip. The doughty captain requested and was given a post of duty; he actually served with distinction at the Battle of New Orleans, January 8, 1815.

After the excitement of the battle subsided, Livingston waited for his chance. In May he had the *Enterprise* seized again by a court order for violating the charter of the Mississippi Steamboat Navigating Company. Captain Shreve was not caught off guard. He was ready with an able lawyer, named A. L. Duncan, who promptly posted bond; then the Captain slithered from the monopoly's grasp on a rapidly rising river. By skillful navigation, Shreve brought his boat back to her home port, Brownsville, Pa., fifty four days after she'd departed, with a journal full enough of adventure stories to satisfy anybody else for a lifetime.

The most important part of Captain Henry Miller Shreve's life, however, was ahead of him.

Shreve immediately went to the designer French with bold ideas for a better steamboat, one which could overcome the hazards he had encountered. But French was obstinate; he was not interested. It turned out to be a good thing for the future of steamboating, for French's attitude resolved Shreve to do it himself.

He set about the task of designing and building his own, improved model of what a steamboat should be. Shreve believed he knew what was wrong with the boats he had seen and operated. The main difficulty, he reasoned, was in the design of the engine, the ponderous flywheels, the clumsy condensers, all of which made them extremely heavy, but by contrast puny in power.

Shreve buried himself in a Brownsville machine shop; months later he emerged with a completely new engine built on entirely different principles. It was horizontal instead of vertical. It had no flywheel and no condenser. It weighed but a fraction of the former engines, and developed 100 horsepower.

Shreve had some ideas of his own about boat design, too. Although the hull and the size of his boat, which now began to rise on the ways, resembled Fulton's *New Orleans,* there were significant changes in the superstructure. The *Washington,* as he called her, had two decks, one above the other; the boiler he placed on the deck instead of in the hold. The whole thing looked so fantastic that the townsfolk joked about it for months. There was no joke when, on its maiden voyage, the boiler exploded killing thirteen of the crew and injuring others. Steamboating might have been set back many decades. But Shreve knew his idea would work and he made repairs.

It would be interesting to know what went on in the mind of Edward Livingston on the morning of October 7, 1816, when he first saw Captain Shreve's *Washington* at the levee in New Orleans. What kind of contraption has this rascal brought down here this time? Then on closer inspection, on seeing its novel, though entirely practical features, he may have exclaimed "Why, I do believe it is far superior to ours!"

Concealing his shock, Edward Livingston assumed a haughty air, as he faced the man who seriously challenged the monopoly.

"You deserve well of your country, young man, but we shall be compelled to beat you if we can," he said.

Livingston immediately had the *Washington* seized and held for $10,000.00 bail. Duncan was ready again, this time demanding through the court that the Fulton-Livingston Company put up a $10,000.00 bond to cover any loss that Shreve and his co-owners might suffer by the detention of the *Washington.*

At last someone had called Livingston's bluff. He was afraid to take the gamble. The suit was dropped and Captain Shreve loaded the *Washington* and chuffed off. The following season, the same little courtroom farce was reënacted, with the same result. So Livingston tried another tack — if you can't lick 'em, join 'em. He offered Shreve a partnership in the monopoly! A strong temptation for one so young, but Shreve refused. Livingston had him arrested. Duncan bailed his client out. The *Washington* sailed a little behind schedule with a full list of passengers and 155 tons of freight.

During Shreve's absence from New Orleans on

this trip, the monopoly matter came to a head. Federal Judge Hall dismissed Livingston's suit against Shreve; this was the beginning of the end of the monopoly. By 1819 the Fulton-Livingston group withdrew its claim to exclusive rights of steam navigation in Louisiana; now the Mississippi, thanks to Shreve, could be navigated by anyone who had the desire and means to build a steamboat. Business boomed from that year on.

Five years later Captain Henry Miller Shreve took on the third and last of the problems he was to solve — snags. The mighty river for centuries toppled huge trees from its caving banks at flood time. Some of these trees would eventually become waterlogged, their roots would become buried in the river bed's sand, their tops waving with the undulating movement of the water. These were the deadly "planters;" "sawyers," just as dangerous, were more loosely set in the stream; the "teeth" of the snags, called also "chicots" by the Canadian flatboatmen, could rip open the wooden bottom of a steamboat in seconds. Boats that didn't explode or burn, snagged.

Captain Shreve, already a legend on the river, put on his thinking cap again. In 1824 he figured out a steam snag-boat and offered the Federal Government a plan to rid the river of these obstructions. His offer gathered dust in some bureaucratic pigeonhole. As often happens, a few years later the government attempted to do the same thing by hand, from barges; Shreve stood by, watching the attempt come to naught.

Then Shreve adopted the lick-'em-join-'em technique. He got appointed a bureaucrat himself. As Superintendent of Western River Improvement, he eventually sold the government on building his snag-boat. The *Heliopolis* was completed in 1829, a monstrous-looking thing. On its first demonstration, it more than proved its worth. Selecting "the most dangerous place on the Mississippi River," Plum Point at the mouth of the White River, he succeeded in just eleven hours' time in removing a veritable forest of formidable snags, many of them six feet in diameter.

In the winter of 1829 and spring and summer of 1830, the *Heliopolis* worked on obstructions in the Mississippi River from the mouth of the Missouri to Bayou Sara. By the end of 1830, the ancient drowned forests had vanished. Snags still caught steamboats, fresh snags from year to year, which were quickly removed

Capt. Henry Miller Shreve.

by subsequent snag-boats. But wholesale snagging had become part of the river's past history.

The last great task for the snag-puller was the removal of the Great Raft from the Red River of the South. A tributary of the Mississippi, the Red tapped an extremely rich portion of Northwest Louisiana. But from time immemorial free passage of its waters had been hindered by a one-hundred-fifty-mile accumulation of logs which choked it, completely blocking navigation and causing overflows.

In 1828, Congress appropriated a paltry $28,-000.00 to improve the Red River, and a party of engineers was sent to explore the raft. Tired and discouraged, they returned to report that it would cost from two to three million dollars to remove the obstruction if the job could be done at all.

The project lapsed for a time. Then Shreve was asked if he could remove the raft. Without hesitation, he took over, in 1833, with an appropriation of only $21,663.00 to do the work. In the first two days he cleared five miles of the timbers. In two and a half months he had cleared seventy miles of the raft and the money ran out. Work stopped.

As money was made available in dribs and drabs, Shreve returned again and again. By 1838, the great raft of the Red River was no more. The cost, $300,000.00, one tenth of the government engineers' estimate! And the Red River was opened for steamboat traffic.

Three years later, Henry Miller Shreve retired from government service at 56. Inventer, snag-puller, trust-buster, he had well earned his rest.

(Above) Explosion on the *Washington*. This was the first explosion of a steamboat on western waters. She was propelled by the new type of engine designed by Shreve. Though she exploded on her maiden voyage, he got her up to St. Louis (after the explosion) on his second try.

(Below) This is a picture of Shreve's *George Washington,* built 1825.

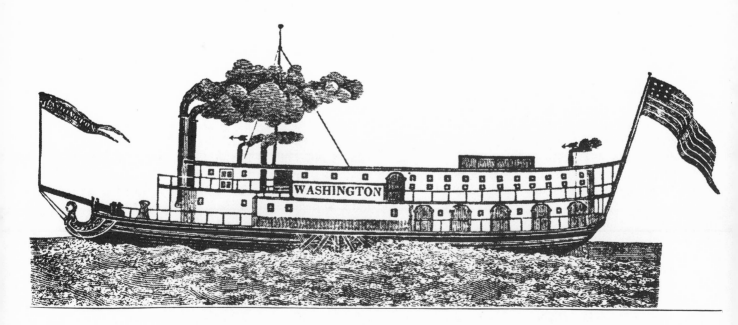

STEAM SNAG BOAT.

U. S.
A.H.SEVIER

U. S. Snagboat. Had a short career: built in 1860, snagged herself to the bottom December the same year.

Snags after the flood.
Sketch by J. Dallas.

Snags

The great Red River "raft". This was an artist's conception of how it looked before being "desnagged."
Log-jam ("raft") north of Shreveport, 1873.

(Right) Snagboat *Aid*, cleaning up
Red River "raft", 1873.

(Below) Another view of the same. 1873.

South Pass, at Mouth of the Mississippi.
After Capt. Eads opened it up in 1879.

THE MAN WHO OPENED

THE

MISSISSIPPI'S MOUTH

THEY called James B. Eads, the self-taught engineer from St. Louis, a crazy man, a fool. The ex-governor of Louisiana and New Orleans' leading scientist both called him half-insane. The Army Engineers massed against him. In effect, they said he didn't know anything about what went on at the bottom of the Mississippi River. Therefore, they cried in unison, before the Congress and before the nation, how could this egghead know how to open up the passes of the Mississippi where it debauched into the Gulf of Mexico? Certainly one had to know what occurred along the bottom to know how to combat the river's bar-forming propensities at its mouth.

Such was their argument when James B. Eads, in 1874, proposed that he could open the river to traffic, thus loosening the bonds which had reduced New Orleans from second to eleventh place as a United States port, and stagnated the entire valley's economy.

What did he know about the action of the river on its bottom? Why, he said, turning the question back at them, what did THEY know

about it; after all, HE had been there! In a diving bell of his own invention, he was said to have "walked every yard of the bed of the Mississippi from Vicksburg to St. Louis."

No one argued the merits of doing something about opening up the river again to trade. The situation at the passes, with the bars resulting from the outflows at the delta of the mighty river, was exasperating. It had been so since the earliest days of New Orleans. In 1726, efforts were made by the French to drag iron harrows over the bars. A hundred years later the Army Engineers, having taken over such projects, proposed to dredge the bars with buckets. They never did.

Not until 1852 did they get around to making any real move and that also ended in talk. Still no channel over the bars. Only the most venturesome ship masters risked the shallow water; only ships of very shallow draft made it. Shippers avoided New Orleans — and the valley's commerce — like the plague.

In 1859, a Chamber of Commerce committee visited the passes. They saw one lone ship blocking the only possible pass, and some 55 ships waiting, either coming in or going out. They estimated that $7,367,339.00 in trade, exclusive of the value of the ships and the expense, was tied up at the mouth of the Mississippi. More, it had been tied up for weeks! And who could tell when it would move?

Nothing was done at the passes during the Civil War, and the bars worsened. In 1868-69, two steam-propelled dredges were built, but by 1873 the Engineers declared them worthless.

So it would appear that anybody with even a half-baked idea for opening a channel would be welcomed as a saviour. Well, almost anybody. Anybody the Corps of Engineers approved of, it seemed. And they didn't approve of brother Eads. Nor his ideas.

Eads was a civil engineer. His great feat had been the erection, almost miraculously, of the giant steel arch bridge across the Mississippi at St. Louis. Prior to that, during the War Between the States, he had worked wonders in building ironclads for the Federal fleet. And before THAT, he had already made a fortune in salvage and in raising steamboats, aided by his diving bell contraption.

At 37, before the war, he had already retired. But now this plan of Eads (for opening up the river's mouth), conceived after exhaustive study and experience, simply called for parallel jetties to be built seaward from the mouth of the pass, thus constricting the channel, causing the stream to flow faster, thereby picking up more deposits and carrying them far out into the gulf. The narrower the jetties, the faster the current, the deeper it would scour the channel. *Et voilá*, a self-perpetuating opening to the mightiest river in North America.

It was an old theorem of hydraulics — the carrying power of a current is in proportion to its velocity. Putting nature to work was the basic idea he proposed. But there was opposition.

The Army Engineers had meanwhile been trying to sell the powers that be on a ship canal from a point a few miles below Fort St. Philip, on the east bank of the river, about twenty miles from the mouth, connecting with Breton Sound, and thus into deep Gulf waters. This plan had been proposed as early as 1837, but had been put aside until 1858.

By the time the Army Engineers had gotten around to it again seriously, the cry for relief from the Mississippi Valley was deafening. So all kinds of surveys were made and committees appointed to promote the canal. Much criticism of the Engineers, for having done nothing in nearly forty years to relieve the problem, was voiced. Here, at last, was a way to get off the hook. Build a canal. Military engineers can build canals.

Such was the climate, then, in May, 1873, when James B. Eads, along with another delegation, this time Congressional, visited the mouth of the river to cluck into their beards about the pity of it all. Talk was about the coming canal, with its granite lock at the river end, 500 feet long, costing a total of eight million dollars, large enough for the biggest thing afloat.

Eads voiced his disagreement. He stated loudly and emphatically that the PROPER way to open the river to commerce was not by a costly and ineffective canal, but by parallel dykes or jetties at the mouth of one of the passes.

That did it. The storm of controversy broke out between the Engineers, New Orleans, and almost everybody else on one side, and Eads, a handful of believers, some St. Louis people, and Providence on the other.

To dramatize his proposal, Eads acted fast. By February of the following year, he went before Congress and offered to bet the United States Government that he could produce and maintain a 28-foot channel at the mouth of the Mississippi. The stake: ten million dollars if he succeeded. If he failed, the government owed him nothing!

The opponents of the jetties plan screamed. General A. A. Humphreys, Chief of Army Engineers, propounded learned reasons why it wouldn't work. New Orleans sent Ex-Governor Paul O. Hebert and Prof. C. G. Forshey, both West Pointers by the way, to Washington to fight for the canal and to silence this upstart. They claimed that the jetties would cause the waters to back up and flood the countryside. They said worms would eat the pilings of the jetties, anyway, and the bars would grow larger and larger.

Heavy guns were brought to bear. Eads answered volley for volley, with such prominent personages as Senator Carl Schurz on his side.

". . . For thirty-seven years they (the Army Engineers) have been planning and reporting upon the matter, and scratching and scraping at the mouth of the Mississippi, and today the depth of water is no greater than it was then . . ." he boomed in the Senate.

The Orleanians fired back:

". . . Would you, can you, honorable Senators,

at such a moment, contemplate or tolerate the half-insane proposition of strangers, who can know nothing of the habits of our inexorable enemy, to dam up his waters at the mouth by jetties or wing dams, that must inevitably send back the flood waters like a tide to the very city of New Orleans, or beyond, and complete the impending destruction? . . ."

Commissions came and went, one to Europe to study the mouths of famous rivers and the effects of jetties such as Eads proposed. Eads went, too. When they all returned, word began to get around that Eads' proposition wasn't as "half-insane" as his opponents thought. Eventually, the jetties bills passed, though on reduced terms; Eads was assigned the job at the narrower and shallower South Pass, instead of Southwest Pass as he had suggested.

Eads was disappointed in the site and the reduced terms, but he was as resolved as ever. At a huge victory banquet in St. Louis on March 25, 1875, he showed himself a God-fearing man of stature:

". . . Every phenomenon and apparent eccentricity of the river — its scouring and depositing action, its caving banks, the formation of the bars at its mouth, the effect of the waves and tides of the sea upon its currents and deposits — is controlled by laws as immutable as the Creator . . . I therefore undertake the work with faith based upon the ever-constant ordinances of God himself; and so certain as he will spare my life and faculties, I will give to the Mississippi River through His Grace and by the application of His laws, a deep, open, safe, and permanent outlet to the sea."

In June work began. The Creator was also smiling on Eads when he selected his associates and his immediate command. They were experts. They persevered against nearly overwhelming odds, there at the barren wastes, in the mosquito-ridden mud flats at the river's mouth.

Although the work to be done was enormous, Eads' plan was comparatively simple — he would first constrict the channel of the river at South Pass by making two artificial banks 700 feet apart and two miles long. The materials would come from nearby forests of pine, for the pilings; and from nearby river banks, for the willow trees, which were in inexhaustible abundance there.

Weaving the willows into gigantic mattresses, weighting them with stones and sinking them to the bottom of the river to be anchored by piles,

Capt. James B. Eads. He re-opened the Mississippi and brought shipping back to New Orleans.

the man-made banks slowly began to rise from the river bottom. The current began to quicken and to dig at its bed.

There was no overnight success. It took eight months to deepen the old eight-foot channel over the bar to thirteen feet, but dig the river did! Then just when the clouds were lifting — the Army again.

Finances were precarious. There was constant needling from the soldier-engineers. Stockholders of the South Pass Jetty Company, formed by Eads and his backers for the interim financing, became restless. An attempt by a large ship to get through the channel ended in failure. At Eads' suggestion, the steamboat *Grand Republic* was hired to bring the stockholders down from as far as St. Louis to inspect the work. When it arrived, he had a 16-foot depth to report. There was jubilation, only to be dampened by the arrival of one Capt. Collins of the Engineers with a chart which he said proved serious shoaling beyond the bar, caused by the jetties. The *Grand Republic* returned upriver in gloom.

But all was not lost. Along came Capt. Gager of the Cromwell line with the ocean-going *Hudson*, willing to bring his vessel in over the new route. Despite a falling tide, Gager pushed the *Hudson* through South Pass, the first deepwater ship to negotiate the passageway.

Before Eads Cleared River's Mouth. Government
ship at work removing the bar at Southwest Pass.
Sketch by Alfred R. Waud.

That summer of 1876, Eads virtually manipulated the entire flow of the river to get certain results he deemed necessary at South Pass. Then, on October 5, the sun-baked men stood breathless as the sounding line paid out in the channel. Twenty feet!

Even then, victory was not in sight. Eads seemed to attract trouble at this point. The Army Engineers had not let up; government payments were withheld as malicious rumors were spread that all was not well at South Pass. In August, 1877, he was forced to telegraph his Chief Assistant, E. L. Corthell, to discharge the whole force unless they were willing to work for certificates of indebtedness. All but two of the 76 men of the force signed up. A narrow squeeze, but the work went on.

Even nature seemed to rebel. A stubborn stretch of jetty bottom wouldn't budge. Eads had to invent a new type of hydraulic dredge, build it, and get it into operation — almost overnight.

Twenty-two feet! Washington relented and sent some funds to pay the men. Then a worse enemy hit. Yellow Fever. Eleven men died of the scourge. In December, Eads capped the jetties

with huge blocks of concrete, some weighing 260 tons. Success was around the corner, in the bag, this time. Or was it? Severe winter storms almost destroyed the whole job. Spur cribs had to be hastily built to stop the racing waves from eating away the year's endeavor.

But Eads' calculations had been solid. Nature was surely on his side, as he had known it would be, and on July 10, 1879, four years after the first pile was driven in the muddy expanse, the middle depth in the channel measured thirty feet at average flood tide, and the bar at the head of the pass had been swept into the Gulf.

In one year after the completion of the jetties, 840 steamers alone had used South Pass; New Orleans again began to assume its place as a leading world port.

What about James B. Eads? Did he slink back into graceful retirement, to bask in the glory of his accomplishments? Not this man, who was called the greatest engineer of his world. Within months, he had convinced Congress of the feasibility and practicality, and was already working out plans, for building a ship-railway across the Isthmus of Tehuantepec in Mexico!

Great Bridge, at St. Louis. Designed and built by Eads. During construction, hot weather expanded some of the steel work so it couldn't be made to fit; but they packed ice-filled gunny sacks around the "recalcitrant" parts, and brought them back to normal size.

Early Pilot Boat. Off the Mississippi's Mouth.
Lithograph by A. St. Aulaire (1835).

Towboat Towing Cotton Ships Up to New Orleans.
Oil painting by J. E. Evans and A. Arnold (c. 1850).

Diving Bell at Bayou Tunica - Mississippi River

T. K. Wharton Dec. 6 1853 12 M.

MATTRESSES PARTLY SUNK.

(Above) Diving Bell at Work in Tunica Bayou. From Sketch by Capt. T. K. Wharton.

(Left) Mattresses of Jetties at South Pass Partly Sunk.

(Below) South Pass While Eads Was Clearing It.

PORT EADS FROM THE GULF.

HOTEL PORT EADS.

Hotel at Port Eads (South Pass) during
construction work.

South Pass Before Eads Cleared It.
Sketch by Alfred R. Waud.

Belle Grove. This beautiful Greek Revival mansion
furnished an outstanding example of plantation living
on the grand scale. It was burned in 1952.

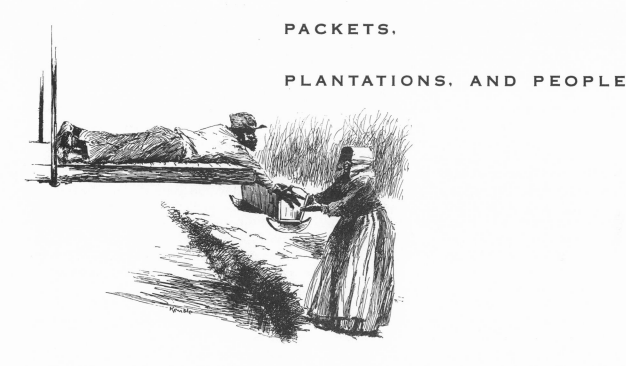

PACKETS,

PLANTATIONS, AND PEOPLE

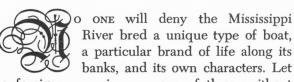

O ONE will deny the Mississippi River bred a unique type of boat, a particular brand of life along its banks, and its own characters. Let a foreigner examine any one of these, without knowing where it came from, and he will be likely to say, "That looks like a Mississippi River boat (plantation house, or gambler)." The Great River left an indelible stamp.

Name another river in the world which has prompted a duel in its honor. Here is the tale as told in an early guide book of New Orleans:

In 1854, a Parisian, the Chevalier Tomasi, visited the city of New Orleans. Tomasi, it appears, was a paragon of knowledge on the subject of hydraulics, and most other topics.

This Tomasi published *A Communication on the Hydraulics of the Mississippi*, which, it appears, was a sneering indictment of the uncouth Creoles of New Orleans, and of Americans in general: An "ignorant tribe expelled from Europe for stupidity or other crimes;" only the Academy of Science in Paris was the authoritative source of information in physics, as the Sorbonne was

supreme in the study of ethics; only he, Tomasi, could control the Mississippi, either stop it entirely, make it deeper, or restrict it within boundaries specified by science.

Well, Americans, and particularly Creoles, can take just so much. At one point in a discussion, while M. Tomasi carried on as above, a Creole ventured to suggest that "the Mississippi is a very headstrong stream, and possibly your calculations were assumed for the smaller streams of Europe and would not be found applicable to so mighty a stream."

"How little you Americans know of the world," Tomasi hissed. "Know that there are rivers in Europe so large that the Mississippi is a mere rill, figuratively speaking."

Inflammatory words there, Tomasi!

"Sir. I will never allow the Mississippi to be insulted or disparaged in my presence by an arrogant pretender to knowledge," exclaimed the Creole in the highest, most polite "code duello" dudgeon, followed immediately by the flick of a glove across the Parisian's cheek.

A duel with swords followed, and the Chevalier Tomasi came off second best.

"A day or two afterwards," goes the story, "the Chevalier appeared in the streets wearing what the surgeons call a 'T bandage' about face and jaw. He wore quite a ghostly aspect, and when asked about it, remarked, 'C'est rien; une égratignure seulement', and stripped away the bandage to show that the sword of his antagonist had duly vindicated the Mississippi by passing entirely across the mouth of the defamer from one cheek to the other."

However, the Chevalier Tomasi got in a last lick at American pride.

"But," said he, replacing his bandage, "I should have killed my antagonist but for the miserable character of your American steel. . . . "

What other great river (save the Mississippi) can boast that a 21-year-old crippled girl has swum across it and back without stopping, at a point where said river is as wide as the Great River is at New Orleans. Yet one Isabel Bentel, crippled, performed the feat starting at the New Orleans side, on Sept. 1, 1930.

Or what impelled a man named Snite to WALK down the river's length in February, 1907? Walk he did, on special buoyant, pontoon-like shoes, to carve himself a special niche in the river's history.

Numerous strange figures dart in and out of that history, but perhaps none are more interesting than two individuals who revealed many fascinating aspects of life along the river's banks during the decade that followed the War Between the States.

One of them is an Englishman, Alfred Waud. Tall, blue-eyed, bearded, Waud was a quick-sketch artist. He had traveled with the Union Army during the war, as an artist for Harper's Weekly, and posterity owes him a great debt for his on-the-spot sketches of the great conflict, long before the days of photo-journalism. Brady, to be sure, was busy making plates in his cumbersome dark-room on wheels. But photo-engraving was yet to come for magazine illustrating, and the sketch artist was the man whose drawing was worth more than reams of wordage.

Waud's brother, William, also an artist for Harper's, had followed the Union fleet up the passes of the Mississippi in 1862. He was with Farragut's ships at the harrowing "running of the forts" below New Orleans, leaving us panoramic sketches of vivid detail. He landed at New Orleans after the surrender, and sent back to Harper's sketches of scenes in the great southern metropolis under the heel of "Silver Spoons" Butler.

A few years later Alfred Waud also came to New Orleans (in 1866). He was then with Harpers' and on this trip he made some memorable sketches of life in the Crescent City in the troublous days of Reconstruction.

In 1871, Alfred Waud came South, now under the auspices of Every Saturday, a staid, Boston-published journal of some popularity in its day. Waud was accompanied on this trip by a reporter who was no stranger to the river and its cities. His name was Ralph Keeler, a man with a keen sense of humor, sharpened years before when, prior to the war, he had been a minstrel with Spaulding and Rogers' showboat, the Floating Palace.

Keeler and Waud were a pair. Adventurous, incisive, intellectual, they sensed a "story" and followed it up, regardless of whether it was important to the "big picture" or just an amusing sidelight. Hence, their series, On The Mississippi is replete with good humor, good sketching and good reporting.

When they came "down the river, down to New Orleans" in 1871, Keeler was an ambitious, restless thirty one; Waud was forty-three and at the peak of his powers. Keeler had just published his first book, Vagabond Adventures, and the assignment to accompany Waud undoubtedly came as a result of his new fame as a journalist. Waud's speed in sketching was legendary, it being said that he could catch a subject in life-like detail before the subject was aware he was being sketched.

Billed as our "Special Artist and Correspondent," Keeler and Waud came down to New Orleans by railroad at a time when railroads were starting to supply the creature comforts which had been standard on steamboats for years. In fact, this was the golden era of the steamboat and perhaps the boys wanted to study the contrast between the two modes of transportation. At any rate, they wanted to start from the mouth of the river and work up, and, from Boston, Massachusetts, the rails offered the quickest route.

Arriving at New Orleans, they merely paused to mention the city, as they were anxious to get to the mouth of the Misissippi. "Of this picturesque city," wrote Keeler, "we shall say nothing until we have come to it regularly in our ascent of the Mississippi."

The two reporters seemed to attract unusual

people; to fall into quaint surroundings; they had many rare opportunities to collect material for their writing and sketching. Right off the bat, in their quest for transportation to the mouth of the river, they happened on a "new steam launch which had just completed a three-mile trial-trip to the satisfaction of its buildiers."

They named her *Great Eastern,* in honor of the hapless British giant of the Atlantic. They loaded her up with stores for the voyage, "with a great many things which we did not need, and forgot a great many things which we did need."

Equipped with a crew which could only be called "motley", the 35-foot boat started down the river in a blast of toots which "sounded like a Cunarder," according to Keeler. "Capt. Fielding was personally acquainted with all the alligators between New Orleans and the Southwest Pass. . . . The alligators seemed to know him, too, for they did not stir from the oozy bank on which they lay sunning themselves."

The engineer was a Maine man who had been in the Haiti Navy and who promptly caught his pants on fire, losing them to the river. The cook, the third and final member of the crew, was also the deck-hand. Keeler said he cooked like a deck-hand, and handled ropes like a cook.

Thus, gliding down the river slowly, pencils moving busily across sketchpad and notebook, Keeler and Waud eagerly absorbed everything they saw and heard. Past the plains of Chalmette they went, with suitable comment by Keeler; down the Lower Coast, past Colonel Stanton's plantation, with accompanying sketch by Waud of the Old Colonel, a Yale man, galloping along the levee, dog at his horse's heeels.

An appropriate quote by Keeler from *Lotus Eaters* says better than Keeler or Waud could, what the Lower Coast looks like:

> In the afternoon they came into a land
> In which it seems always afternoon.
> All around the Coast the languid air did swoon,
> Breathing like one that hath a weary dream.

Shadows of cypress trees and Spanish moss, in the distance. Lonely echoes sent back from the banks, of the little toot of the *Great Eastern.* The river was high, and one actually looked down at the countryside, an effect which still startles the stranger. "A large, rusty English ship passes us by in silence; a feat which we held, I hope, in sufficient contempt."

Sugar House Point, river "tows", and then the party arrived at Woodland, the sugar plantation

Unloading Cotton on the Levee, New Orleans.

Roustabouts. Sketch by Alfred R. Waud. The horseman emblem (upper right) was carried by the Rob't. E. Lee on her jackstaff.

"The Parting Song". Sketch by Alfred R. Waud.

Memphians, in Front of Hotel Peabody, Memphis.
Sketch by Alfred R. Waud.

Passengers (First Class, in modern parlance).
Sketch by Alfred R. Waud.

Deck Passengers (Equivalent of steerage).
Sketch by Alfred R. Waud.

of Mr. Bradish Johnson, one of several he owned, but his favorite.

Waud and Keeler made the most of this visit. Johnson was absent, but his overseer, a Mr. Forsythe, rolled out the carpet. The reporters studied plantation life minutely, from such details as the pay received by the ex-slaves, to the probable success of Mr. Johnson's experiment with importing Chinese hands, to the details of sugar-making, to methods of causing sickness by voodoo (hiding dried lizards under the house).

The Negroes couldn't quite understand what Waud and Keeler were doing, poking into the plantation's nooks and crannies. They followed the pair around curiously, as did "stray mosquitoes and two or three dogs." Finally, the fireman of the draining machine at the sugar house solved the mystery by anouncing to the crowd that Waud and Keeler had "come to build another engine house."

More mosquitoes, an encounter with an alligator, a fond "Farewell," and the *Great Eastern* pushed on down the Mississippi, past "miles and miles of almost continuous villages" consisting of sugar houses, pretty residences, and Negro quarters. Then, the scene of the naval battle of a scant nine years previous, when Farragut ran the guns of Forts Jackson on the West bank, and St. Philip on the East. Gaunt skeletons of the gallant ships and mortar boats still lay half buried in the shallows. Here was the *Varuna*, which took six Confederate boats with her to glory; the *Morgan*, a "large side-wheeled steamer casemated with cotton and transformed into a Confederate gunboat." Upon the remains of the *Morgan's* smoke stack, the U.S. Corps of Engineers had erected a flagstaff for surveying purposes. Reflecting upon this, Keeler stated:

"Thus it happens, oddly enough, that one of the most heroic wrecks of the Rebellion is used by the government to measure its strength, or — as that phraseology is somewhat fanciful — is at least made to do the State some service." Mr. Keeler was writing for a Boston publication.

The Great Eastern tied up at Fort Jackson, still manned by the military in 1871, though a dismal post, to be sure.

"The United States soldier is probably never consigned to a worse place than this," Keeler wrote. Everywhere, water. The entire garrison dwelt on stilts like a Venice in the wilderness. This fort, Keeler explained, together with Fort St. Philip across the river, was under one command. Fort St. Philip was built during the Spanish occupation.

The forts were, of course, in Union hands at the war's outbreak, but surrendered to the Confederates shortly afterward. Later they surrendered again, this time to the Union forces of Farragut. But the story of the first surrender is worth telling.

The story was told by "one of the victorious besiegers," a member of the proud New Orleans battalion, the Washington Artillery. Three days after the secession of Louisiana, a detachment of "these warriors" went down by steamboat to take possession of the forts in the name of the Confederacy.

The forts were in "command" of an old U.S. Army Sergeant named Bill Boswell, who, it appeared, spent most of his time in New Orleans. On hearing of the expedition, he hastened to his post, arriving somehow ahead of the beseigers. Let Keeler tell it:

"The detachment landed in due time, leaving their arms on board the boat. Confronting them at the sally-port stood Sergeant Boswell with an old sabre and the challenge:

" 'Who goes there?'

" 'We demand the surrender of this fort in the name of the State of Louisiana.'

"To which the sergeant replied, elevating his drawn sabre, 'I will never surrender.'

" 'Then we will charge upon you.'

" 'Come on,' cried the doughty Boswell.

" 'Stormers, to the front'; and at the command, the column advanced, each man with a bottle of champagne extended in his right hand.

"Down went the sergeant's sword. Surveying the ranks of the besiegers for a moment, he said, 'Gentlemen, I surrender at discretion.' "

The lonesome officers of the fort treated the journalists royally; and the pair retaliated by staging a moonlight ride on the *Great Eastern* for their hosts and their hosts' ladies. Next day, Waud and Keeler pushed on down toward the passes.

They found that below Fort Jackson there was very little to see, outside of a few shacks occupied by "poor French Creoles and poorer Negroes." Sugar fields disappeared, and rice fields were seen. Finally, nothing but marsh, and then first on one side, then on the other, the Gulf. At the extreme end of the river, they came across the domain of one Dick Cubit, described as "half man, half-alligator," in the Mike Fink tra-

Clerk of the *Natchez* Off Duty.
Sketch by Alfred R. Waud.

Cape Girardeau. Boasted one permanent hotel and one intermittent one. Sketch by Alfred R. Waud.

dition. But evidently Cubit was real, although our reporters did not meet him personally. Yet in Cubit's kingdom, perhaps the remnant of the Balize, his word was law. Actually, he was the law, a sort of Judge Bean of the passes. He dispensed his own peculiar brand of whiskey and law, being a bar-keep and Justice of the Peace. Keeler tells one story of Cubit's bench-side manner:

"An Englishman and an Italian had gotten into a fight down at Pass a-l'Outre, and the Englishman, badly beaten, appealed to Judge Cubit. The judge took a couple of drinks, removed his hat, and said that court was open. Having heard the stories of each man patiently to the end, Dick fined them fifteen dollars apiece.

"'I shall appeal,' exclaimed the aggrieved Englishman.

"'Appeal, hell, you've got to pay the fine first!' said Dick; and so justice was maintained."

At the very mouth of Southwest Pass, Keeler and Waud encountered the fleet of pre-jetty dredges, keeping the passes open. They were the *Essayons,* and the *Achilles,* "which the pilots and other people of the passes pronounce in various unclassical ways." A buoy marked the wreck of the courageous Confederate iron-clad *Louisiana,* and Keeler paused in his narrative to tell its long, bloody story.

The reporters discovered the strange phenomena called mud lumps, small islands of mud which mysteriously rise out of the marsh around the river's mouth, still not sufficiently explained by geologists, and still the object of considerable study. The reporters edged out into the gulf to reach an island on which a tottering old lighthouse was still maintained by an aged German. He first threatened them with a gun, and then invited them into his rude shack and regaled them with songs and accordion accompaniment. This old fellow, an ex-soldier, was indeed the last man on the Mississippi, for beyond his hut there is nothing but water.

Back to the U. S. Engineers and the *Essayons,* and the intrepid pair turned upriver once again. At Pilottown, the base of the "bar" and "river" pilots who take the big ships into the river from the gulf, and then up to the river ports, they examined the quiet existence of these skilled men, and it is much the same with them today.

Living in clean, comfortable quarters, the pilots talk, sleep, play cards, and eat, while waiting for the observer in their watchtower to report an incoming ship with signal raised indicating a pilot is awaited. A tightly-knit little group, then as now, Keeler reported that the "bar-pilots associate themselves in independent companies of five or six, and each crew has its headquarters before which its boats are moored. . ."

Waud and Keeler were fascinated by the pilots and their tales, by the carefree life at Pilottown. They dismissed the *Great Eastern,* since the pilots promised to put them aboard an incoming steamer shortly expected, bound upriver for New Orleans.

The men wandered around the town, found it to be another set of houses and walks perched on stilts. A parrot greeted them with "O, you robbers!," and while enjoying a copious dinner — these dinners served up by the pilots are still famous — they heard harrowing stories of pilots turned blockade-runners during the war.

The steamship *Victor* finally came and took Waud and Keeler away from Pilottown, and after an overnight trip, they arrived back in New Orleans. More excitement awaited them there — there was a crevasse upriver at Bonnet Carré plantation.

Post-haste they took passage on a little steamboat for Bonnet Carré, about 30 miles above New Orleans. Bonnet Carré had once been proposed by the wealthy philanthropist, John McDonogh, as the ideal site for a spillway into Lake Pontchartrain above the city, to relieve the latter in time of threatened flood. This area was the closest approach of the river to this lake, above New Orleans. The flood of 1871 proved that it was useful as a spillway, but not until 1931 did Congress finally appropriate the necessary funds, and the Bonnet Carré spillway today protects New Orleans from being flooded. It has been opened three times, and has worked admirably, just as McDonogh said it would, back in 1824.

To Bonnet Carré plantation, then, Keeler and Waud hurried, encountering the cast of unusual characters they always ran across. There was the "Creole pedagogue," right out of Irving's "Creole Village," wrote Keeler, who could speak no English, and sat reading the popular French Newspaper of New Orleans, *L'Abeille.*

"'Nobody,' he said to Keeler who understood French, 'nobody reads les Journaux Americains because they are in favor of the Prussians.'" The Prussians had just licked the French, and here in this remote former colony of la belle France (of 1803), was a schoolteacher, loyal to the last.

Keeler described the scene of devastation, while Waud sketched furiously, barely missing being swept into the torrent when the levee on which he was standing gave way and fell into the river.

They are struck by the impassive attitude of the people at the crevasse. No one hurries, no one in tears, no excitement, no complaints in spite of the total loss to so many. The planter in Waud's picture has been ruined three times in this manner.

Before a rainstorm drove them back to the steamboat, they met on old darkey who offered to bet a hundred dollars he could "stop dat water." There being no takers, he stalked off saying, "Well, I lose a heap dis year — corn. But I don't ce-are, for I'se a horse-doctor. Dey may stop dere own crevasse."

Far more exciting to Waud and Keeler was the return trip on the steamboat. For want of passengers, or just the plain ennui, the crew had taken to drink and decided to make a "picnic excursion" of the voyage.

Just before sundown they spotted a deer swimming in the middle of the river, and a deer hunt was on. The pilot gave chase.

"It was unanimously resolved to take the deer alive, and our boat coming up to him, about a dozen drunken men, deck-hands, cooks, and what-not, tried slipping nooses everywhere about the poor animal, except his head."

The deer got away and the boat "crowded on all steam" after it. The skiff was put out, with a couple of more drunks aboard, and "there began one of the most ludicrous chases that could well be imagined." It ended up with one of the men stripping, jumping into the river, and swimming after the deer, which quickly outdistanced him. The skiff was lost. The man's clothes were lost, and the deer escaped completely. The only winners were Keeler and Waud who got it all on paper delightfully.

The "Special Artist and Correspondent" next turned their attention to New Orleans. Their description of the levee and the people who frequented the docks constitutes as graphic a picture of that period as the researcher can find. They also covered every phase of the city's life, from the cock fights to the St. Louis Cathedral masses.

Striking out upriver for Baton Rouge, Natchez, Vicksburg and St. Louis, Waud and Keeler give these cities the same close scrutiny. They passed the *Rob't. E. Lee* and the *Natchez,* it being one year after the great race, and excitement was still running high over the outcome. They made part of their upriver journey on the *Natchez* and Waud sketched Capt. T. P. Leathers. They cover, again in detail, "A Day on a Mississippi Steamboat." Aboard the *City of Cairo* they had the exciting experience of a minor explosion. At St. Louis, they examined the wineries, and journeyed by train for visits to Iron Mountain and Pilot Knob.

They liked St. Louis, and the city returned the feeling. An artist for a German-American newspaper there turned the tables, and sketched them. One of Waud's cleverest contributions is a page of sketches of St. Louis faces, similar to the one he had done of New Orleans personages.

The climax of the trip came when they received news of the Chicago fire, and were rushed by their editor to that city. Two vivid sketches of the fire, plus Keeler's very vivid description, are their contributions to the story of that disaster, and are the climax of their trip.

Waud explored other fields thereafter, living until 1891, when, while on another assignment sketching the battlefields of the South to illustrate a series of war stories, he died at Marietta, Ga. Keeler was less lucky; he did not die in bed peacefully. Sent to Cuba as a correspondent for the *New York Tribune* in 1873, he mysteriously disappeared from his ship while en route. It was thought that he had been murdered and his body tossed overboard.

These two, observing, asking, sketching, caught many glimpses of life along the river of the gracious mode of living that is all but gone. However, never lighting long anywhere, they missed some of the finer facets of plantation life.

The river was the focus of existence, for it was the artery of transportation before the railroads spread their steel networks, and the roads their ribbons of concrete. In the lower Mississippi Valley, sugar and cotton accounted for the enormous fortunes built up in the plantation country.

Many of the plantations stemmed from early grants to colonial families. Others were bought as Americans moved into the Louisiana territory after its purchase in 1803. Through the normal course of buying and selling, inheritance and crop failures, not to mention the vicissitudes of the Civil War, great land holdings were consolidated into larger tracts, or divided up into infinitesimal slices and then gobbled up by wealthier neighbors. Few of the original large planta-

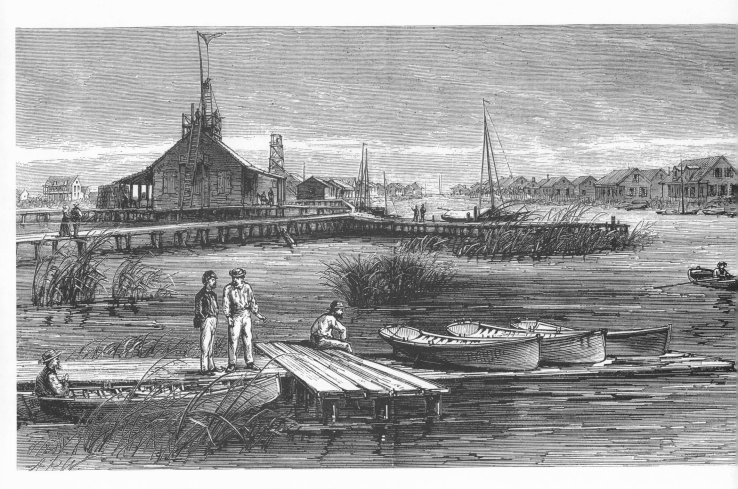

(*Above*) Pilot-Town and Telegraph Station in Lower
Reaches of the River. Sketches by Alfred R. Waud.

La Fourche Packet Landing, New Orleans.
Sketch by Alfred R. Waud.

Looking Toward Jackson R. R. Depot, New Orleans.
Sketch by Alfred R. Waud.

Helena, Arkansas. Sketch by Alfred R. Waud.

Napoleon. Here the famous free-for-all occurred (see p. 16). Sketch by Alfred R. Waud. Keeler, Waud's companion, notes Napoleon "used to have the reputation of the wickedest town on the Mississippi."

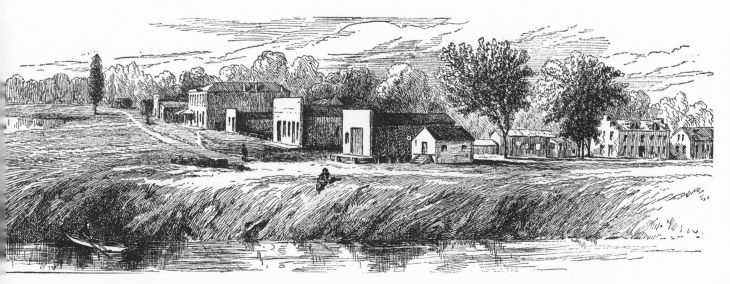

(*Above*) Slab Hut: A Mississippi Residence.
Sketch by Alfred R. Waud.

(*Below*) Memphis. Sketch by Alfred R. Waud.
On such wharfboats as this, Devol, the great
gambler, set up his games (see p. 195).

Beer-Garden, St. Louis. Sketch by Alfred R. Waud.

Hailing a Steamboat. Sketch by Alfred R. Waud.

tions remain intact today, and even fewer in the hands of descendants of the original owners.

The center of operations on a typical plantation was the big house, usually taking its name from that of the entire plantation. The decade of the 1850's was an era of plantation-house building on an elaborate scale. John Hampton Randolph, of the Virginia Randolphs, built "Nottaway" in 1857; and John Andrews, another Virginian, who had migrated to Louisiana, built "Belle Grove" that same year. As an example of Mississippi plantation living on the grand scale, "Belle Grove" was it.

His was a 6000-acre tract fronting the river. Andrews hired from New Orleans an outstanding architect to build a Greek revival mansion second to none. No extravagance was spared in furnishing it with the best European tapestries, curtains, furniture, and other accoutrements. Its spacious grounds, private race track, gardens and other buildings were the talk of the plantation age, and its fame spread beyond the boundaries of Louisiana.

William Edwards Clement, whose family plantation, "Retreat" was nearby, writes of "Belle Grove" in his interesting memoirs, *Plantation Life on the Mississippi* (Pelican Press). He describes the fabulous wedding of Emily Andrews to Edward Schiff of Paris, France:

"There were fifty house guests who stayed a week and 500 additional guests who came just for the wedding, all with their maids and valets who arrived by steamboat. Imbert, the famous New Orleans chef and caterer, came with his entire staff a week in advance to prepare his daube glacés, his pyramids of nougat, and his incomparable salads and bouillons, and remained throughout the entire season of fetes.

"The great green porticoes of Belle Grove were hung with a thousand lights which shone far out into the river, dancing cloths were laid over the lower floors and the chambers were all festooned with flowers. The feast was so bounteous that the very boatmen on the Mississippi who brought 'the dear five hundred' up the river to Belle Grove landing came in for their share. . . ."

Belle Grove, like many another mansion, passed from its original owner to a neighbor, and was to see even greater splendor before it, too, became an economic unreality in the 1920's. For years this imposing, empty spectre of a bygone age stood proudly, with the river moving ever closer to its columns. Once it stood a mile from the levee; now scarcely a hundred yards separates it from its inevitable watery grave. One by one, the massive oak trees had to go, as the river moved closer. Then, on March 15, 1952, a fire raced through the "noble ruin" and hastened the end. Although some of the walls remain standing, all the woodwork was consumed.

By contrast, the family plantation of one of the authors of these *Tales* stood on a several-hundred-acre site at Tunica Landing, (La.), above Baton Rouge. A small cotton planter, Grandfather made a fine living from the soil, on a less pretentious scale by far than Belle Grove. His plantation didn't even have a name, although his store and the Tunica Landing, which he tended, were familiar landmarks along the river.

He shared one thing with the Andrews of Belle Grove and their successors. He, too, had the river eating away at his plantation. In the late 1880's there finally was no choice. The old house had been moved back until there was no longer anywhere to move it. And still the river came, and the floods. The sons can still remember, as youngsters, catching crawfish and shrimp through the fireplaces when river water lapped at the floorboards. They can recall steamboats rescuing the family from housetops, and the thought of the small "mail-boat" packets, their sternwheels churning across flooded fields far inland on rescue missions, still gives them a light-hearted chuckle, as it did to their boyish souls 60 years ago.

One day in the early 1930's, son and grandson journeyed back to Tunica Landing to look for the site of Grandfather's plantation. Very little had survived out of those happy days of boyhood memory. Standing on the edge of the river's bank, Father pointed to a sandbar across the river.

"There's all that's left of the old place," he said. "Like the darkies used to say, 'The ribber done come an' took it away.' "

A moment or two later, an old colored man came strolling across the field. Father hailed him. "Do you know who used to live on this place?"

The old fellow, with hair and beard the same color as the gray moss swinging from a nearby oak, scratched his head as if to stir up his memory.

"Why, dis here was Mistah Charlie Samuel's place," he said.

"Did he have any children?" asked Father.

Another pause. "Oh, yes. He had a little boy named Mister Joe, and another little fat boy named Mister Ernest," replied the old man.

Belle Grove. Built 1852; burned 1952. No extravagance was spared in furnishing it. Its fame spread beyond the boundaries of Louisiana.

Sugar House, Belair Plantation (c. 1890).

Cane Shed, Same Plantation.

Old Negro. Probably remembered slave days, since this photo was taken in c. 1890.

Belair (c. 1890). The levee ran back almost to porch of house. One more move by the levee and no house!

Old Slave Quarters at Belair.

"Well, I'm Mister Joe, Uncle," said Father, tears streaming down his face. After much hand-pumping, mopping of eyes on both sides, and a gift of $10 for "old time's sake," the old man hobbled off into oblivion.

Life at Tunica Landing, before the river came and took it away, had many pleasant moments. The trips in to St. Francisville, a long journey by oxcart, and the even longer ride to the nearest railroad to go to the big city, when for some reason that was more expedient than the steamboat, were outstanding events.

Then there was the time when Grandmother Samuel was giving birth to the youngest of the four children. Captain Blanche Douglass Leathers held the sternwheel *Natchez* against the dock at Tunica Landing, and waited there until all was well, in case there was need for a speed run to New Orleans. In gratitude, Grandmother named the young daughter Blanche, and Blanche will tell you about it in person today, if you ask.

Sometimes a plantation owner made a couple of good crops and decided to build a larger, more imposing home as befitted a prosperous planter. George Lorio of Star Plantation, across the river and above New Orleans, raised a fine mansion with a porch all around the house. He sent to Europe for fine stained glass with which to make a decorative effect in the roof.

Up in the attic, Lorio pére had his own private tobacco-curing establishment. Lee Lorio, his son, still recalls "Papa's long leaves of tobacco hanging up there." Then one hot day, the sun came beaming into the attic through those fancy stained glasses and set fire to some of Papa's tobacco-curing gear. Before help could arrive, the pride of the Lorios was burned to the ground.

The balls, the gay dancers waltzing through marbled halls, the smiling butlers with trays of juleps were part of the scene along the river; romantic novels and movies got that much straight. There is lots of documentary evidence to substantiate the old story about the planter who lost his plantation at cards going down the river on a steamboat — and won it back on the return trip upriver.

Tales of war heroism, the real thing, abound in family annals, of staunch plantation matrons holding the Yankees at bay, while faithful old Mammy hid the plate in the cistern; of romances between neighboring sons and daughters ending in marriages — or in duels. As with any such system of close-knit family domains, strung out side by side, there were bound to be feuds, and the Mississippi spawned some brutal ones. Such as when the river got high, and it was easier to row across the river in the dead of night and cut somebody else's levee, than to take a chance on the crevasse opening up on one's own place. So in times of high water, planters posted guards armed with shotguns and pistols along these levees and this resulted in more than one pitched battle, and caused feuds which have never healed.

Perhaps the most picturesque and quaint revelation of plantation life concerns one of the oldest, the holding of Jean Etienne de Boré, situated according to a rough calculation in a part of what is now Audubon Park at New Orleans, exactly six miles above the French Quarter, and fronting on the Mississippi River.

The description of the Boré plantation was written by his grandson, Charles Gayarré, venerable dean of Louisiana historians, who as a boy lived there. Bridging the gap from colonial Louisiana to the twilight of the 19th century, Gayarré served to kindle the spark of interest in that almost forgotten era of which we can barely feel the warmth today.

Writing in *Harper's* in 1887, he described "A Louisiana Sugar Plantation of the Old Regime." Boré was the patriarch around whom gathered the members of his family, his sons-in-law and their families. Gayarré was the son of Boré's youngest daughter. Boré had been a "mousquetaire", or member of the royal bodyguard of France; Gayarré's paternal grandsire was a "real contador", one of those sent by the King of Spain to take possession of Louisiana in 1769.

So the young boy lived in a setting of importance. And he saw historic personages come and go at the Boré plantation and was known and liked by a frequent visitor, Gen. Andrew Jackson. Before this time, Boré had played host to the Duke of Orleans and his two brothers, the Count of Beaujolais and the Duke of Montpensier, in the large, airy rooms of the plantation house.

In one paragraph, Gayarré sets the tone of the place:

"This plantation was sagaciously and tastefully laid out for beauty and productiveness. The gardens occupied a large area, and at once astonished the eye by the magnificience of their shady avenues of orange trees. Unbroken retreats of myrtle and laurel defied the rays of the sun. Flowers of every description perfumed the air. Extensive orchards produced every fruit of which the climate was susceptible. By judicious culture,

there had been obtained remarkable success in producing an abundance of juicy grapes, every bunch of which, however, when they began to ripen, was enveloped in a sack of wire to protect them against the depredations of birds. The fields were cultivated with such a careful observance of the variable exigencies of every successive season that there was no such thing as a short or half crop, or no crop at all. This was reserved for much later days. But under the administration of Etienne de Boré, during a period of about 25 years, from the first ebullition of the sugar kettle in 1795 to the time of his death in 1820, every crop was regularly the same within a few hogsheads . . ."

And Gayarré adds: "When, however, he ceased to exist, this seat of order and prosperity became a chaos of disorder and ruin, and the estate finally passed away from the family into the hands of strangers."

Boré was the first Louisiana planter to granulate sugar. But, besides this profitable sugar crop, the plantation produced bountifully of meat, fowl and vegetables, both for its own use and for sale to other establishments. Each morning, wagonloads of the plantation's produce were dispatched to New Orleans, where they were turned over to "Agathe and Marie, who were the occupants and guardians of the town house of Boré . . . Josephine, a handsome, strong-limbed, and light-footed Mulatress, with another female assistant of darker color, sold the milk and butter with wonderful rapidity, and both were back at the plantation by 10 a.m. with the mail, the daily papers, and whatever else they had to bring . . ."

Gayarré recalled that each morning before going to the fields, a bell rang and all the Negroes came and knelt for prayers. The same ceremony took place in the evening after work was over. It was a thrill for the young boy, the first time he was asked to preside at the prayers.

It is interesting to note that the plantation's master never raised hogs. This was left to the slaves, and they were paid handsomely by the master for the nice, fat porkers. From the Mississippi River they also caught fish and drift wood, for which later the master also paid. But the fish they cooked for themselves, in their own humble quarters, and regaled the nostrils of young Gayarré with a "savory smell."

Gayarré relates that the plantation was run with military precision and discipline, as befitted the household of a former "mousquetaire."

Sentries patrolled the boundaries and guarded the gates and sensitive areas, where "depredations might be committed." This did not stop the stealing of a magnificent pair of new carriage horses, spirited away without a trace, one night. So slick was the job, that the Negroes attributed their disappearance to "Zombi or Bouki, who rank among the spirits in which they believe."

Two impressive rows of pecan trees lined the avenue from the river road back to the plantation house. The house and the other buildings had the appearance of a "fortified place," complete with a sort of revetment and moat. The enclosure extended about 300 feet on each side of an entrance gate which opened into the courtyard. It was reminiscent of a French chateau, and evidently was so intended, to make M. de Boré and his guests and family feel at home.

Gayarré remembered the rumblings of the devastating New Madrid earthquake of 1811. He recalled clearly the excitement attending the Battle of New Orleans, the anxiety of the plantation folk as conflicting rumors drifted upriver, and the day before his 10th birthday, he heard the cannonading of that memorable conflict of Jan. 8, 1815, when his friend, Gen. Jackson, turned back the pride of English arms at Chalmette. What a thrill, when Boré finally returned and calmly said to the group in the parlor:

"Dismiss your fears; the Americans are victorious."

At eight o'clock breakfast, at two dinner, and seven p.m. supper, the Boré table was open to visitors, travelers, or even peddlers who might find themselves in the neighborhood at the time. In fact, Boré was offended if they did not stay for a meal, or spend the night.

The house was abundantly and comfortably furnished, Gayarré says, but was very plain "compared with the exigencies of modern times." This simplicity, he said, prevailed in the dwelling of the wealthiest planters. This was before the days of "keeping up with the Boudreaux."

But the table, that was something else again! The food and wines were superb, Gayarré wrote. Such dishes were concocted by "black Pierrot and yellow Charlotte"! Delicacies of which "the best cooks in France have dreamed." He told how Sambo cooked rice in an iron pot.

"I say iron, because it must be nothing else, and that rice must come out solid, retaining the exact shape of the pot, with a golden crust around its top and sides . . . Who but Sambo ever made

'grillades de sang de dinde,' looking and tasting like truffles? What a sauce! . . ."

This was life on a Mississippi River plantation of the old regime. A delectable life, based on a system which, alas, had barely a half-century more to exist.

NEGROES ALONG THE RIVER

But there was a shadow side, too, to this idyllic life on the plantations and steamboats along the great river. The Negro roustabout, of the "befo' de wah" era, shuffling on and off boats, loading heavy freight mostly on his "shoulder bones," had the same occasions for sorrow and sadness as his plantation counterpart. Not the least of these was the risk of being bought and sold out of hand, like any other commodity; indeed, he often figured as the stakes in a gambling game, or even as the prize in a raffle.

This happened to an unfortunate Negro, one Bill, whose master, finding himself in financial difficulties, sold chances on his human chattel, at ten dollars per chance. But Bill had a unique stroke of luck. A stranger who bought the last available chance, gave it to the boy to throw the dice for his freedom. Bill tossed the lucky throw, and found himself free. But then, realizing that there was money to be made this way, proceeded to sell chances on himself, to the amount of 590 dollars. Whereupon, he had another stroke of luck. It was his old master who won the raffle, and to cap the series of happy strokes of fortune, the master, touched by Bill's fidelity, promised to set him free when he, Bill, became twenty-one.

But this was an exceptional coincidence of good luck. Most of the Negroes along the river had their full share of grief, gruelling hard work, and little happiness. Despite this, they found time to express their joys and sorrows in melody and dance strumming the banjo, shuffling feet as they "jumped Jim Crow", and expressing their emotions, sad and joyful, in songs. The spirituals of the river plantation Negro, the coonjine, of the steamboat roustabouts, reflect these various moods, high and low.

The roustabout while at work loading and unloading the packet boats, improvised rhythms to the bouncing of the gangplank. This gave birth to the "coonjine," a merry chant which helped to ease the heavy labors.

Most roustabout songs have perished with the passing years, but fortunately for posterity,

Along New Orleans Docks.

Cotton Floats at New Orleans Docks. (c. 1890).

Crap Game Aboard the *Natchez.* (c. 1910).
Picking a pocket to get the wherewithal to
join in the game.

Just Waiting.

The Pie Woman (c. 1890).

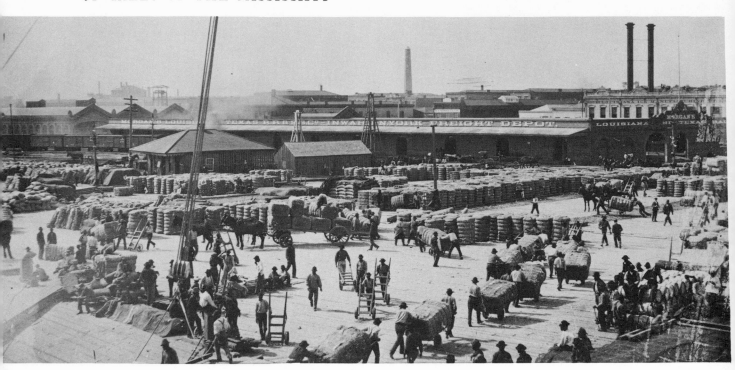

Unloading Cotton at New Orleans (c. 1890).

Miss Mary Wheeler, a trained musician, felt that an effort should be made to preserve them. Some years ago she coaxed a number of older Negroes, who had once been on the boats, to sing the songs they remembered for her. She faithfully recorded the words and the melodies. More than sixty river songs were rescued through her efforts.*

Though the work was hard, the life of a roustabout suited the Negro to a T. He could travel and see the world, he got three meals a day and a place to sleep and there was practically no responsibility to bother him. The steamboat on which he worked was to him practically a thing alive. Quite naturally the names of boats were woven into some of his songs.

THE MACOMBREY QUEEN
Hear the boat a-whistlin',
Comin' roun' the bend,
Hear the boat a whistlin',
Comin' roun' the bend,
With its tank pipes painted,
Bringin' my true love back agin.
So I got to git ready,
We're goin' to New Orleans,
So I got to git ready,
We're goin' to New Orleans,
On the purtiest steamboat,
It's the Macombrey Queen.

THE KATE ADAMS
Oh, I thought I heard the Kate Adams when
she blowed,
She blowed jes' lak she ain't goin' to blow
no mo'.
The reason that I lak the Kate Adams so,
She carries a chambermaid an' a watch below.
Come on boys with yo' neck out long,
Show me what shoulder you want it on.

Many of the river songs were plaintive; this one was probably composed by a tired and homesick man:

I'M WUKIN' MY WAY BACK HOME
I'm wukin' my way back home,
I'm wukin' my way back home,
I'm wukin' my way back home, Baby
I'm wukin' my way back home.
Timber don't git too heavy fo' me,
An' sacks too heavy to stack,
All that I crave fo' many a long day,
Is yo' lovin' when I git back.
Oh, fireman, keep her rollin' for me,
Let's make it to Memphis, Tennessee.
Fo' my back is gittin' tired,
An' my shoulder is gittin' sore.

* "Steamboatin' Days", Louisiana State University Press, Baton Rouge, La., 1944. Songs reproduced are with the permission of the copyright owner.

The Docks at New Orleans (c. 1890).

Down in the Mississippi to Gulf uv Mexico,
Down below Natchez,
But ef the boat keep steppin'
I'll be seein' you soon.

Not all of the songs sung by the roustabouts were labor songs or boat songs — sometimes they sang spirituals. One of these is *Red Sea*, which was sung for Miss Wheeler by an old Negro who had once served on one of the last of the lower river packets, the *Tennessee Belle:*

RED SEA

When Moses wuz leadin' the Israelites,
Red Sea,
Pharoah tried to ketch them jes' fo' spite,
Red Sea,
Oh, Pharoah he got drownded, drownded,
    drownded,
Oh, Pharoah he got drownded in the Red
    Sea.
I nevuh shall fo'git the day,
Red Sea,
When Jesus washed my sins away,
Red Sea,
I nevuh shall fo'git the day,
Red Sea,
When Jesus preached among the po',
Red Sea.

Roustabouts had their love songs, too. Much of their time was spent away from those they loved

and this separation produced some very sentimental ballads.

ALBERTA, LET YO' HAIR HANG LOW

Alberta, let yo' hair hang low,
Alberta, let yo' hair hang low,
I'll give you mo' gold than yo' apron will hold,
Ef you'll jes' let yo' hair hang low.
Alberta, what's on yo' mind?
Alberta, what's on yo' mind?
You keep me worried, you keep me bothered,
    all the time.
Alberta, what's on yo' mind?
Alberta, don't you treat me unkind.
Alberta, don't you treat me unkind.
'Cause I'm worried, 'cause I'm bothered, all the
    time.
Alberta, don't you treat me unkind.

Colin Robinson was a roustabout on the *City of Bayou Sara* when she burned, December 5, 1885. Years later he recalled the awful calamity which destroyed a fine steamboat and took eight lives.

"Some o' them rousters wuz sleeping so heavy we nevuh got 'em out in time."

Taken aboard the *Arkansas City*, the survivors immediately composed a song about the disaster.

On the Docks at New Orleans.
Sketch by Alfred R. Waud.

B'Y' SARA BURNED DOWN

Way down the rivuh an' I couldn't stay long,
B'y' Sara burned down.
She burnt down to the water's edge,
B'y' Sara burned down.
The people begun to run and squall,
B'y' Sara burned down,
When they begin to look they wuz about to fall,
 B'y' Sara burned down.
Look away over yonder, what I see,
B'y' Sara burned down,
The captain an' the mate wuz comin' after me,
 B'y' Sara burned down.
Tere's two bright angels by my side,
B'y' Sara burned down,
'Cause I want to go to Heaven when I die,
 B'y' Sara burned down.

And here's a song defying Satan

"I fink I hea'd de preacher say
 Oh how, how oh!
You never git to heben less you pray,
 Oh how, how oh!
W'en Satan come into de room,
 Oh how, how oh!
We'll bang him wid a hick'ry broom,
 Oh how, how oh!
'Roun' de room we'll gibe him chase,
 Oh how, how oh!
And frow de kittle in he's face,
 Oh how, how oh!
De w'ile temptation we defy,
 Oh how, how oh!

The *America* taking on cargo during a falling river.

Home of Zachary Taylor near Baton Rouge.

HE KIDNAPED A PRESIDENT

ATE and the Mississippi joined in a conspiracy to keep Zachary Taylor from becoming President of the United States. The conspiracy almost succeeded.

General Taylor, hero of the Mexican War, was an old man at the time he was being considered for nomination to the highest office in the gift of the American people — and a tired one, no doubt. That will perhaps account for the summary manner in which he handled the mass of letters he received from his many admirers — that, and the fact that in those days letters came postage collect. At any rate, the old man just returned all of this mail unopened. Now, included in a batch of such letters, was one asking him to accept the Presidential nomination. Not hearing from Taylor, his supporters seriously considered withdrawing his name.

However, he *was* nominated and, thereafter, duly elected. The time now approached for his inauguration. He was at Baton Rouge on Jan. 23, 1849, when advised to proceed to Washington.

The weather was cold, the river was high, but the old warrior was in good health. The city had turned itself inside out to fete the President-elect, the first man from Louisiana to reach the high office (though he was born in Virginia.)

The side-wheeler *Princess*, Capt. Truman Holmes, arrived on Jan. 24 to take the general to his plantation at Spithead Point, just above Baton Rouge. On the 31st, the elegant steamboat, *Tennessee*, was to arrive from New Orleans with a delegation to pick up Gen. Taylor and to take him as far as Nashville.

But a brash young steamboat captain, Tom Coleman Jr. of the *Saladin*, had other ideas. There was a sharp rivalry between the *Saladin* and the *Tennessee*, with the latter receiving the slight edge in speed. When the *Tennessee* was selected for the honor of carrying the President-elect, despite the long-standing friendship between the Colemans and the Taylors from Kentucky days, young Tom, then 24 years old, took the matter in hand. The two steamboats were tied up at New Orleans. He quietly slipped away and headed the *Saladin* under forced draft for Spithead Point. The *Tennessee's* captain saw her go, but figured it was only a routine departure. Later that evening, he, too, got under way.

The quiet of the morning at Spithead Point was broken by the long blasts from the *Saladin's* whistle. The sleepy-eyed President-elect and his hastily dressed party got to the wharf as the *Saladin* was tying up. From far down the river, the chugging of the *Tennessee* could already be heard.

His prize aboard, Capt. Tom signaled the engine room for its greatest effort. Soon the *Saladin* was flying toward Vicksburg at full speed. Gen. Taylor and his party had gone back to sleep in the comfortable cabins.

The *Tennessee?* By that time she was blowing long and loud at the Spithead Point landing — and fruitlessly, for nobody showed up to see the banners and decorations, to hear the speeches of the New Orleans delegation.

The following dialogue, substantially as reported by a Kentucky daily, ensued when the mistake was discovered aboard the *Saladin:*

"What in tarnation boat is this, suh?" blazed the escort committee's chief.

"I . . . I . . . I'll call Capt. Coleman," stammered a frightened mate.

"Capt. Coleman! *The Saladin?* My God, stop the boat! Turn around! Stop quick! Here, all of you, we are on the wrong boat!"

Other members of the escort party, once more hurriedly dressing, came milling from their cabins. They screamed for Coleman, fire in their sleepy eyes.

Capt. Coleman, cool and collected, arrived in the cabin, echoing with oaths and demands for an explanation.

"Good morning, gentlemen. Is there something I can do for you?"

The men of the escort went crazy. One of them drew a pistol and threatened the young captain.

"Do you know, sir," he said excitedly, "do you know, sir, what you are doing? Your are kidnaping the President of the United States!"

"And do you know, sir," answered Coleman, "that the President of the United States is riding my boat without my invitation and without my permission?"

There was no response. He continued: "He came on here of his own free will and accord, and certainly I am not going to put the President of the United States off my boat unless he asks

Capt. Tom C. Coleman.

to be put off. Now, gentlemen, there are only two men in the world who can stop this boat — the President and myself. I won't stop her. It's up to the President."

There was silence. The cabin soon began to hum as the committee members whispered among themselves. Then Gen. Taylor appeared, looking very solemn.

"Tom," he said, walking up to the captain, shaking his finger in the young man's face. "Tom, you scamp. What do you mean by getting me into this?"

Then he turned to the angry, sulking committee: "Gentlemen, I reckon about all we can do now is take a drink."

Gen. Taylor was tendered a large banquet and ball at Vicksburg, and left the celebration at midnight to return to his steamboat, presumably the *Saladin* still, since *The Picayune* of Feb. 7 states, "We are informed that this boat was not the *Tennessee.*"

Evidently the *Tennessee* did finally overhaul the *Saladin,* and take aboard the *Saladin's* distinguished passenger and party near Memphis. But that chosen steamboat was to suffer further ignominy. Before she reached Memphis in triumph, she broke her rudder! On Feb. 6, the *Tennessee* was towed into port by the *Mohican*, and tied up at Shaw's wharf-boat. The temperature was sub-freezing, and a sleet storm was in progress.

Quick repairs having been made, the *Tennessee* steamed up the Cumberland river to Nashville. After celebrations in that fair city, Gen. Taylor boarded the *Daniel Boone* for Louisville.

But well-meaning welcoming delegations continued to harass the President-elect and delay his progress. A crowd from Louisville had come downriver on the *Courtland* to welcome him to that city. So he had to transfer from the *Daniel Boone* to the *Courtland*, presumably mid-stream.

More celebrations, and then Gen. Taylor got aboard the *Sea Gull* and went up the Kentucky river, where the usual treatment awaited him, at Frankfort; later he returned on this boat to Carrollton. There he caught the *Ben Franklin*, which carried him to Cincinnati.

The aged man was certainly a Spartan. From Cincinnati, he set out for Wheeling aboard the *Telegraph No. 2*, owned in part by Capt. Tom Coleman Sr., father of the "kidnaper." More trouble. The boat was stopped near Moundsville, W. Va., by ice and low water.

The general had to get off and WALK through the snow to Moundsville, where he could get a sleigh for Wheeling. A sleigh ride over the National Pike to Washington completed the journey.

"This was a hectic trip," comments Capt. Frederick Way Jr., an authority on steamboat lore, "for one of the four oldest men ever elected to the presidency, and particularly inasmuch as he was acclimated to the balmy Southland, where he had been for some years. But the cold didn't kill him. The Washington heat did."

After his death, the body of the President was brought back to Kentucky. It was a long journey. The first stage was overland to Pittsburgh. Here the casket was transferred to Captain William Dean's shallow-draft boat, the *Navigator*, for it was summer low-water time on the Ohio. The *Navigator* bumped and scraped over shoals some six hundred miles to Louisville for the burial of the President's remains. And Old Whitey, Zachary Taylor's horse, followed down the Ohio a few weeks later.

Capt. Coleman's steamboat *The Saladin*, which "stole" the President-elect.

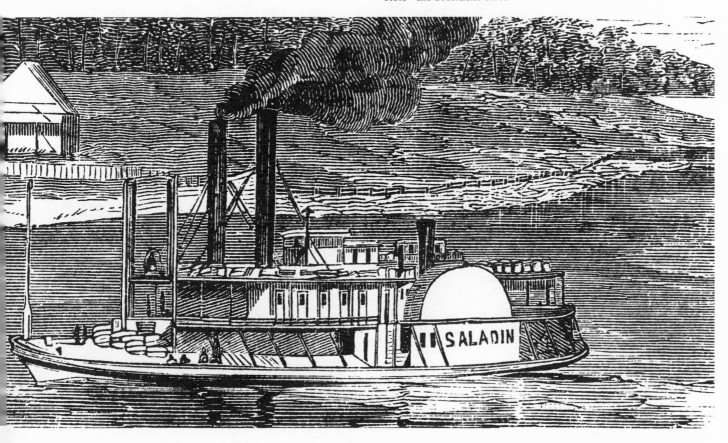

Gen. Zachary Taylor.

(Above) Funeral Cortège of Gen. Zachary Taylor, President of the United States.

(Right) Funeral Cortège showing the General's white horse "caparisoned and led."

The Great Steamboat Race Between the
Rob't. E. Lee and *Natchez.* Currier & Ives. Actually,
the two steamboats never got as close together as
this lithograph would indicate.

THE RACE OF THE GIANTS

HE date is June 30, 1870.
Ten thousand people crowding the upper wharf, just above Canal Street, are focusing their attention on two steamboats, one of them tied up two boats away from the other. We recognize the lower boat immediately as the celebrated speedster, *Rob't E. Lee*. It is the palatial packet belonging to and masterminded by Capt. John W. Cannon.

The other, with its red smokestacks, is certainly the champion steamboat *Natchez*, pride of Capt. Thomas P. Leathers, the sixth and grandest boat of that name he has owned.

Both boats are leaving at 5 P.M. for the same destination: St. Louis.

They are living, breathing, seething monsters. Men hustle around the decks. Officers shout orders. Roustabouts shuffle on and off the gangplanks on last-minute details. The massive side wheels of the steamers turn lazily in the muddy water, steam pipes hiss, and black plumes of smoke rise in ebony clouds from the towering smokestacks. Like thoroughbreds, shifting uneasily in the starting gate, tense, high-strung, they await the moment when every ounce of their strength will send them shooting ahead.

On the boiler deck of the *Lee* stands a well-groomed man, wearing a suit of hand-woven "Tuckapaw" topped by a Panama hat. This is Capt. Cannon. His opposite number on the *Natchez*, Capt. Leathers, stands on the hurricane deck, peering over the side. He wears his usual black suit, and the familiar lace-frilled, puff-bosomed shirt front. A giant diamond cluster in it catches the afternoon sun.

The wharf is alive with humanity. Hawkers sell "wharf pies," gingerbread, candies and cakes. The sporting element is out in force, waving handsfull of greenbacks.

"Even money rules, gentlemen . . . so if you like you can bet any size package in chunks — hedge and seesaw if you wish to plunge, for we can take or place a cool million" . . . "Eleven *Natchez* money to nine she makes Harry Hill's Gate in the first hour's run" . . . Nine to ten the

Lee makes Vicksburg in the first twenty-four hours' run" . . . "Any size bet to ten thousand here at nine to ten the *Lee* reaches Memphis in less than fifty hours . . ."

Loud-bellowing, hard-cussing Ed Cummings, mate of the *Natchez*, is selecting his crew of rousters with care. No danged slow-walkers this trip. The burly Negroes run about frantically, looking for "podners" to "ship up."

"We wants de honah ob de trip, boss," they say, and Cummings gives them a quick lookover. To those passing his scrutiny, he pushes shipping tickets and shouts at them to "stan' by the lines," accompanied by an oath.

Each boat's partisans crowd closer. About 4:45, those standing by the *Lee* notice her wheels begin to spin a little faster. The steamboat strains at her bow lines. Two rousters stand by with axes. Then, suddenly, shortly before 5 o'clock even, tension at the wharf increases.

"Launch stage," shouts the mate of the *Rob't E. Lee*. Black, sweating muscles give a quick lurch, and the rousters on the *Lee* heave the gangplank so that it shoots in across the deck. The bell rings. Down come the axes on the bow lines — and "Hoppin' Bob" backs out into the Mississippi, as thousands loose the pent-up energy of their throats.

"Hurrah fo' de 'Hoppin' Bob'!" "Hurrah for the *Rob't E. Lee!*"

As she lunges into the stream stern first, battered hats wave from the fo'cstle, and somebody strikes up a tune on a banjo. The few passengers on the *Lee* wave at the wharf. The big boat, slowed, heads round upstream. With a groan as her buckets dig into the current, she shoots away like an arrow from a bow.

Capt. Cannon sets her head for St. Louis, and the *Lee* is off. As she passes St. Mary's market, the official starting place for all steamboat timing, a thousand watch cases snap open. Their owners look for the puff of white smoke to come from the *Lee's* cannon.

"Bang" goes the little signal piece. Five-oh-three," note the countless timekeepers.

All eyes then turn to the "Big Injin." Capt. Leathers rings his bell only after the last piece of freight has been hustled aboard, the last passenger safely across the stage. With a mighty heave, the wheels of the *Natchez* back, as she widens the gap between her bow and the wharf. Hitting the current, there is a pause, a long, maddening pause for the *Natchez's* backers. Then the wheels dig in, the rudders begin to take effect, and the *Natchez* shoots after the *Lee*.

The watch cases snap open again. "Bang!" say the "Big Injin's" guns. Five-oh-six is the time. The *Natchez* is three minutes behind her adversary, but nobody, least of all Capt. Leathers, gives it a second thought.

Rounding the Carrollton bend, the two giants of the river are within sight of each other still. Then the *Lee* begins to widen the distance. Some who stand on the levee shake their heads.

"The *Natchez* ain't in it. She won't see the *Lee* again 'til she reaches St. Louis."

On board the *Rob't E. Lee*, the seventy-five passengers begin to relax and enjoy what is rapidly turning into a routine run instead of a touch-and-go race. The ladies drift into the music room and play the piano. The men chat on the guards, and poker games spring up in the saloon, the clink of chips being the loudest sound above the purr of the engines and the steady swoosh of the paddle wheels.

It's a different picture on board the *Natchez*. As the "Hoppin' Bob" becomes only a cloud of smoke around the next bend, gloom settles on the "Big Injin." Capt. Leathers descends from his famous perch atop the hurricane deck and sits moodily in a chair on the boiler deck, deep in thought. No one speaks to him, and he offers no conversation. "Old Push" just sits.

Bonfires light the levees as night comes on, as the boats pass plantations and country towns. Faint cheers echo across the water.

The first big community to await the steamboats is Baton Rouge. Telegraphers sit anxiously at their receivers all up and down the river, waiting for that flash out of Baton Rouge, the first report of the positions of the two charging racers. At the Louisiana capital city, Baton Rouge, the levees are jammed. The passengers on the *Lee* go out on deck to see the lights and look for the *Natchez's* smoke.

At midnight, the *Lee* passes Conrad's Point, foot of the long reach below Baton Rouge. By the time the *Natchez* gets there, the *Lee* is already four miles above the city and nine miles ahead. The "Hoppin' Bob" is really showing her heels to her rival!

And then it happens — one of those breaks which make any kind of racing uncertain until the finish line is crossed. Passengers see a commotion among the *Lee's* officers. Men run up and down whispering, pointing. The *Lee* begins to slow down. At Proffit's Point, July 1, 1870, the leader in the race bursts a steam pipe!

Capt. T. P. Leathers, nicknamed "Old Push" of the *Natchez*.

Capt. J. W. Cannon, of the *Rob't. E. Lee*. From a portrait owned by his daughter, Miss Cardie Cannon Forster.

The boilers will have to cool down while repairs are made. The engineers go to work. Minutes stretch into one hour, two hours, and the *Natchez* is creeping up.

Some of the officers go to Capt. Cannon, who stands expectantly in the engine room, watching Bill Perkins' engineers in the sweat and steam, working like demons. The officers suggest falling out of the run, and returning to New Orleans.

"That's all right," replies Capt. Cannon. "We'll have it repaired after a while. If we can get through before the *Natchez* catches us is all I care for."

Those watching on the hurricane deck soon see the *Natchez's* big, black columns against the starry night downstream around the bend.

"She's creeping closer," they say, glancing up at the Lee's quiet stacks.

At 4 a.m. the huge propulsion machinery begins to heave to life. The wheels start revolving slowly, then faster, and the "Hoppin' Bob" hops ahead once more. The *Natchez* is only three minutes behind!

This accident, which nearly costs Capt. Cannon the race, does cost the *Lee's* supporters thousands of dollars in bets, since many wagers have been made on her time to various points; or on the times she would beat the *Natchez* to certain places. But, from here on, things are different on the *Lee*.

"Perkins," says the captain, addressing the perspiring engineer, "don't crowd or shove this boat any more. We are not running for time. We can beat that boat easily; you know that. So let her go along moderately. Just keep ahead of her; that's all I want to do."

"All right, Cap'n Cannon, we'll stay ahead of her," is Bill Perkins' sorrowful reply.

The *Rob't E. Lee* swings by the city of Natchez at 10:15 the next morning. The crowded wharf boat hopes against hope that the *Natchez* will catch the *Lee*, and a band is on hand to serenade Capt. Leathers. The musicians are so irritated they don't play a note. But the famous deer horns of the record-breaking steamboat *Princess*, which had hung proudly on the wharf boat, challenging any boat to beat her time from New Orleans to Natchez and "take the horns," are lowered and sent out to Capt. Cannon in midstream.

Capt. Cannon sounds his whistle and fires the cannon. The crowd comes to life for this display of sportsmanship. Two coal flats await the *Lee* in the river and she lashes onto them under way,

Cards published in the *Daily Picayune* by Cannon and Leathers. Assured the public that there wouldn't be a race.

while rousters work furiously to stow the choice, lump, Pittsburgh coal. The mate directs the placement of every bag, to keep his boat in trim. When the final bag is dumped, the flats are cast off and the *Lee* speeds ahead again. As she rounds the bend above the city, the *Natchez* comes into view downstream.

The *Natchez* stops at the wharf boat, losing little time in unloading and taking on freight and passengers, then darts ahead after the *Lee*. After leaving the town of Natchez, there dawns a glimmer of hope for Captain Leathers' steamboat, which, at this point, picks up a little on the *Lee*. Then suddenly, this hope is dashed. At Milliken's Bend, the *Natchez'* cold water pump goes dead. The boat is tied up at Buckhorn Landing for thirty-three minutes. And later, the *Natchez* begins to exhibit peculiar symptoms in her course. At Island 93, she "runs off" (goes out of control) and has to be halted to keep from piling up on the bank. These vagaries are to plague Capt. Leathers from now on during the race.

The "Hoppin' Bob" is not to be caught. She passes Vicksburg at 4:42 p.m. of the same day she passed the town of Natchez — and not even the smoke of the *Natchez* is visible.

Now, in the bends of the river above Vicksburg comes an incident which is to mar Capt. Cannon's otherwise clean victory, in the eyes of many enthusiasts. He had sent his good, lifelong friend, Capt. John W. Tobin, ahead to arrange for fuel, and Capt. Tobin has loaded his own fast packet named the *Frank Pargoud* with 100 cords of pine knots. When the *Lee* approaches, the *Pargoud* lights out upriver at full throttle, and, as the *Lee* edges up alongside, the two steamers are lashed together. While the pine knots are transferred, the two powerful engines run as one.

(That, howled many bettors later, was a foul.)

The levees and wharves at Memphis await the racers with barrels of tar, cannon and fireworks. There is still a measure of excitement over the outcome of the race, although the news that the *Lee* is generally the faster boat thus far dims the enthusiasm somewhat. But when the shout goes up, "Here they come," all hell breaks loose. The tar is lighted, the battery of cannon boom, and skyrockets fill the air.

But it isn't the *Lee*. It isn't the *Natchez*, either. It's the steamboat *Thompson Dean*, on a routine upriver trip. The embarrassed captain toots his whistle respectfully, and the Memphians on the levee reload their cannon, and quickly scrounge around for unused fireworks. They don't have to wait long. At 11:04 the *Lee* heaves into sight. More noise!

The *Natchez* is doing pretty well, too. She is only an hour and three minutes behind at Memphis; but the *Lee* runs between her prearranged coal barges and continues upstream, while the *Natchez* stops at the wharf. She had laid by thirty-six minutes at Helena, Ark., repairing a defective pump, and, taking that delay into consideration, she does well for herself.

All that night, and the next day, on the run to Cairo, the river still is crowded with flag-draped steamboats, cheering levee throngs and excursion boats. The *Lee* sets a new record to Cairo, arriving there at 6:30 p.m. July 3, three days and one hour from New Orleans. The *Natchez* is one hour ten and a quarter minutes on her heels.

"From here on," announces Capt. Cannon to the assembled passengers, as the *Lee* speeds by Cairo without stopping, "the trick is piloting, not speed." Indeed, he had taken on from the coal flats at that point something else besides coal —

(Above) Another Old Print Showing the Race.

(Below) The Great Race. Depicted by an
anonymous artist.

two experienced pilots who knew every drop of water, every inch of bottom from there to St. Louis.

Even then, about six miles above Cairo, the *Lee* slows down, stops, goes ahead again; more backing. Some of the passengers, worried, go to Capt. Cannon, who calms them with:

"Don't be disheartened and give up. No boat can run 'full tilt' in shoal water. We are a long ways ahead of the *Natchez*. She'll never again catch us. I have instructed the new pilots to let her go along at half steam. The race for speed with the *Natchez* has been won. It is with the pilots from now on."

The rousters on the deck below sing:
Shoo fly, don't bodder me!
You can't catch up wit de *Robt. E. Lee.*

But Capt. Thomas P. Leathers isn't of a mind to bother the *Rob't E. Lee*. When the shoal waters are reached, and an enveloping fog aggravates his navigation, he ties up the *Natchez*. For nearly five hours his boat sits still, while the *Lee* slithers on far ahead, over and around the shoals to St. Louis.

The ovation which the *Lee* receives at St. Louis is legendary. At 11:33 on the morning of Independence Day, exactly three days, eighteen hours and thirteen minutes after leaving St. Mary's market, she crosses the finish line.

That evening, the *Natchez* steams in, too, at exactly 6 o'clock.

De *Lee* an' de *Natchez* had a race.
De *Lee* t'rowed water in de *Natchez*' face.

The race between the *Natchez* and the *Rob't E. Lee* is perhaps the biggest thing that ever happened on the Mississippi River from the standpoint of national interest. Bets were made on the other side of the Atlantic. Millions of dollars changed hands.

The background of the two boats and the men who built and owned them is important. Both Capt. John W. Cannon and Capt. Thomas Paul Leathers, natives of Kentucky, were river titans. Before the War Between the States, both operated in the New Orleans-Vicksburg trade and other runs.

Cannon was a friend of Gen. Grant, and it is possible that he named his boat the *Rob't. E. Lee* to head off resentment because of his known sympathies.

Captain Leathers, on his part, always claimed that he had defied Union General Butler at New Orleans, and he boasted that his fifth *Natchez* had been burned while fighting the Federals. But it is also established that he was once arrested for Union sympathies and then pardoned by his close friend, Jefferson Davis.

After the war, both men recouped their fortunes and resumed river trade. They once were interested in a steamboat together, the *Gen. Quitman*. But the pair quarreled over business matters, the surly, tough-speaking, powerfully built Leathers being diametrically opposite in temperament to slighter-built, soft-spoken Cannon.

In the spring of 1866, Cannon went to New Albany, Ind., where in the sand on the banks of the Ohio he sketched with his walking-stick the plan for the steamboat he wanted built. No cost was spared to make the boat the fastest, most luxurious.

After the *Lee* was launched, crowds gathered at the Indiana shipyard. They became hostile when they saw whose name was being painted on the paddle boxes. So the *Lee* was towed across the river to the friendly Kentucky shore, and the painting job was finished there.

The *Lee* arrived in New Orleans in October, 1866, and set about making speed records, capturing important passengers and shippers — and making Capt. Leathers furious. In November, 1868, news reports tell of a fist fight between the two captains. The report notes, "Very little claret, was drawn."

Leathers got a Cincinnati shipyard to build a new super-*Natchez* (the sixth by that name) for him in 1869. There is no doubt he built it to beat the *Lee*. Both the new *Natchez* and the *Lee* had eight boilers, although the *Lee* had 40-inch-diameter cylinders and the *Natchez* 34-inch ones. Size and build of hulls were comparable. Certain features which might give one an advantage were outweighed by certain features of the other. They were about evenly matched.

In June, 1870, after cotton shipping season, Capt. Leathers took his *Natchez* on a trip to St. Louis to try and beat the old *J. M. White's* record — three days, twenty-three hours, twenty-one minutes. She clipped a sensational hour and twelve minutes from that record.

Rumors of a race started circulating. Cannon was against a race because he knew the *Natchez* was good, but he also was interested in recovering his speed supremacy. Leathers told his friends to lay all their pennies on the *Natchez*.

But *The Daily Picayune* carried notice "cards"

Rob't. E. Lee. From an old print.

from both Leathers and Cannon saying the rumors were not true. These cards ran right next to each other, even after the race started!

For the race, Leathers accepted a full passenger and freight load. The *Lee* carried no freight, a select list of seventy-five passengers only, and stripped herself of excess weight and wind-resisting objects to prepare for a speed run. Leathers' *Natchez* had to stop for coal, while Cannon's *Lee* arranged nonstop fueling from barges. The tying in of the *Frank Pargoud*, which was not a barge, but a fast steamer, for this kind of refuelling, was decried by some as unsportsmanlike, but showed the generalship exhibited by Cannon in his anxiety to best Leathers.

A study of the times the boats made — deducting the loss by the *Natchez* at landings and in the fog at the shoals above Cairo — leaves little doubt the *Natchez* was at least the equal of the *Lee*.

But the *Rob't. E. Lee* won, and all the "ifs" and "buts" can't take away the glory.

When the *Natchez* did arrive at St. Louis, the architect of the Cincinnati firm which designed and built the *Natchez* made his way through the crowd to Capt. Leathers.

"Captain," he asked, "how is it the *Lee* beat you?"

"Thunderation, man, do I not owe you $90,000?"

"What's that got to do with it, Captain?"

"Do with it?" shouted the captain. "Come with me." They went to the steamboat's office. "Mr. Ayres," he said to the clerk, "what's our earnings this trip?"

Sam Ayres slowly looked over the books and reported the net earnings as several hundred dollars over four thousand for the trip.

"Pay the gentlemen four thousand. I guess we can get along on the rest. Racing? That's the sort of racing I have been doing, sir."

(Above) *The Frank Pargoud.* It refuelled
the *Rob't. E. Lee* above Vicksburg, and gave
rise to accusations of unsportsmanlike
conduct on Cannon's part.

(Right) Cover Carried by the
Frank Pargoud.

(Below) Freight Bill from the
Pargoud.

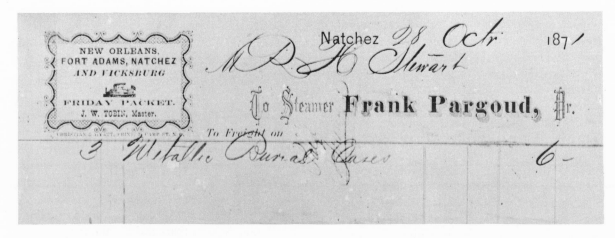

(Above) Building steamboat cabins had become a
fine art by the time of the Civil War.

(Below) Interior of *Rob't. E. Lee II*. Burned at
Yucatan Pt., Oct. 30, 1882, with loss of 30 lives.

Rob't. E. Lee II in Gala Attire.

NEW ORLEANS,
Natchez & Vicksburg Packet.

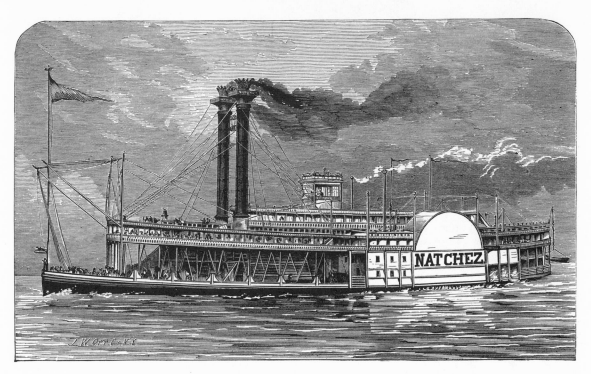

The Natchez.

"Brag card" of the *Natchez.*

STEAMER NATCHEZ,

CAPTAIN T. P. LEATHERS, MASTER.

Length of Hull, . . . 307 Feet.	Eight Boilers, 34 feet long ---
Width of Beam, ... 44 "	40 inches diameter and 2 Flues.
Depth of Hold, . . . 10 "	Two 34 inch Cylinders, 10 feet Stroke.
Diameter of Wheel, . . . 44 "	Extreme Height, 119 feet, 6 inches.
Length of Bucket . . . 16 "	Capacity for 5,500 bales cotton.

THE GREAT CAPTAIN LEATHERS

That gigantic figure of a man seated in a broad-bottomed rocking chair atop the roof of the texas of the puffing steamboat suddenly arose. He sniffed the midnight air, and shouted to the pilot:

"Pep her up a bit more, Mr. Strong. Here comes the fog now."

This apparent contradiction of usual navigational precautions brought an anxious "What did you say, Capt. Leathers?" from the man at the wheel.

The enormous man, Capt. Thomas Paul Leathers, dean of river-boat titans, answered calmly, "I said, sir, to increase your speed. We are running into fog." Then, to answer the pilot's next query before it was spoken, "It is better to hasten the danger than to linger in its shadows."

Suddenly, two tall smokestacks appeared ahead, towering above the fog, and bearing directly down on the *Natchez*.

"Back her!" shouted Capt. Leathers.

'Back her!" roared another voice from the fog, as if in echo. "By the Lord Harry, back her hard!"

The mighty *Natchez* trembled. She shuddered from her jackstaff to her stern. The rush of water, as the massive buckets released their tons of "forward" load and bit into reverse, caused the gold-plated chandelier in the cabin to dance as if possessed.

The other boat, the *J. M. White*, did the same at the command of her master, Capt. John C. Swon. The river dreadnaughts slowed up and stopped, bow to bow, so close the two captains could have stepped from one boat to the other. They exchanged views by calling across from their perches on the texas decks.

"Leathers! By the Lord Harry, you are always on the watchout at the right time. Had that not been you, Leathers, by the Lord Harry, we'd all be enjoying a morning swim right now, and it's devilish cold for a swim, devilish cold!

"And by the Lord Harry, I doubt, Capt. Leathers, whether many of us would be in a condition to do much swimming afterwards."

The passengers slept on. Capt. Leathers never revealed, in telling this, his favorite story, how he answered Capt. Swon. But in telling it, he revealed much of the character of one of the most colorful men who helped build the Missis-

sippi valley, and who lived to see it grow beyond the need for his beloved steamboats, a fact he never admitted.

Capt. Leathers was the man whose word was enough for him to order the building of boats costing tens of thousands of dollars, without even a note to back it up. This red-headed, red-bearded, massive man of unquestioned integrity lived through the most exciting era in the history of the United States and played a dramatic part in it. Here was a man who embodied all that goes into the expression "Southern gentleman."

There were Leathers who were prominent in the first colonization of the New World, stout English traders who fought Indians in Virginia. In 1812, John Leathers, the captain's father, came to New Orleans to look around. He hired an Indian guide to take him to Kentucky, where he bought plantations near the northern boundary of the state, and began to raise tobacco. In time, he made "a neat little fortune."

John married, and eventually there were young Leathers, five boys and two girls. The fourth son, who was to become the red-bearded giant of the Mississippi, was born in 1816 and named Thomas Paul. As a child, he was noted for his marksmanship. He remained in Kentucky and, as a man of 21, he voted for Martin Van Buren. At that time, his father was having trouble with Ohio "jayhawkers" who preyed upon his extensive slaveholdings, selling the Negroes to owners elsewhere in Kentucky after snatching them across the line. So he sent Thomas on an exploration trip to find a new home, intending that his son should look in the North.

Thomas had other ideas. His brother John was already a steamboatman on the lower Mississippi, and toward him the young Thomas gravitated by natural instinct.

"I had found a land," Capt. Leathers stated in later years, "where was reared a race of gentlemen, where a man's word was his bond. I received the courtesies that might have been extended a prince, and such were the courtesies always extended a gentleman regardless of the condition of his purse . . . I told my father it would be insane, in the very nature of conditions, to go north, when such a people dwelt in the South."

The first family steamboat venture was a small steamer named the *Sunflower*, manned by the Leathers brothers. With Tom as mate, it first took a load of cotton from Grenada, Miss. This was the era in which Thomas Paul Leathers was receiving his schooling, learning the rudiments of the profession he was to master.

Meanwhile, with another brother (William) and with several other persons (including Cassius D. Sandford), Tom began in 1839 to build the first of the series of steamboats to be named the *Princess*. By the time the fourth *Princess* was built, Capts. Tom Leathers and Truman C. Holmes were the owners. The *Princesses* made Leathers a king; by 1845 he definitely could branch out for himself and build the first of the great *Natchez* steamboats.

The story of the *Natchez* series really is the story of Leathers, and the story of the development of the Mississippi for nearly 45 years.

Capt. Leathers' first *Natchez* was built "at the mouth of Crayfish bayou." She ran as a fast, Saturday packet in the New Orleans-Vicksburg trade until 1848. But trade was growing so quickly that Leathers sold her and built another, larger and faster, with more attention to passenger comfort. This one also soon was outgrown. The public clamored for bigger, speedier, more elegant "floating palaces."

The third *Natchez* brought sadness amidst the glory. While docked at New Orleans in February, 1854, she went up in flames along with twelve other boats. Capt. Tom barely got himself and his young wife off in time, but one of his brothers, James, perished.

Undaunted, the fourth *Natchez* followed quickly, and by early 1855 she was carrying the mail between New Orleans and Vicksburg every Saturday.

The fifth *Natchez* was a beauty. To make her the finest thing afloat or ashore for comfort and elegance, and the last word in luxury, specially woven carpet was ordered from Belgium. Bright chandeliers made by skilled craftsmen, plus a glass dome, ornamented the interior. It was something of which he could be proud, and Capt. Leathers showed her off, but not for long, alas!

She arrived at New Orleans shortly before the War Between the States. When war broke out, she was sent up the Yazoo to escape Federal seizure. In 1863, with 2000 bales of cotton stacked around her as protection, she was used as a ram, and was burned.

Another *Natchez*, sixth of the name, was begun 1869, and she lived to become the most famous of them all. With the *Rob't E. Lee* she was the most renowned and most familiar of all river boats, for she was the great racer who lost the river speed title in that by-now legendary tale of the great river. But she lived ten long, useful, profitable years, and ended up in retirement as a wharf-boat at Vicksburg.

River trade was starting to ebb in 1879, when Leathers put his greatest effort, the seventh *Natchez*, on the river. She was a beautiful sight with her hand-painted transom lights depicting Indian chiefs. Gorgeously equipped, she operated successfully at first, but she was just too late for the big time. By 1887, Capt. Leathers laid her up for two years, after which she sank.

This was the end of Capt. T. P. Leathers' *Natchez* boats, but it was not the last boat of that name to ply the river. An eighth *Natchez* was being built in 1891, by his son, Bowling Leathers and his wife Blanche, it is said. The old man had no interest, financial or otherwise, in the eighth *Natchez*. The railroad whistles had already sounded taps for the great days of river trade, and the Admiral of the Mississippi was busy with another boat, the *T. P. Leathers*, his last personal venture.

There wasn't too much about the eighth *Natchez* to remind oldtimers of her predecessors except her name; but it seemed that while Capt. Leathers lived there would be a *Natchez* on the river. And this sternwheel *Natchez* was on the river on June 1, 1896, when the venerable captain was crossing St. Charles Ave. at Josephine, one block from his fine home at Josephine and Carondelet. It was nighttime. From out the dark came a hit-and-run bicyclist. The man who had lived through the turmoil and excitement of an era, the victor of duels and fisticuff encounters, fires and storms, was injured fatally by a bicycle! He lingered until Jan. 13, when he died.

This memorable man left behind one story which has nothing to do with the river, only with his character and presence of mind.

One day he was crossing the Ohio river at Cincinnati, where one of the *Natchez* boats was being built. A man sidled up to him on the ferry.

"Let me give you a piece of timely advice Leathers. There is going to be a run on the Bank of Commerce tomorrow, and I want to advise you to go and draw out your money."

This bank had been courteous to Leathers, and although not a depositor, he was a Southern gentleman. He went immediately to his own bank, withdrew $4500 in one dollar bills, rolled them up and put a $500 bill on top. He elbowed his way into the crowded lobby of the Bank of Commerce and walked up to the cashier.

"Deposit this to my credit, please," he fairly

(Above) The *Natchez. Harper's Weekly,* Nov. 12, 1870 — Says the Editor: "So far there hasn't been an accident. But no one would be surprised to hear any day that one or both of them (Rob't. E. Lee and Natchez) had been blown to fragments."

(Below) The *Natchez.*

(Above) Natchez VII. This was the one wrecked by Capt. Bowling Leathers, "Old Push's" son.

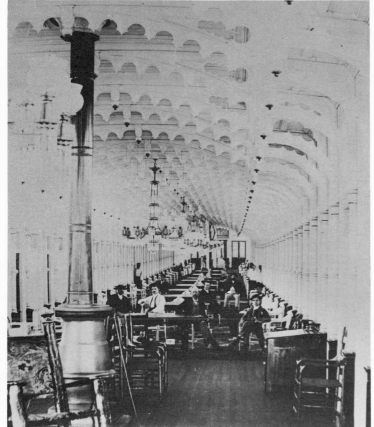

(Left) Cabin of Natchez VII. Note Capt. Leathers' commodious armchair in foreground.

(Above) Natchez VII. Under Steam. Sunk at
Stack Is., Jan. 1, 1889.

(Below) Natchez VIII (1891-1918). This was the
stern-wheeler built by Bowling Leathers and his wife.

shouted. "I shall return later when you have had time to count it. Good day."

The crowd began to buzz. How could the bank be folding if Leathers was entrusting it with such a wad?

For years afterwards, when a Cincinnati bank got into trouble, the slogan was: "Send for Capt. Leathers. He'll straighten it out."

AN ACCOUNT OF AN
EXTEMPORANEOUS RIVER RACE

Our reporter was named Frederick Law Olmstead. He came to the United States to write articles for British journals. He examined life in various sections with a magnifying glass, and turned out a Boswellian job. He was particularly interested in the slavery question. Hence his protracted tour of Louisiana — and the incidental steamboat ride.

Olmstead made a trip upriver and his account of this adventure gives a detailed picture of river travel at midcentury. First of all, he had one devil of a time getting under way.

He wanted to go from New Orleans to Shreveport, so he looked in *The Picayune* and found an ad stating that two steamers, the *Swamp Fox* and the *St. Charles*, would be leaving a 4 p.m. He went down to the levee and looked them over. He decided on the *St. Charles,* went aboard, and engaged the last stateroom. He checked out of the St. Charles hotel and took himself and baggage aboard at 3:30 p.m. The steamer had fire up in the boiler. The great bell rang, freight was being hustled over the gangplank . . . and nearby, the S*wamp Fox* was doing the same.

At 5 p.m. they were still at the wharf. By 6:30 p.m. the captain had still not come aboard. Olmstead asked the clerk if she would be leaving that night, and he said no, there was too much freight. How about in the morning? Naw, not much chance of leaving until Monday noon. Back to the hotel.

Bright and early Monday morning Olmstead eagerly scanned *The Picayune's* steamboat columns. Sure enough. There it was. The ad said that both the steamers would leave that day at 5 p.m. But what's this? An editorial in the same edition stated:

"The floating palace, the *St. Charles,* will leave for Shreveport at 5 p.m., and if anybody wants to make a quick luxurious trip up the Red river with a jolly soul, Capt. Lickup is in command."

Then the editorial continued: "If any of its friends has business up the Red River, Capt. Pitchup is a whole-souled veteran of the trade, and is going up with that remarkably low-draft favorite, the *Swamp Fox,* leaving at 4 p.m."

Olmstead got worried about this departure time discrepancy, so he went down at noon to ask around. Four p.m. was right, he was told, for the *St. Charles.* So Olmstead checked out again and came aboard at that time. The boilers were fired up, the bell rang (likewise aboard the *Swamp Fox*). At 6 p.m. they were still tied up.

At 7 the fires went out, and the stevedores went home. Back to the hotel. Same Tuesday. Wednesday was different. There were more encouraging signs of departure, but there was another disappointment. His stateroom was occupied by a huge character "with a longer knife than mine," and no inclination to listen to reason.

What would you do today in such a fix? Exactly what Olmstead did. He went to the clerk and raised Cain. Hardly looking up from his desk, the clerk snapped:

"Since you didn't stay on board, and since you didn't pay in advance, I had no way of knowing you were still making the trip. Now, I'm very busy and arguing won't get you anywhere. The boat's leaving at 4 p.m. If you want to pay passage, I'll do the best I can. You can put your bags in my cabin."

"Are you certain that we're leaving at 4?" insisted Olmstead, wishing he was on a first-class channel boat to Le Havre.

"Not the smallest doubt. We're ready now, but we cant' leave because of our advertisement," was the amazing reply. Olmstead, mad as a hornet, could still be amused at this fine "technical point of honor."

At 7 P.M. the *St. Charles* and the *Swamp Fox* were making fancy plumes of black smoke, blowing steam, and ringing bells. Each one was trying to leave before the other, and the captains were impatiently pacing the texas, or hurricane deck.

The steamer was crowded with peddlers. "I had confidence in their instinct," he wrote. They hadn't been there before. They were selling "shells," oranges, bananas, newspapers, and trinkets. One man was surreptitiously selling copies of "Uncle Tom's Cabin," while another tried to push a thing called "Bible Defense of Slavery" on him. He bought neither.

At 7:30 Capt. Lickup scanned the levee in all directions. Then, he uttered the magic words:

"No use waitin' any longer, I reckon; throw off, Mr. Heady."

To the singing of Negro boathands on the lower deck, the *St. Charles* backed out, winded round, and breasted the current. They were off, at last! But the *Swamp Fox* didn't leave until three days later.

> "Ye see dem boat way dah ahead?
> De *San Charles* is arter 'em,
> Dey mus' go behine . . .
> Oh! We is gwine up de Red ribber, oh!"

It would take too long to relate all the charming aspects of Olmstead's "quick and luxurious" trip. But it should be said that he still found no berth, and the clerk was a downright stinker about the whole thing, saying he didn't know where Olmstead could sleep, he didn't care, and the luckless passenger would have to look out for himself.

What would you do in this case? Exactly as Olmstead did. He complained to the captain.

"The clerk knows his business. I have nothing to do with that," growled Capt. Lickup, and walked away. Olmstead finally got a place to sleep in an improvised kind of a bunk along with some hundred and fifty others in the same situation. The man next to him, however, was "so strong" that Olmstead couldn't sleep. So he moseyed around the boat, topside and below, asking questions, making notes, until he found out that none of the other men, trying to sleep nearby, could stand the smell either, and they had ejected the offender. After that, they all went to sleep — until midnight.

Which brings us to the "race." At the stroke of twelve, there was a sudden jar in the boat. They all woke to the noise of excited talking on deck. On the gallery, Olmstead saw another boat just abeam, "head-and-head," very close. This was the *Kimball*.

The crews were shouting across to each other, exchanging wagers and uncomplimentary re-

Race between the *Baltic* and *Diana*, from New Orleans to Louisville, Ky. 1,382 miles, the longest river steamboat race on record. The *Baltic* won. A passenger on the *Baltic*, George F. Fuller, painted the scene, and his painting was reproduced in litho, 1859.

marks about the other's speed. The firemen were crowding the furnaces.

"Shove her up, boys! Give her hell!" was a typical shout.

"She got to hold a conversation with us before she gets by, anyhow," was one Negro's remark.

"Ye har that'ar whistlins!" a white man asked Olmstead. "Tell ye, thar ain't any too much water in her bilers when ye har that." Nervous laughter from Olmstead.

The *Kimball* slowly drew ahead, and as if to add insult to injury, crossed the *St. Charles'* bows. The contest was "given up."

"Ef I could pitch a few ton o' dat freight off her bow, I bet da *Kimball* would be askin' her de way mighty quick. De ole lady is jus' too heavy."

(Right) Stokers Threw Rotten Meat into Fire Boxes to Help Get up Steam.

(Below) The Wm. Carig. Built 1904. Won a race "against time" against the *Delta King* and *Delta Queen* on the Sacramento River in 1939.

Delta Queen. Built in Stockton, Cal., troop transfer
ship during World War I, crated and brought through
Panama Canal and up the Mississippi, and to
Pennsylvania where she was refitted; her new owner
was the Greene Steamship Line.

(Below) Latter-day Steamboat Race, between the
Betsy Ann and the *Greene* (1930).

The J. M. White, Mistress of the Mississippi. She broke many speed records. From the oil painting by Chas. Morgenthaler of St. Louis.

PAIR of deer antlers was the most-prized possession a Mississippi river steamboat could wear, mounted high up between her stacks. It was the symbol of speed supremacy.

Only one steamboat, winning the antlers, was never successfully challenged for their possession, and that was the *Rob't E. Lee*. But almost everybody conceded that there was one other Mississippi greyhound which could have "stripped her antlers." That was the *J. M. White*.

"Greatest, fastest, costliest." These were the adjectives usually applied to the *J. M. White*. If by greatest is meant largest, the *Grand Republic* was actually about thirty feet longer. If by costliest is meant actual cost of construction including all her "trimmin's," the *Thompson Dean* is said to have set her builder back $400,000. The *White* cost $250,000 (same as the *Lee*).

As for being the fastest, there is little doubt that this was so. But as for the *White* being the most glamorous steamboat ever built, there is no doubt at all. She was the "grande dame."

There were actually three *J. M. Whites*, the first two named for a St. Louis merchant. The first was built in 1842 at Elizabethtown, Pa., and sank the next year. The second, known as "the Old White", was built in 1843 at Pittsburgh. She was designed by Billy King of St. Louis, who deserves a special place in the nautical hall of fame.

King was among the first to put side paddle wheels on a steamboat slightly aft of amidships. He noticed that the "bow wave" dipped in the middle third section of the hull, and then rose to its crest again as it slid by the aft third section. So he concluded that by placing the paddle wheels in the after third section, they would catch the crest of the "bow wave," thus allowing the "buckets" to dig more water.

This worked fine. The "old White" began to break all records for speed and maneuverability. Other boats followed suit, the paddle wheels moving further and further back.

The third — and last — *J. M. White* incorporated this and just about every other refinement

117

of steamboat design. She was built in a yard famous for its floating palaces, the Howard Shipyard located in Jeffersonville, Ind. Her keel was laid on Sept. 15th, 1877, and she was launched April 3, 1878. She was 325 feet long, with a 47′ 9″ beam. Her cotton guards extended twenty feet on each side, so that her main deck was actually ninety-one feet wide. She was named for Capt. J. M. White, a famous river man of his day.

The *White* was really put together! No effort was spared to make her the mightiest steamboat afloat. She was an engineer's dreamboat, a pilot's paradise, and a passenger's idea of elegance.

Here are some features: She had steam-driven capstans and winches, a roustabout luxury. She had a five-tone whistle. Her feather-crowned chimneys were eighty-one feet tall, and her jackstaff topped them by twelve feet more. Her steering wheel was twelve feet in diameter and required two men to operate it.

The filigree woodwork in the main cabin was made entirely of natural cherry, with inlaid arches. On each side of the wide cabin, which could seat 250 passengers at table when set up for the delectable meals, were twenty-three staterooms. There were also two luxurious bridal suites, or "chambers". Above, on the texas, as the top deck was called, there were fifty staterooms, with two spacious rooms forward for the captain, plus a hall and rooms for the officers.

The staterooms were exceptionally large — ten by fourteen feet, and the smaller ones eight by ten. The appointments and furnishings could not be matched in any hotel in the world, it was said. There were promenade decks outside the staterooms. On these, and the fore and aft galleries, 400 people could be accommodated comfortably. Inside the long cabin, twelve ponderous chandeliers with ornate candelabra swung on gilded iron rings. All stateroom doors were handpainted, the inside surfaces being walnut. Paneling was curly walnut veneer.

The furniture, all imported from France, was unique — heavy walnut with an inlay of contrasting lighter wood forming the boat's initials within a holly wreath. All chinaware, designed especially for the *White,* had her picture handpainted and burned in. The silverware was the finest money could buy, and each piece had the boat's picture engraved on it. The finest linen from Ireland, with the boat's initials worked by hand, made up the napery.

The skylights were stained glass.

Who could have built such a steamboat? It was the pride of Capt. John W. Tobin, an Alabaman who came to the river, and at his peak, owned and operated sixty-three packets.

He brought his masterpiece to New Orleans in July, 1878, and placed her in the New Orleans-Vicksburg-Greenville trade. Capt. Tobin knew he had a thoroughbred on his hands, and he treated her right. He had a specially trained fire-fighting crew. She cut a magnificent figure when under way, but it was never known exactly how fast she would really go. So powerful were her engines that Capt. Tobin was afraid to open her up. But without trying, she broke all records between New Orleans and Vicksburg numerous times.

It was not solely because of her engines that Capt. Tobin wouldn't let her out. There was a nice sentimental reason behind it, too.

His officers continually clocked the *White* between certain points, and compared them to the *Rob't E. Lee's* time. Then they'd beg Capt. Tobin to "make the trip from New Orleans to St. Louis and strip the antlers off the *Lee.*"

He always said no. They couldn't understand. Some years later, his son, John W. Tobin, Jr., explained the captain's secret reason:

"My father was a close friend of Capt. John W. Cannon, the *Lee's* owner, and Capt. Cannon was nearing the end of an illustrious career. He was having hard luck, too. Those antlers on the *Lee* were his dearest possession. It would have broken the old gentleman's heart to have lost those antlers, especially to his best friend."

Anthony P. Medine of New Orleans, one of the *White's* pilots, told this story:

"One night we were snoring calmly upstream from New Orleans. Capt. Tobin was asleep in his cabin. I was in the wheelhouse, thinking, as we all did, of those antlers. So I suddenly decided to signal the engineer to 'let her out'. We raced faster.

"Well, the vibrations woke the captain. He knew what was going on. He pulled on his clothes and climbed up to the pilot house.

"'You're ahead of schedule, aren't you' he asked me. I said we were. 'Then throttle down. Forget about those antlers. We'll never take them off the *Rob't E. Lee* while I live.'

"And we never did."

Like Capt. Cannon, of the *Rob't E. Lee,* Capt. Tobin was a bitter enemy of Capt. Thomas P. Leathers of the *Natchez.* Cannon and Tobin also ran the *Ed. Richardson,* a fine large boat, but no match for the racer *Natchez.* One of Leather's favorite tricks was to let a rival boat pull out a little before he did from the New Orleans levee, then pour on the coal and pass the boat, to the delight of his passengers. This he did one day in 1878 to the *Ed. Richardson,* adding insult to injury by firing a small cannon he carried, when he passed the *Richardson.* Capt. Tobin was aboard the *Richardson* in that trip and he resolved to beat Leathers at his own game. A short time afterwards he brought his new *J. M. White* to New Orleans; one day both the *White* and the *Natchez* pulled out almost together and headed upstream. Leathers gunned the *Natchez* ahead; a minor accident slowed the *White* while repairs were being made, but soon after, the *White* came boiling along, caught up with the *Natchez,* passed her and disappeared from sight. To save face, Leathers resorted to an old trick — he made a fake landing. Just before he was about to be passed, the *Natchez* turned to shore as though answering a hail. The swinging stage was lowered and a rouster rolled a barrel ashore, an *empty* barrel. Result — a new New Orleans-Baton Rouge record, this time by the *J. M. White* of seven hours flat, faster by forty minutes than the best time of the *Rob't E. Lee.*

Although Tobin's mate, Mike Carbine, was famous for his fighting and for his vocabulary, the *White's* owner ran a boat that was completely safe for the most delicate lady. He allowed no gambling, George Devol's memoirs to the contrary, notwithstanding, and everything was kept spotless. As for the matchless food, Tobin instructed his steward to feed the passengers the best of everything, and as much as they wanted. The bill for fruit and nuts alone, one trip, was $700 a week.

"Her giant silver water cooler — deeply engraved — was massive and impressive," wrote Dr. Pierce Butler (in *The Unhurried Years,* LSU Press), who traveled on her as a boy, "and there were eighteen heavy silver cups swinging on the sides of the cooler by means of a heavy silver chain." He recalled that near the stern, the *White* even had a nursery for the children. Also on the texas, he said, was a lavishly furnished "Freedman's Bureau" for the more prosperous Negroes.

Dr. Butler described a typical scene as his family boarded the *J. M. White.*

"Capt. Tobin, quite calm and unhurried as always, came down from the hurricane deck whence he had supervised the landing.

"'You're in luck, Jim [Dr. Butler's father]. I wondered what crazy man thought I would stop this boat at Hutchins, and then I saw the ladies and the boys. Just had to tell old Pearce (the pilot) to round her in, even if we lose money on you.'

"'Glad you saw us, Tobin, and I won't worry about the money.'"

Capt. Tobin took the Butler boys up to the pilot house, a rare treat, as any Mark Twain fan knows.

"We stood in awe of grim old Pilot Pearce, but he was very kindly. When we presently met an Anchor Line steamboat below Glasscock, he said 'Buddy, blow that whistle for me.'"

It is said that the *J. M. White* consistently lost money. In the eight years of her life, insurance premiums alone amounted to $100,000. Not that she didn't try. Here's a contemporary account:

"The steamer *J. M. White* arrived in port [New Orleans] a little after 6 o'clock one morning with 6000 bales of cotton, and 4000 sacks of cotton seed on board. At 11:45, this immense cargo was discharged, and that evening at 5 o'clock, the magnificent steamer was on her way upriver with another load." In her heyday, she is said to have netted $15,000 a week.

In December, 1888, she was listed as being owned by Tobin, E. Conery, and Albert Baldwin, and was valued at about $60,000. She was insured for only $27,000. This had been reduced $2500 in the first week of that month, and the owners were considering cancelling all of it due to the high premiums they were forced to pay. The glamorous lady was a liability in her eighth year, it would appear. In fact, she was under charter to other operators.

Even her proud owner had premonitions that the *J. M. White* was too lavish. Shortly after his arrival with her at New Orleans, he was quoted as saying to a friend:

"Charley, I'm afraid she's a little too fine."

On Monday night, Dec. 13, she was proceeding downriver from Vicksburg. She had paused as scheduled at all the usual stops, including Natchez. At about 9:30 she nosed up to the Blue Store landing, at a plantation in Pointe Coupée parish, about five miles above, and within sight of Bayou Sara. She had 3600 bales of cotton aboard, 8000 seed sacks, 400 barrels of oil, and about forty passengers. What a comedown from her capacity days!

She had hardly made fast, when sheets of flame leapt out of her main deck, from among the deck passengers, and before warning of the danger could be given passengers and crew, the "grande dame" was enveloped in fire.

The captain, James F. Muse, was ill in his stateroom, and barely got out with his life. Only a few of the passengers in the staterooms could be routed out in time. Deeds of heroism and scenes of horror vied for space in the newspapers the next morning. A sailor named Andrew Piersen was singled out for high editorial praise. Capt. Floyd Walsh, a passenger, lost his life saving others. About twenty-eight perished, it was estimated.

Among the casualties was a gigantic ox named Otoe Chief, billed as the "largest in the world," weighing 3980 pounds. He had been exhibited throughout Dixie, and was on his way to be a "feature of the forthcoming Mardi Gras parade."

Strange was a statement given by Frank Barnes, a watchman on the boat. He said the entire crew had been suspicious of disaster. During the trip there were whisperings that the last trip of the steamer was being made that night. He said that when he was relieved by watchman Gus Hunter,

the latter said to him: "If anything happens, for God's sake, wake me up. I am filled with forebodings of evil tonight, and something tells me there is going to be trouble."

He later said: "I am satisfied that the fire was caused by the carelessness of deck passengers smoking near the cotton."

Among the tragic episodes was that of a little boy who held onto a log and floated a mile below the wreck. He was rescued by a Negro woman. But no clue could be found to his identity. His parents were lost. When asked: "Whose boy are you?" he could only reply, "Mama's."

"Everything about the *White* was of the finest," said *The Picayune's* reporter dispatched to the scene. "It can be said safely that another such boat will never be built for a western river."

Capt. Tobin, fifty-nine years old at the time, mourned the loss of his "Aladdin's palace," as a father would for a lost child. He died two years later in Louisville. The great river has never seen the equal of his great boat since.

The J. M. White, the Mistress of the Mississippi (Launched 1878). Note two men painting her smokestacks. She was equipped with every known luxury of the period.

Grand Stairway of the *J. M. White*.

Head of stairway of *J. M. White*.

Huge Mirror at End of the *J. M. White's* Cabin.

Detail of the Cabin of the *J. M. White*.
Note the inlaid floors.

Stalactite Interior
of *J. M. White's* Cabin.

Spittoon Row of the *J. M. White.*

The *Old White* (1843) was one of the fastest pre–Civil War steamboats.

Another View of the Mistress of the Mississippi.

Confederate Guerillas Attacking Mississippi
Steamer *Lebanon*.

WHEN THE MISSISSIPPI RAN RED

ED ran the river in March, 1862. The tawny waters were red with fire and the blood of Yankees fighting Confederates for the grand prize of the War Between the States — control of the Mississippi.

The life of the Confederacy was at stake. To control the river was to keep the Confederacy intact. To lose it was to split the South. But President Lincoln had ordered his armies and navy to wrest control of the Mississippi in its entire course, so that it might "roll unvexed to the sea."

The whole world watched the river in these grim days of 1862 when Grant was attacking "the Gibraltar of the South."

But at the time of the great battle along the Mississippi's banks at Vicksburg, there was another struggle taking place on the river 250 miles downstream, at a small but powerful bastion which is little remembered now. The tiny river town of Port Hudson, La., saw the river war at its bloodiest and bravest. And unlike Vicksburg,

the defenders of Port Hudson — the last desperate hold of the South on its all-important river — never were subdued. And what is even less known, there below the bluffs, from the turbulence of the naval battle, emerged the figure of a man who was to become one of America's great naval heroes. At that fierce but forgotten fight, George Dewey got his baptism by fire — and also by muddy Mississippi water.

The two fortresses of Port Hudson and Vicksburg were prickly thorns in the side of the Federals. The Union forces held Memphis to the north, Baton Rouge and New Orleans to the south. In between, bloody but unbowed, stood Port Hudson and Vicksburg which, defying the Union Navy and Army, continued to vex what Mr. Lincoln wanted "unvexed" — the free roll of Union supplies and forces to the Gulf.

Admiral Farragut bravely ran past these forts several times, losing ships and sailors, soldiers and supplies each trip. The gunners high up on the bluffs showered iron down on the Federal fighting ships. On land, Union General Nathaniel

P. Banks assaulted the tough breastworks of Port Hudson almost continuously between May 24 and July 9. The Confederates' Gen. Frank Gardner beat them all off. It became obvious that only a long, costly siege, first at Vicksburg, and then at Port Hudson, could remove these two obstacles. Both were tough nuts to crack.

Perhaps Port Hudson's greatest trial by combat came on May 27, when the Federals attacked heavily from land and sea. Gen. Banks and Admiral Farragut unleashed a combined assault, but succeeded only in slightly weakening the defenders and smashing several guns, at a heavy cost to their own forces. On June 10 and June 14, the Northerners stormed again, only to realize that the stubborn, grimy, hungry defenders, displaying superhuman courage, were not to be taken.

It was during the earlier blockade-running, past the eager guns of the Confederates at Port Hudson, that a new name in naval history came into prominence. On March 14, Admiral Farragut lashed his flagship, the *Hartford* to another gun-boat, the *Albatross*. These were covered by the *Mississippi*, a powerful "war steamer." With them came the *Monongahela*. Gen. Banks was to arrive from Baton Rouge, twenty-two miles below, and attack at the same time.

Besides the vessels named, the Farragut fleet included a number of smaller supply ships and troop carriers. It was a formidable flotilla.

Port Hudson sits high on the bluff, on the river's east bank. Eighty-five feet was the highest point, and along the edge, its heavy batteries commanded excellent range in both directions. Farther down the bluff, forty-five feet from the river's edge, was the "water battery" prepared for three guns, but with only one 32-lb. rifle in place. Other batteries fronted the river. One light unit was the famed "Capt. Fenner's Louisiana battery," called the "most efficient battery of the port" by the Confederate chief of ordnance. Some said Port Hudson's defenses were better than Vicksburg's. Later events proved this.

The fighting Admiral, whose remark, "Damn the torpedoes, full speed ahead!" became a Navy motto, was confident that he could get past Port Hudson. Could the man who ran the fire and iron hail of Forts St. Philip and Jackson, near the river's mouth, and subjugated New Orleans, fail?

Night fell on the river on March 14. There was the ominous silence that precedes a storm. The men in gray stood at their guns as the faint chugging sound of vessels in motion up the river became audible.

By 11 p.m., Farragut had ordered full speed ahead. The batteries of Port Hudson began to train on the lead vessels. Fifteen minutes passed, then suddenly it began. Guns blaring, the *Hartford* and the *Albatross* rushed through the cauldron taking hits, but passing miraculously unscathed. Behind them, the *Monongahela* at that crucial moment, developed engine trouble. Being right under the central batteries, she turned quickly and fled downstream. The *Mississippi* caught the full brunt of the Confederate fury.

For minutes in which the issue hung in balance, she lingered under the Confederate guns as they poured shells into her. Then with a jolt she struck ground. From the bridge, the executive officer, George Dewey, was thrown over the railing and fell into the water.

The twenty-six-year-old lieutenant commander hit the water with a splash. When he came to the surface, dazed, he began to swim instinctively toward the shore. Then, as the cold water cleared his mind, he grasped the situation, turned and swam back to his ship, then starting to go up in flame!

The gunners were still manning their pieces when the "exec" climbed back aboard, but the *Mississippi* was littered with dead. She had been under broadside fire for thirty-five minutes, and the Confederates on the bluff weren't letting up. Her crew was ordered to make sure the flames could not be controlled, and finally to "abandon ship." The executive officer remained until the last man was off. He then signaled the captain, and they crawled ashore. Admiral Farragut, watching from upstream, cursed in anguish as he saw the *Mississippi's* flames lighting up the river. When the fire reached her engines, she blew up, scattering debris all over the waters.

In due course, the admiral received the official report. Said the captain, in his report:

"I consider that I should be neglecting a most important duty should I omit to mention the coolness of my executive officer, Cr. Dewey, and the steady, fearless, and gallant manner in which the officers and men of the *Mississippi* defended her. . . ."

As for the Port Hudson defenders, it is said that "they received each broadside of the attacking fleet with laughter."

Port Hudson beat off attack after attack from the river and held at bay the land forces encircling it.

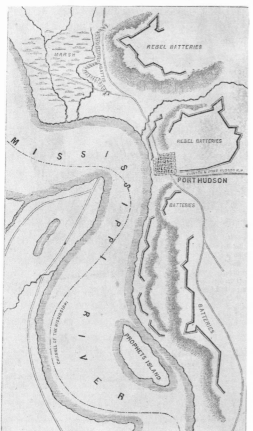

(Above) Union Gun-Boat *Essex* destroying Rebel
Ironclad Ram, *Arkansas,* in the Mississippi.

(Below) The Burning of the US ship *Mississippi,*
during Farragut's Attempt to Run Past
the Forts at Port Hudson.

(Left) Map of Port Hudson Fortifications.

Lieutenant Commander George Dewey.

Bombardment of Port Hudson. Hundred-pound
Parrott gun of the *Richmond.*
Sketched by an officer of the navy.

Then, on July 4, the news of Vicksburg's surrender got through. With little prospect of aiding the waning cause any longer, with the mighty Mississippi almost completely in Federal control, the men who couldn't be shaken from their defenses by force of arms, voluntarily surrendered.

THE GAUNTLET OF THE GUNS

If you rode a steamboat up the Mississippi in 1861-63, you took a chance of getting your fool head shot off.

If you could even get a steamboat to take you upriver then — and that was difficult unless decked out in blue uniform — you must be mighty desperate to get somewhere. Few people were that desperate, and thanks to the state of war raging up and down, from below New Orleans to well beyond the junction of the Mississippi and the Missouri, few steamboats moved in civilian occupations.

No one could blame the folks for staying off the river. Why, on July 23, '63, about forty guerrillas fired on the steamboat *J. P. Penny* on the Tennessee side opposite Island No. 40. Rifles cracked from the banks, two rounds were fired.

Eight days later, the prized steamboat *Sultana* was rounding Council Bend near Memphis with three top-ranking Yankee generals aboard. Thirty armed men banged away at her, using Minie rifles and Enfields, badly damaging her upper works.

On Aug. 22, the *Gladiator,* running from Helena to Memphis, was nearing Hamson's Landing when guerillas opened fire. One ball went clean through the clerk's office just as that gentleman stepped out of it. Twenty bullets pierced the wheelhouse. The boat was crowded with passengers.

A week later, the steamboat *Julia* carrying troops, and under guard of the gunboat *Champion,* was peppered by 500 Confederate guerillas from the shore.

But by far the most harrowing experience of a steamboat during this period was that of the fine passenger ship, the *Empress.* Early impressed by the Federals for running troops and supplies between New Orleans and St. Louis, she was a great source of annoyance to the Confederates then occupying sectors along the river.

When it was learned that Gen. McNeil, U. S. A., was a passenger, anxiety rose in the Southern ranks. Some cavalrymen, and gunners enough to man eight 12-lb. guns and one 10-inch

VIEW OF SPRINGFIELD LANDING, BELOW PORT HUDSON, LOUISIANA—A DÉPÔT OF SUPPLIES FOR BANKS'S ARMY.—From a Drawing by Mr. J. R. Hamilton.—[See Page 446.]

SIEGE OF PORT HUDSON—GENERAL PAINE'S HEAD-QUARTERS AT CHAMBERS'S SUGAR-HOUSE.—[See Page 446.]

THE SIEGE OF PORT HUDSON—HEAD-QUARTERS OF GENERAL BANKS AT RILEY'S PLANTATION.—[See Page 446.]

(Above) Page from Harper's Weekly illustrating Port Hudson Siege.

(Below) Farragut's fleet running past the forts below New Orleans, April 1862.

Naval Combat Off Ft. Wright, May 8, 1862.

General Banks' army marched into Alexandria, Louisiana on the Red River on May 4, 1863. After its defeat at Mansfield, the army retreated past the city, burning much of it.

Capture of Vicksburg. Arrival of
Admiral Porter's Fleet.

Steamboats served as army transports in the
battles for the Mississippi River.

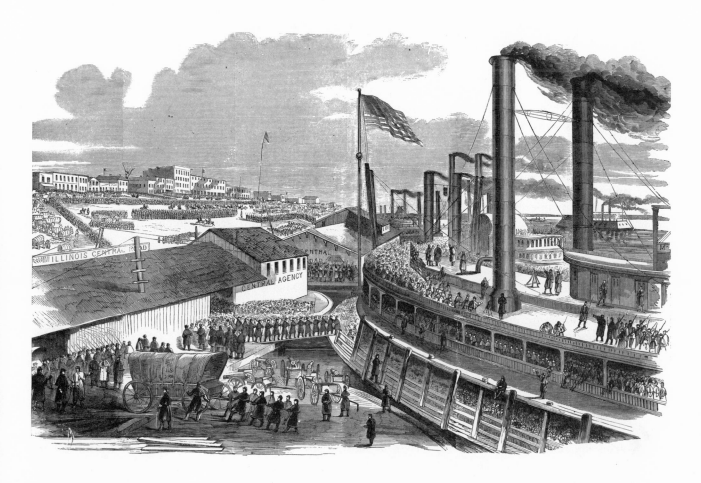

mortar, were dispatched to the river bank, and carefully placed at a strategic turn which would force the *Empress* into easy range, and keep her there long enough to blow her up.

The *Empress* had a record of fifteen miles an hour upstream. She relied on her speed and the gunboats, or "tin-clads," stationed at intervals along the river, for protection. She carried no guns herself, and was unarmored except for some boiler iron on the pilot house.

She had left New Orleans in early August, 1863, and by the tenth of that month, was scurrying upriver. As she approached a bend in the stream, a few miles below Gaines' Landing on the Arkansas side, she entered a narrow where a swift current slowed her down somewhat. It was then that the Confederates, on a high point of the bank, less than a quarter mile away, opened fire.

A masterfully aimed shot nearly clipped the drive shaft of the shoreside paddlewheel, and also disabled the important "doctor" engine which supplied water to the boilers.

The captain, in his office at the moment, ran for the ladder to the texas deck. He turned to shout an order to the pilot. Just then the concussion of a second volley shook the trees on the bank. As the sound of the shot reached the boat, the whining ball from a 12-pounder tore off the captain's head.

The pilot, seeing that to drift downstream would put him right where the batteries wanted the target, tried to make for the opposite shore where less swift water might let him get around the bend.

But the current caught him first and surged him toward the hostile bank. Now he was coming in range of the cavalrymen's firearms, and bullets began to pepper the pilot house. Suddenly he made one of those command decisions so important in war. He gave the wheel hard over and steered directly for the bank where the Confederate guns were stationed. He figured on getting so close that the cannon would fire over him.

As the *Empress* edged closer, he looked around, and sure enough, the balls were falling harmlessly in midstream.

But danger was by no means past. If the pilot let her drift downstream any more, she would again fall within range. Any attempt to make headway upstream would likewise court disaster. So he held her there, with just enough power to keep her steady in the current, while the small arms fire raked the *Empress* from stem to stern,

while the one good wheel churned the muddy water, and while sounds of repairwork echoed from below.

The engine-room crew struggled to slip a new shaft into place. "How long will it take to fix her?" called the pilot down the speaking tube.

"Gimme another ten minutes,'" called the chief engineer.

"We'll hold her here," replied the pilot looking through the broken glass of the pilot house. He could easily see the gunners working to depress their pieces to bear on the helpless steamboat. A trial shot whizzed over the *Empress* and caught the guy wire holding one of her tall stacks.

He looked again and saw the bank abeam of the boat lined with cavalrymen all firing at the pilot house. Glass shattered, bullets rained, planks splintered. The pilot ducked below the iron plate protection, clutching the wheel with now-bloody fingers.

The cannons became still again, evidently re-sighting on the spots above or below where the *Empress* must soon pass. The fearsome "Rebel Yell" echoed again and again from the bank. Then the pilot heard the bell from the engine room ring. He crawled to the speaking tube and raised his head to its mouth, "Ready?"

"We're ready down here," was the reply.

"Then, full steam ahead!"

The *Empress* trembled, slowly forged into the current. Six hundred yards ahead lay twenty minutes of death and then safe water 'round the bend. Two black columns of smoke way upriver marked the approach of a gunboat coming to the rescue.

What was left of the door to the pilot house opened and the night pilot, Gridley, crawled in. "I thought you might need me," he said to the bloody man clutching the wheel.

The *Empress* was going full speed when she reached the spot on which the cannons were zeroed in. Each gunner had picked a particular part of the steamboat for a target — boiler, paddlewheels, pilot house, smoke-stacks. With the first volley it seemed as if Satan himself had grasped the *Empress* and shaken her. The starboard paddlewheel went flying into a thousand pieces; the loosened stack came crashing across the deck. Boiling water spurted from broken pipes, wood planks crashed and splintered.

Gridley took the wheel, as the other pilot crumpled dead at his feet. Lashed by cannon balls, reduced to half speed, the *Empress* inched forward. The scourge of fire pounded her for the

(Above) Burning of Steam Boats, New Orleans Levee,
Night of May 27, 1864.

(Below) Rebel Attack on Sugar Steamer *Empire Parish*
44 miles below Baton Rouge.
The boat escaped through courage of the
Captain who, however, was killed.

full twenty minutes, ripping her to shreds. But miraculously she made headway, and by super-human effort, crawled around the bend to safety.

A total of sixty 12-lb. cannon balls were picked up on the *Empress,* or pried out of her boards. During the fight, a 10-inch shell fell at the feet of a fireman as he opened a firebox.

The *Empress* was immediately rebuilt and returned to her former duties. On Sept. 23, an ad in *The Picayune* announced that she would "leave New Orleans at 5 p.m., for St. Louis, Memphis, Cincinnati. . . ."

If you were still fool enough to ride her, all you had to do was contact "A. G. Cunningham, Clerk."

THE DARING EXPLOITS OF AB GRIMES

The cry, "Here Comes Grimes!" echoed through the ragged camp of the dirty, homesick, war-weary Missourians at Rienzi, Miss., in April, 1862.

The whole camp came to life as if a bugle call had summoned them to a royal feast after months of hardtack, beans and salt back.

Mail from home! Soldiers swarmed around the grimy, dusty Maj. Absalom Grimes as he unbuckled his old carpetbag and alighted from his buggy. "God bless you, Grimes," was the murmur as the mail was distributed, the unclaimed letters sadly returned to the pouch.

Downing a quick meal with the men, Grimes passed out paper and envelopes for them to write. Soon the mail bag was full again. With a wave of his hat and a rebel yell, Grimes was off again, back through the Federal lines to St. Louis.

This scene was repeated many times during the War Between the States, by numerous brave men who knew what a letter means to a soldier's morale, and to morale on the home front. But no accounts of individual intrepidity have come down through the years to rival those about Maj. Grimes, "official mail carrier of the Confederate Army."

Missouri in 1861 was one of the border states, its people bitterly divided. Many of its sons were fighting in the Confederate Army, but early in the war the Federals gained control of the state and maintained their power (with occasional interruptions) until the war's end.

When the North came into control there, nearly all the Missourians in the Confederate Army turned southward to fight, almost as if they were soldiers in a foreign war. Their homes were in

enemy possession; they couldn't visit loved ones, nor could they communicate by mail, except by underground. Thus, in April, 1862, former steamboat pilot Capt. Absalom Grimes, living near Hannibal, Mo., appointed himself to the extremely dangerous job of "running the lines" and carrying the mail.

Grimes was suited ideally to the task. A licensed Mississippi river pilot, he knew his way around the stream. He knew his way around the Federals, too, for when the war broke out in 1861, Grimes and a pilot friend, Sam Clemens (Mark Twain), had been ordered to report to the Federal Army for pilot duty at St. Louis. Grimes later recalled that he and Clemens were waiting to see the general when that officer left to talk to some pretty ladies. As the general talked, the two pilots walked — leaving the Yankees.

Capt. Grimes went south, where his sympathies lay. He joined the Confederates, was captured toward the end of the year, and imprisoned in the old Myrtle St. jail in St. Louis. In March, 1862, he was put aboard the steamboat *City of Alton* for transfer to the penitentiary at Alton, Ill.

Major Absalom Grimes, C.S.A.

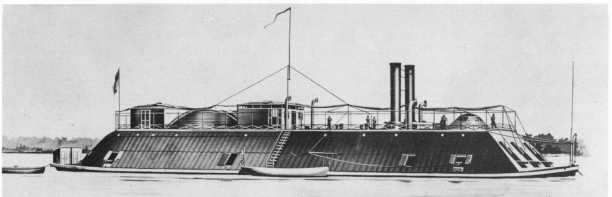

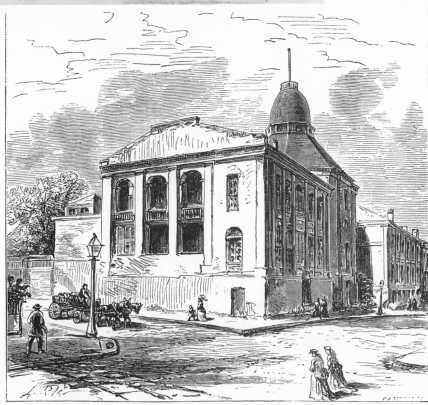

(*At top*) Steamboat Van Phul on which
Grimes made Honeymoon Trip,
from St. Louis to New Orleans shortly
after the war ended.

(*Center*) The U.S. Iron-Clad *Essex*
which Grimes tried to blow up.

(*To Right*) Gratiot Street Prison,
St. Louis, where Grimes was jailed.
By Alfred R. Waud

He knew the ship's pilot, engineer and assorted crewmen. When the other prisoners solemnly marched off the boat at Alton, Grimes was still aboard, busily oiling the engine. Guards searching for stragglers failed to spot the man who looked like he had been oiling engines all his life. The next morning Grimes walked aboard an adjoining steamer. Its pilot also being a pal of his, he returned to St. Louis and freedom.

In St. Louis he realized the need for a shifty man to carry mail through the lines. His friends secretly gathered hundreds of letters, and his first trip to the Missouri soldiers in Mississippi took him six days. He returned to St. Louis with a pack full of letters from the soldiers.

The women of his postal underground, who helped him gather letters, got busy. Taking advantage of their voluminous, ruffled hoopskirts, they sewed in double linings in which to hide letters. It was said that there was one woman who could conceal a thousand letters!

His next trip was grim. He left the steamboat *Far West* when she got sixty miles below St. Louis and took to a skiff. He floated past Federal gunboats at that point, his skiff camouflaged with willow branches. Falling into the fighting going on, he detoured into Arkansas. He was recognized and captured, but not before he was able to hide his bag of mail in a hollow stump in a swamp.

Grimes was confined in the jail at Cairo. The river rose and flooded his cell. With a knife he had sewn in the lining of his coat lapel, he carved a hole in the wooden floor, and when the water subsided, he let himself out. At Cairo Landing he boarded the steamer *Planet*, bound for Tennessee with Federal troops. He was not detected, was fed, supplied with fresh clothing, and helped further in his escape — the engineer of the *Planet* was an old friend of his father!

Grimes finally made his way to the Confederate camp at Corinth, Miss., where the disappointment of the soldiers matched that of the letter-carrier. The letters still were in a stump in Arkansas.

Loaded with mail for the return trip again, Grimes blithely took passage to Cairo on the *Skylark* (the captain was another friend of his). While the steamer approached, landed and departed Cairo, Grimes was hidden under an overturned lifeboat. On June 4 he brought the Confederate soldiers' mail into St. Louis.

Sometimes Grimes worked alone; on other trips he had partners. The Federals were incensed at him, since Grimes also acted as a military courier. Northern fighters and secret service men everywhere were seeking him. Civilians, too, were looking for him.

A hotel clerk in St. Louis betrayed him, and Grimes was taken aboard the ferryboat *Christy* after hurling his bag of letters into the river. Fished out, the evidence jailed him and he was sentenced to be shot in December, 1862.

Carefully imprisoned in the dreaded Gratiot St. jail in St. Louis, Grimes calmly planned his escape. On the night of Oct. 2, he and another prisoner politely walked out. Grimes gathered more mail, and took it to the soliders at Holly Springs, Miss.

Confederate Armies gradually gave way before the relentless power of the North, however. By 1863 Vicksburg was besieged. Getting the mail there was Grimes' next job, one which required his utmost cunning.

With a co-worker named Bob Louden, Grimes had a tinsmith make four metal boxes in which the mail was placed. The boxes were soldered shut, water tight. Louden and Grimes got two frying pans, wired the boxes and a pair of oars inside a skiff and sank the craft until water was within three inches of the gunwales. On a dark night in May they floated past the entire Federal fleet, paddling underwater with the frying pans. Safely past the guns, they came up, used the pans to bail with, and then rowed into Vicksburg!

But when names were called for soldiers to receive their letters, many did not reply. The shock of so many of the boys being gone forever unnerved the man with nerves of steel. He and Louden were discouraged, ready to retire from mail running. It took three generals together to persuade them to continue. So, donning Union uniforms and fastening the metal boxes full of return mail to the bottom of their skiff, they boldly rowed past the enemy again.

One day Grimes arrived at the St. Louis waterfront and saw the mighty Federal gunboat *Essex* tied up there. He resolved to blow her up.

With the help of friends he made a crude bomb, put it in a carpetbag, and walked aboard the *Essex* with it. He sedately told the guard he had some baggage for the captain. There was a delay, and Grimes couldn't find a good place to deposit the bag. Meanwhile, inside it the lighted fuse hissed.

He turned around and calmly but quickly left the boat, expecting momentarily to be blown sky high. Safe from sight of eyes aboard the *Essex*,

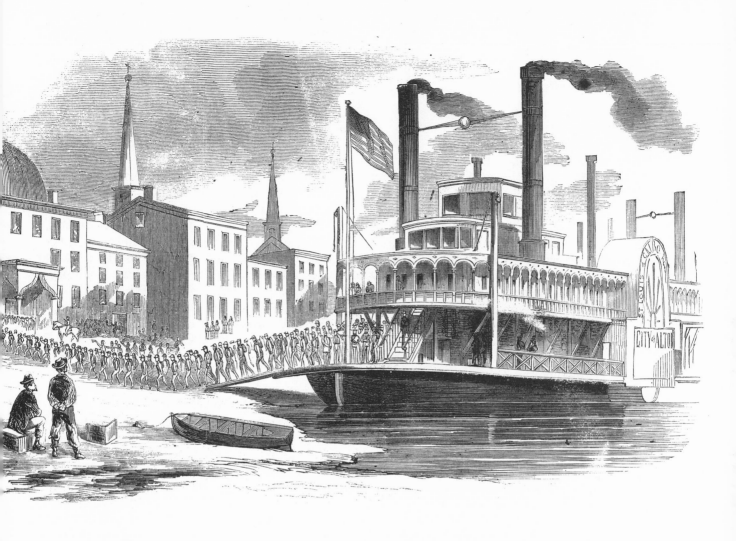

City of Alton debarking 22nd Indiana Volunteers at
St. Louis. This was the steamer
Grimes escaped from in March, 1862.

he opened the bag and grabbed the fuse.

It had just four inches to go!

Grimes also concocted a daring plan to capture a steamboat at Memphis to bring food to
the Confederates starving at Vicksburg. The boat
was one already loaded by the Federals with
commissary stores. Everything was prepared for
this audacious scheme when another craft came
upriver with a large canvas sign nailed to her
hurricane deck: "Vicksburg has surrendered."

There were more close escapes, some of them
while he was visiting his fiancée, but finally the
net closed in on wiley Ab Grimes. He was captured again, was heavily guarded in a strong cell
at Gratiot Street in St. Louis, went to trial and
was sentenced to hang June 18, 1864. He was
soon in the thick of another escape plot.

Ingenious as ever, he had an elaborate plan,
including a wood pile in the prison yard, a check
on the exact moment when guards were changed,
and split-second timing on the part of Grimes
and his fellow escapees.

Just at the ticklish moment, one man stumbled
and the wood pile crashed in a heap. The guards
came running, shooting Grimes twice, killing
three other prisoners and fouling the entire plan.

It looked like curtains for the dare-devil. But
on Dec. 1 he was granted a full pardon — by
Abraham Lincoln.

The four harrowing years behind Grimes left
him little the worse for wear. The foremost mail
carrier of the Confederacy lived to the ripe old
age of seventy-eight.

RURAL ROUTE #1

The Mississippi was the great natural post road for the U. S. Mail — but the early days were hard ones for the Post Office Department.

$500.00 in gold!

That was the prize that the Post Office Department offered to the captain whose steamboat made the first trip between New Orleans and Louisville within six days. The first boats took eighteen to twenty-five days to make the trip but improvements in design had cut the time of the trip considerably — still six days was something to shoot at. In 1838 several boats tried to win the money. In April the *Empress* made the trip in six days, nine hours, only to be beaten a few months later by the *Monarch* which negotiated the 1,480 miles course in six days, one hour. The prize went to Captain Frank Carter in July, 1838. Carter put the *Diana* over the course in five days, twenty-three hours and fifteen minutes.

Speed was one thing and regularity of service another; no captain in the early days of steamboating apparently had the faintest idea about running his boat on a fixed schedule. He would often put an advertisement in the local paper stating that "the splendid steamer *Crowfoot* will positively depart Saturday at 5 p.m. for Natchez and all intermediate landings;" but the following Monday morning might well see our friend's boat securely moored to the levee, still awaiting a paying cargo before departing. Such goings-on made postal officials reluctant to use the steamboats to transport mail under contract. True, steamboats had been carrying mail almost from the time the first one started to run out of New Orleans in 1812, but it wasn't until after the famous run of the *Diana* that the Department got around to making contracts with the steamboat operators. Even then, things didn't work so well; the boats blew up with alarming frequency, collisions and snaggings were common, fog and ice, high water and low water hampered operations and the populace just didn't patronize the mails.

"Saving postage" seemed to have been one of the outstanding pastimes of everybody along the river from merchants to schoolgirls. For years apparently everybody on the steamboats carried the mail — all except the United States — the captain and the clerk often had bags of letters to deliver to customers along the way; passengers carried letters for friends. Even after some rather strict laws were passed, for a long time a good part of the river mail never saw the inside of a postoffice.

Cities, and hence postoffices of any size, were few and far between in the 1,200 mile stretch of river from St. Louis to New Orleans. To this great agricultural section, the Mississippi was the natural post road and the steamboat the mail carrier of what soon came to be Rural Route #1 of the nation. And the steamboat with all its drawbacks was well fitted for the task. Most boats would stop at the wave of a handkerchief from shore to pick up passengers or freight; whether or not the boat had a mail contract, her clerk would pick up letters and take them along to the city where he would receive a small payment for each from the postmaster. On many such letters the steamboat clerk would place a rubber handstamp which would give the name of the steamer, very often its master's name and sometimes the name of the clerk and the trade in which she ran. These handstamped letters were an eloquent form of advertising, especially if the boat had made a quick trip.

After a series of trials with contracts, the Post Office Department soon realized that because most steamboats were owned by individuals — and rugged individualists at that — that the most feasible way to handle the mail between New Orleans and Natchez, Vicksburg, Memphis, St. Louis, Cairo and Louisville was to have contractors engage passage for the mails by the trip. For many years — all during the 1840's and early 1850's this makeshift method was used. Surprisingly, it worked fairly well. True, the ever-increasing volume of mail coming into New Orleans made it necessary to designate a man "Agent, Post Office, New Orleans" and assign him the duty of meeting each incoming steamboat, where he paid the clerk for the "Way" mail and even delivered it to waiting representatives of commercial firms without benefit of the postoffice. This man, E. A. Dentzel, operated as a postman's postman for about seven years (1850-1857). He even carried and used a "Paid" handstamp bearing his own name.

The country was growing and New Orleans trade was reaching new heights with each passing year. A new and better way to handle the river mail had to be found because the merchants were complaining of the poor service at the postoffice and even poorer arrangements for the carriage of the river mail. (One postmaster even advertised that the river mail was due "every time it gets here.")

In the midst of the hurly-burly and rush of the crowded riverfront, a partnership of two captains was coming into prominence. For a number of years Captain Thomas P. Leathers and Captain Truman C. Holmes had been operating boats in the Vicksburg and Natchez cotton trade on fixed schedules. Their boats, Leathers' *Natchez* and Holmes *Princess*, were renowned for their safety, punctuality and speed; when either captain tapped the big bell on the hurricane deck for the order to back her out, you could set your watch at 5 o'clock for that day.

In the fall of 1854, the Post Office Department, goaded by New Orleans business interests, cancelled the existing "mail by the trip" arrangement and gave Holmes and Leathers a contract to carry the mail from New Orleans to Vicksburg and return, service to be three times a week and the pay $40,000.00 a year. A happier postal arrangement was never made. Leathers and his partner carried the mail from early 1855 until the outbreak of the Civil War. Three times a week the boats were "on the track," plowing the 397 muddy miles between the two cities with regularity.

Encouraged by the success of the Holmes and Leathers contract, the Post Office Department late in 1855 awarded a contract for what was known as "The Great Through Mail," a 1075 mile trip from New Orleans to Cairo, Illinois, where the Illinois Central Railroad, then newly opened, would take the mail bags for Chicago. The price was a handsome $329,000.00 a year. What happened to the contractors in 1856-7 was to spell the doom of the steamboats as long-distance mail carriers. Everything went wrong — the river froze in the winter and boats couldn't move because of ice jams; the next summer there was such extremely low water in the Ohio that the bigger boats grounded. The contractors hired ten steamers on charter, but bad luck continued to plague them as one after another was snagged, sunk or damaged by grounding. Government fines ate up nearly $200,000.00 of the contractors' compensation and they were forced to withdraw. Post Office officials, becoming exasperated, began to

Advertisement of U.S. Mail Line. Note the assurance that this "is the route for Southerners" since "passing through Slave Territory, travellers are free from annoyance" in connection with their servants.

cast their eyes on the growing stretch of iron rails which was soon to connect the Ohio River with New Orleans.

The Civil War is popularly supposed to have spelled the doom of the steamboats of the Mississippi. Actually, such was far from the truth. After the war many new boats bigger, stronger, faster were built and Uncle Sam continued to give mail contracts to them, even while he was giving contracts to their rivals, the railroads. There was even a contract (at a greatly reduced figure) for the New Orleans-Cairo route in 1865. By 1876 the railroads had made vast inroads into steamboat traffic, but the three erstwhile river rivals, Captains Leathers, Tobin and Cannon, were carrying the mail between New Orleans and Vicksburg and receiving $35,000.00 a year for their trouble.

In 1887 Captain Leathers was still carrying the mail, under contract, from New Orleans to Vicksburg. In an open letter to the people in his "trade," the old man proudly wrote on July 16, 1887:

The *T. P. Leathers* [he had laid up his *Natchez* because of slack trade] is the only through United States mail packet from New Orleans to Vicksburg, and between these points every mail landing (37 in number) is made each trip up and down. . . . There is a regular mail delivery by the *Leathers*, in charge of Mr. H. F. Wilson, a duly authorized and commissioned route agent, one of the most reliable and best known of river clerks.

For more than fifty years I have been steamboating in this trade, and for forty years, except during the war, no Saturday has passed without a boat of mine leaving New Orleans on that day for Vicksburg — boats noted for speed, safety and excellence of accommodations for both traveler and shipper.

But not even Tom Leathers, river giant that he was, could stay the inexorable march of progress. The steamboat as a carrier of the mail had seen its day and with the coming of the new century the great white boats which proudly flew the pennant "U.S.M." were seen no more on the tawny waters of the great river that had spawned them a century before.

The *Princess* Wooding Up. Her engineer declared he'd reach New Orleans on schedule or blow up. He blew up below Baton Rouge, Feb. 27, 1859. Currier & Ives.

Tecumseh (Built 1826) made a "lightening" run from New Orleans to St. Louis, of a bit more than 8 days, delivering New Orleans newspapers and mail much faster than would have been possible by overland route.

Mail Bill of the *Atlantic*, June 20, 1854.

ST. LOUIS TO NEW ORLEANS.

MAIL-BILL.

Steamboat *Atlantic* Capt *Cutter* is to convey the mails made up for this route at the offices in the left hand column, and deliver them into the offices respectively in the right hand column, as entered in this bill. Boat is to leave SAINT LOUIS on the 13th day of June 1854 and reach NEW ORLEANS in seven days. Price for the service is Twenty Dollars, to be paid by the Postmaster at NEW ORLEANS in full performance in all particulars. $20.

I swear to support the Constitution of the United States, to perform the duties of Mail Carrier, and to abstain from every thing forbidden by the Laws establishing Post Offices and Post Roads.

H. H. Eggers Clk

Ed. Milligan A.P.O.

Natchez.	Vicksburg.	Napoleon.	Memphis.	Hickman.	Cairo.	St. Louis.	Numbered Mail Bags Sent from to	Postmasters or Agents, will sign their names opposite their Offices in this Column, if they have received all the Mail Bags sent; if not, they will specially note the deficiency on this Bill.
						None	Cairo.	
							Hickman.	*G. _____*
						1	Memphis.	*Geo. A. Smith*
			3			2	Napoleon.	*J. A. _____*
		1				1	Vicksburg.	*Wm. _____*
		1				1	Natchez.	*A. H. _____*
One		2	1			2	New Orleans.	*F. A. Bentze*

Received said *Twenty* Dollars of the Postmaster at New Orleans this 20th day of June 1854 *Charles Cutter* CAPTAIN.

INSTRUCTIONS.

The *Southerner* was the last Mail-Boat down.—Should your Bo at break, get aground or be detained from any other cause, ship the Mail by the first boat going down; give her your mail Bill, and take her receipt for the Mail. It is very important that the Mail should be at the Post office as soon as possible after the arrival of the Boat. You will, therefore, immediately on reaching the landing, despatch it by some RESPONSIBLE OFFICER of the Boat to the Office. All Letters deposited in your letter-box, or coming within your control on the Boat, must be taken with the Mail to the Post Office; and, in order to enable the Postmaster to charge the proper postage on them, write the name of the place at which they were received on the letters.

(Above) The Belle Creole (1845-52) and the Music (1850-59). From painting owned by Mrs. E. C. Chadbourne, Washington, D.C. The Belle Creole sank in 1846, was raised and put back in service, and exploded in 1949, and repaired again, ran 'till end of 1851.

(To Right) Freight Bill of the Belle Creole.

Envelope Carried by the Belle Creole.

Envelope Carried on the Duck River. Note the "hand" stamp, used to advertise the steamer.

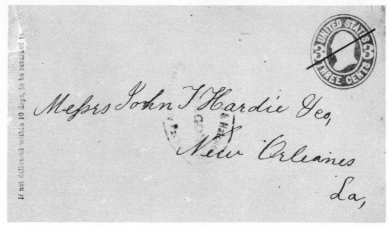

(Above) The *Wild Wagoner* Mail Packet.

(To Right) Envelope bearing stamp of *Wild Wagoner*.

(Below Left) Envelope Carried by the Holmes & Leathers' *Natchez*, Nov. 20, 1858.

(Below Right) Natchez Post Office, Sunday Morning. Sketch by Alfred R. Waud, 1871.

(Above) The Tragic *Sultana* crowded with Soldiers.

(Below) An Artist's Sketch of The Great Disaster.

THE FLOATING TORCH

AND

THE FLAMING COFFIN

HESE days, when man-made catastrophes can wipe out thousands at one stroke, it is difficult to appreciate the tremendous impact which steamboat disasters had on citizens of the mid-nineteenth century.

Here was a new-fangled method of transportation — steam-propelled boats which carried passengers and freight swiftly and cheaply. The rivers soon became crowded with the graceful, puffing, white steamers gliding effortlessly along the muddy waters, brimming with song, romance and wealth. This was living!

But from the earliest days of the steamboats, nearly all had one dreadful characteristic in common — they exploded. Early engines were crude; boilers often were defective. They just didn't know how to build them safely yet. Engineers who ran them, too, just plain didn't know. It was all so new. The demand for more, bigger and faster engines far outdistanced the technological advances.

Then there was the almost universal mania for racing. It was natural to want to travel on the fastest boat. The owners could hardly resist cater-

ing to this whim, for it meant more revenue to best a rival to a landing. This all culminated in a long series of steamboat explosions and burnings in the period roughly between 1835 and 1865. Those fateful thirty years, while often called the "Golden Age of Steamboating," might also be termed the "Boom period," with every emphasis on the grim pun.

Growled *The Picayune* of that day in its restrained rhetoric: "We think it full time that a stop should be put to events of a nature so revolting to the mentalities of man . . ." And an old steamboat captain wrote to the editor of the same daily in November 1840:

> Want to know why boilers bust on leaving shore? Steamboat men and even passengers have a pride in making a display of speed. To do this they hold on to, instead of letting off, steam. The flue gets hot and the water low, and the first revolution brings the two elements in contact and causes a collapse. . . .

Every edition of the newspapers carried outcries for protection, while news columns carried doleful reports of new tragedies. The New Orleans *Bee* as early as May, 1837, cried out that this type of tragedy was "all too common on Western waters." *The Bee* was indignant about the *Ben Sherod* disaster which is described as "a scene of horror beggaring all description," and which will figure further along in this story.

The 1830's had been the worst decade for carnage on Western waters, and there had been a slight slacking off in the early '40's' But, as the mid-century approached, the boilers began to let go as if to celebrate the occasion. There were approximately forty-eight explosions in the 1836-1840 period. From '46 to '48, there were twenty-eight, killing about 259 people.

Two events, twenty-eight years apart, serve to point up the tragic consequences of carelessness with a new toy and the urge for speed.

Two names which stood for many years as synonmous with Inferno — *Ben Sherrod* and *Sultana*.

Young Pilot Davis of the *Ben Sherrod* placed his foot on the rail of the bar in Loubet's Saloon, near Monkey Wrench Corner at Canal and Royal Streets, New Orleans. The only topic of conversation anywhere on the river that day was the awful explosion of the steamboat *Tennessee*.

"If ever I should be on a boat that takes fire," he drawled, taking another pull at the stein of cold beer, "and I don't save the passengers, it will be because the tiller ropes burn — or I perish in the flames."

His companions remembered young Pilot Davis' remark. A week later, at the wheel of the *Ben Sherrod*, he seemed to be about the only member of the crew with such high ideals, as the boat sped through the night.

For down on the boiler deck, a Bacchanalian brawl was in progress. Capt. Castleman, the master, was slowly overtaking a rival steamer, the *Prairie*. Ordering pine knots and resined coal heaped on the already overcharged fires, he retired for the night, comfortable in the knowledge that he would deliver his mail ahead of the *Prairie's*, cocky with the thought of his passenger's surprise on awaking the next morning, miles and hours closer to their destinations.

In keeping with the Captain's mood, the firemen were stoking themselves out of a whiskey barrel as enthusiastically as they were the boilers. The hotter the boilers got, the drunker the firemen became. "Beastly drunk," charged an eyewitness later.

Then, at 1 a.m. on the night of May 8, 1837, fourteen miles above Fort Adams, Mississippi, the overheated boilers set fire to sixty cords of resin-dripping pine wood, stacked nearby, and in a flash the boat was a flaming torch.

Most steamers in like circumstance got it over quickly. They exploded and sank. Not so the *Ben*, which preferred slow torture. Passengers and crew went crazy. There was no thought of "women and children first." It was every man for himself.

"To the shore, to the shore," shrieked nearly four hundred terrorized souls. It was weird and dreadful. To Pilot Davis' credit, he attempted to steer the burning boat shoreward, but as he had predicted, the hempen wheel ropes burned in two. There was only one thing left for him to do — "perish in the flames."

The *Ben Sherrod* was still under steam. She headed upstream again. The ropes holding a crowded yawl burned, drowning all its occupants, mostly crew. Others began to throw themselves into the crimson-tinted darkness of the river. The steamboat was leaving a wake of shouting people and flaming debris. Then the miserable wretches floundering in the water had something more to contend with in the form of the well-meaning steamer *Alton*, racing to the rescue. Stupidly, she plowed her way through the victims, "drowning many persons in the water."

The monster in command of the racing *Prairie*, now far ahead, ordered his vessel to go on its way leaving the *Ben Sherrod* in flames, merely reporting her afire when he arrived at Natchez.

Other rescue boats did better, picking up dozens of survivors. By then, however, the *coup de grace* was ready. The *Ben's* fire finally enveloped, ironically enough, the barrel of whiskey that had inspired the stokers' recklessness. It went off like a cannon. Next went the long overdue boilers, roaring to be delivered of their giant head of steam. But the worst was yet to come.

When the fire reached forty barrels of gunpowder, the "fearful" explosion was heard "many miles." One hardened onlooker stated: "It was the grandest sight ever seen."

There were instances of heroism, but for sheer urge to self-preservation, for panic, and greed, the *Ben Sherrod* disaster has rarely been equalled. People pushed each other off floating planks, fought for bobbing objects, threw women aside.

Seventy-two people perished. The blackened hulk of the *Ben* finally settled to the bottom, out of sight, above Fort Adams.

But from this tale of infamy — the drunken firemen, the callous crew, the *Prairie's* captain, the blundering *Alton* — there emerges a figure whose despicable character records an all-time low. Let Mr. Cook, a survivor, pillory the "scoundrel" for all time:

"As I and others were floating downstream, I managed to hail a man I saw standing on the shore. He came out in a yawl, picking up baggage and boxes and looking into debris. As he reached us, he asked with the utmost *sang froid*, 'How much will you give me?'

"We entreated him for help and he replied, 'Oh, you're well off there; keep cool, and you'll come out comfortable'. And he paddled away."

THE SULTANA DISASTER

No one could see it, when the *Sultana* pulled out of New Orleans for Cairo, but a skull and crossbones flew from the jack-staff. It wasn't visible, but it was there just the same. The Grim Reaper was commanding the voyage. Death rode the *Sultana* in April, 1865.

He gave his first warning of what was to come before the steamer reached Vicksburg. The *Sultana* developed a leak in one of her four boilers. A big new boat, she was enrolled at 1719 tons, licensed to carry 376, including her crew. It took thirty-three hours to repair her boiler. A reprieve — nothing more. The stage for the last act in the macabre drama was all set.

At a camp near Vicksburg were hundreds of paroled Union prisoners of war, mostly from Ohio, Indiana, Michigan, Kentucky and Tennessee. The Civil War at long last was ended; they had been released from the living hells of Cahaba and Andersonville prisons.

Weak, suffering from wounds and lean from starvation, they longed for home, and the Federal Army Officers at Vicksburg were bent on sending them upriver to Cairo, homeward bound, a thousand to every steamboat.

For several days the work of transporting these living skeletons progressed. The *Henry Ames* appeared and took off 1300; the *Olive Branch* left with about 700. Scarcely had she pulled away, April 23, when the *Sultana* hove into view with her leaky boiler. While it was being repaired, those thirty-three hours of grace, she was designated by the military to take aboard from 1200 to 1500. By midday of the 24th, her boilers were working again, but for some reason only a few soldiers had come aboard.

There was a rumor that somebody was paying off certain officers to detain the men until the *Sultana* had cleared, so they would have to go on other boats. The rumor reached the commanding officer, Major General N. J. T. Dana. Fur began to fly. Although two other steamboats were docked at Vicksburg, the officers ordered *all* the men left at camp aboard the *Sultana!* That would still the tongues accusing Army officers of taking bribes!

Thus began the fearful overloading of the floating coffin. The clerk of the *Sultana* told one soldier that if the boat arrived safely at Cairo, and he already had serious doubts, it would be the greatest trip ever made on Western waters, there being more people aboard than had ever been carried by one boat on the Mississippi River. He stated that there were 2400 soldiers, 100 civilian passengers, and a crew of eighty — in all over 2500, or six times her capacity!

One officer later admitted that he knew about the leaky boiler, but didn't inspect the repairs. Another had grave doubts about the boat's capacity, even reported it to a superior who did nothing. Only after the *Sultana* had taken the last of her emaciated cargo aboard and steamed off did the commanding general realize she had over 2000 men aboard. But he did nothing either.

She left Vicksburg at 1 A.M., April 25. Six hours later she landed at Helena, Arkansas, where a photographer on shore took a picture of the *Sultana,* with nearly every member of her human cargo at the rail, bent on having his face discernible in the photograph.

"Smile please," said Death.

The steamer arrived at Memphis at 7 P.M. the next day, after a smooth trip. Some of the men helped unload her cargo of sugar. Later that evening, she steamed across the river and, after taking on coal from some barges, headed upriver.

"Here," said Death. "Now!"

A boiler exploded with terrific force. Shrieks, cries, prayers and groans in the darkness. Crashing smoke-stacks, staterooms torn apart, mangled, scalded human forms heaped and piled amid the burning debris of the lower deck. Raging flames shooting from the hull, rising through the rift which cut cabin, roof and texas in two.

Within twenty minutes after the explosion, the whole boat was enveloped in a sheet of flame. Many of the passengers were blown into the river by the force of the blast; others, pinned down by the wreckage, were burned where they fell. Whole groups jumped blindly into the water, pulling each other down as they struggled.

A survivor said: "Men were rushing to and fro, trampling over each other in their endeavor to escape. All was confusion . . . I stood for a few moments and listened to that awful wail of hundreds of human beings being burned alive in the cabins and under the fallen timbers . . ."

The struggle for survival both aboard what was left of the *Sultana* and in the river, was intense; people were fighting, kicking, grasping to hang on. One man remembered, as he surged through the burning boat toward the rail, a pet alligator in a large wooden box under the stairway in a closet. He got it, bayoneted the alligator, threw the box overboard, paused to take off everything but his drawers, jumped in after the box, and managed to pull himself into it. Naturally, others wanted it, but he kicked them off.

"If they would have got hold of me, we would both have drowned," he added.

Soon the intense flames of the burning *Sultana* died down and the hundreds still struggling in the water were in total darkness. To add to their misery, it was a rainy night and the Mississippi was at flood stage. The river was three miles wide where the *Sultana* blew up; only the good swimmers made it to the shore unaided.

Many survivors were rescued by other steamboats. The official count of the dead and missing was set at 1547.

The whys and wherefores of this explosion were argued for years afterwards. A post-mortem on the salvaged boilers showed it was not the repaired boiler which let go, but one of the other three "good" ones. It finally came down to the construction of the boilers, an expert saying they were "an experiment on the Lower Mississippi." This type of boiler was quickly taken out of other steamboats.

WHEN THE LOUISIANA EXPLODED

A few minutes past 5 p.m. on Thursday, Nov. 15, 1849, the proud steamboat *Louisiana*, Capt Cannon, exploded her boilers at the foot of Gravier St., New Orleans. A piece of flying metal cut a mule in two, and Mayor A. D. Crossman had his pocket picked.

Every house in New Orleans was shaken on its foundations, and a bereaved father had a scene of the tragedy cut in marble for the family tomb in memory of his son.

Steamboats on each side of the *Louisiana* — the *Bostona* and the *Storm* — were leveled to the water. A twelve-foot piece of metal of immense weight was kicked all the way to Canal and Front Sts., about five blocks away, knocking over a popular coffee house on that corner.

People standing as far as two hundred yards from the *Louisiana* were mowed down by flying debris. Yet, a man standing on her texas deck, almost above the boilers, was uninjured. The *Storm*, what was left of her, was blown fifty feet out into the river. Her pilot, who was in the wheelhouse, thought it was his own boilers, and flattened himself on the deck. A dead man came sailing through the window, and landed on top of him.

Mayor Crossman who had just left the dock ten minutes before, hurried back to help — and to have his pockets picked by one of the many vandals who also hurried to the scene to loot the bodies and hustle away cargo.

The *Storm* had just landed all her passengers upriver at Lafayette (now part of New Orleans); the *Louisiana* was to pick up 200 German immigrants at the Third Municipality landing (below Esplanade Avenue).

The clerk of the *Storm*, Mr. Moody, was sitting at his desk, then located about twenty feet from the Louisiana's boilers next door. The explosion riddled the walls around him as if with grapeshot, tearing them away. He was uninjured. His wife, though, was standing at the stern of the boat, and was killed instantly. Their child was found next morning, safe and sound.

The *Louisiana* disaster was one of the worst steamboat disasters of the time, with an estimated eighty-six (slightly exaggerated, perhaps; but no count could ever be made exactly) killed, and scores mangled and wounded.

New Orleans had seen other steamboat tragedies at first hand. Only one month before, on Oct. 8, no less than five steamboats burned at the foot of Poydras — the *Falcon*, the *Marshal Ney*, the *Illinois*, the *North America*, and the *Aaron Hart*. Two more boats were moved into the stream just in time, to escape with little damage. The bill was $250,000, but the loss of life was nil.

"For St. Louis — The new and elegant, fastrunning steamer *Louisiana*, John W. Cannon, master, is now receiving freight and will leave as above, on Thursday, the 15th inst., at 4 o'clock p.m. . . ."

This was the usual ad run by steamboats, and the one which announced the departure of the big noisemaker. Although she was slightly later than her announced departure time in backing away, that one-hour delay was pretty good, considering the contempt which most captains had for keeping schedules.

As it happened, both Capt. Cannon and his chief engineer, John L. Smith, were ashore when the big sidewheeler edged from her wharf, took a turn of the drive shaft, and let go. This absence of the two top men in command was not unusual, however. They were making certain arrangements for the trip, and the second in command would bring her over to the Third Municipality landing where the passengers waited. But it looked bad to the public and to the examiners who later questioned the absentees on charges of manslaughter.

Capt. Cannon was a very popular steamboat figure — the man who, twenty years later with his *Rob't E. Lee,* was to outfox the wily Capt. T. P. Leathers and beat the *Natchez* to St. Louis. The *Louisiana* was a distinguished steamboat of her day, and always left with a good payload and enthusiastic passengers who liked her speed and her famous, bountiful dining table.

To the citizens of New Orleans, and especially to those in the business section, the sudden explosion came as a terrific, frightening phenomenon — the deafening noise, the awesome concussion, followed by shattered glass, swaying buildings and shouting people. The smoke and flames rose from the wharves, the cries of the wounded raised a horrific din. Wrote *The Daily Picayune's* reporter [it was] "utterly impossible to describe all the revolting sights." But he did.

Reading of the great pillar of smoke mushrooming over the river, today's atomic explosions come to mind. In fact, an eyewitness 100 years ago described the steamboats as having been "shattered to atoms."

The *Louisiana's* hull sank from sight ten minutes after the explosion, carrying more people down with her. One line in the newspapers said, in the first story, that "Mr. Barelli's son [Joseph A. Barelli, Jr.] has been found and it is expected will recover."

Then, next day: "We regret to learn that Mr. Barelli, son of the much-respected Sicilian Consul [he represented the kingdom of Two Sicilies, which then took in much of Southern Italy] is still among the missing. Last night's intelligence brought to us that he had been found, we are extremely sorry to say, was premature. The finding of his watch on the levee had previously inspired the most painful foreboding."

Thus it was that the scion of the Barelli family disappeared in the confusion, as did numerous persons whose bodies were never recovered. The senior Barelli was a leading citizen, who had come from Como, Italy, in 1801. An "honorable merchant and noble man," according to his death notice nine years later, he was also Consul for Portugal and was "the father" of the Italian Benevolent Society. He resided at 61 Common St.

So it was not surprising that this distinguished gentleman, mourning the loss of his son and heir (whose body was never found) should send to Italy for a marble memorial. The scene depicts the explosion of the *Louisiana,* with young Barelli being lifted from the mortal flames into Heaven by an angel. It is said to have cost $2500. It can still be seen, weathered by wind and rain, in St. Louis Cemetery No. 2.

Not only Barelli but the whole city went into mourning. Mayor Crossman asked boat captains and business houses to lower their flags to half mast. Days later, the authorities were still finding bodies, and scooping up cargo out of the river.

Two inquiries were held, to determine the cause and to fix the blame, if any. The coroner's jury met at the Verandah hotel. One of the jurors was F. A. Lumsden, an owner of *The Picayune.* The jury found the second engineer, Clinton Smith, "grossly, culpably, and criminally neglectful and careless of his duty . . .", and that Capt. Cannon was "censurable and highly culpable" in allowing a man like Smith to be in charge. It therefore charged that Cannon and Smith, "to these extents" were the "cause and causes of said explosion."

The other inquiry was held before Recorder Baldwin, whose remarkable and amusing decisions echo through the court records to this day. He was also billed as "U.S. Commissioner," and in that capacity, examined Capt. Cannon and John Smith, the chief engineer, on the manslaughter charge brought by one William Moales. After listening to numerous witnesses, testifying to the characters of the accused, and to the *Louisiana's* condition, and steamboat practices, Recorder Baldwin acquitted both men.

Through the testimony runs the undercurrent that the steamboat's boilers were old and defective. She had acquired them from an older steamboat which had been dismantled, and it looked as though the machinery was already in bad shape when installed on the *Louisiana.*

There was also reason to think that the men in the steamboat's engine room were not doing their duty, not watching their valves and gauges. Actually, the inquiry did lead to reforms in steamboat operations.

What about the mayor's pocket getting picked? While Mayor Crossman was assisting in identifying bodies, somebody handed him a gold watch from one of the dead. He slipped it into his coat pocket.

"In an instant," said *The Picayune*, "a hand from the crowd dived into the aperture, seized the timepiece, and made off with it unperceived. The mayor's surprise may be conceived when, a few moments afterwards, he felt for the property just deposited with him and found it gone.

(Left) Explosion of the *Moselle*. The engineer hung three heavy wrenches on the safety valve.

(Below) The *Henry Frank*.

(On facing page) Four illustrations of John Hay's Famous Ballad: "Jim Bledso of the *Prairie Belle*. Illustrated by S. Entinge, Jr.

Jim cried:

> " 'I'll hold her nozzle agin the bank
> "Till the last galoot's ashore'. —
> "And Jim Bledso's ghost went up alone
> "In the smoke of the *Prairie Belle*."

I CAN'T TELL WHAR HE LIVES.

HE WERE N'T NO SAINT.

A NIGGER SQUAT ON HER SAFETY-VALVE.

I'LL HOLD HER NOZZLE AGIN THE BANK.

(Above) Collision of the *Western World* and *H. R. W. Hill.* Some 30 people on the *Western World* lost their lives.

(Right) Burning of the *John Swasey* at New Orleans. Most of the passengers escaped by jumping onto the dock.

(Below) Explosion on Mississippi Steamboat. Sketch by Alfred R. Waud. Explosion caused by bursting steam pipe.

Steamship Graveyard. Finale for the *Mississippi*.
Drawn by Chas. Graham.

(*On facing page, above*) Burning of the *Rob't E. Lee II*, Oct. 30, 1882. 30 lives were lost. She was a successor to the *Rob't E. Lee* of the famous race (see "Race of the Giants").

(*On facing page below*) Burning of Steamers at St. Louis.

(*Above*) Collision at Mingo of the *Scioto* and *John Lomas*, July 4, 1882.

(Above) *The Grand Republic* built 1881. Destroyed by fire. (See *The Slickest Rascal on the Mississippi*).

(Below) *Grand Republic's* Cabin. Luxurious Victorian Gothic.

(Above) *The Lafourche,* burned Sept, 20, 1907.

(Right) Another View of the *Lafourche.*

The Imperial. She succumbed to shrimp.

THE IMPERIAL SUCCUMBED TO SHRIMP

XCEPT for an excursion steamer here and there, and only one lone, special "cruise" paddlewheeler, the glory that was steamboating has passed into oblivion. But as long as those who remember the good old days still live, the memory of steamboatin' will continue to capture the fancy of the present generation. The majestic boats, puffing and wheezing at the wharves of the Mississippi, Red, Ohio, and Missouri rivers, made the entire Mississippi valley bud and blossom, setting the stage for the prosperity of this age.

Let's look at some of the steamers which plied the Red and Mississippi rivers. N. Philip Norman, writing in the *Louisiana Historical Quarterly* of April 1942, compiled an amazing amount of data on the boats which were familiar sights along the levees from the earliest to the last days of the steamboat trade.

For instance, the nicknames! The "One Arm John" was the *John D. Scully,* so named because she only had one chimney. The *Valley Queen* was called the "Statesman's Boat" because her master was named George Washington Rea, and her clerk was Henry Clay Boazman.

The "Dirty Belle" was *La Belle,* and she got this label because she consumed an enormous amount of fuel, and deposited a corresponding amount of cinders and dirt on her passengers and cargo. The "Fourth of July" was the *Independent,* for obvious reasons, and while on the subject of names, Capt. E. Parker, master of the *Piota,* called his boat by that name because the letters stood for "Parker Is Obliged To All."

Roustabouts, who loved fantastic names, christened the *Wheelock,* "Starvation," the *Danube,* "You be dam," the *Alvin,* "Calico Jack," the *Ouachita,* "Oyster Loaf," the *Paul Tulane,* "Two Days and a Half," the *T. P. Leathers,* "T. P. Mule," and the *G. W. Sentell,* "Broken Back."

Names meant much to the masters and operators of steamboats. The owners of the *Franklin Pierce* went to court to change her name to the *Texana* because the boat's original name was hexed, or "unlucky." In those days (1855), by some legal quirk, the U.S. government had to be sued in order to make such a change, and Congress passed a special act, the first of its kind, allowing the switch. Unhexed by act of Congress!

More names? The *Lioness,* an early (1832)

159

La Belle, otherwise known as the "Dirty Belle", carried 2,699 bales of cotton with her to the bottom.

boat in the New Orleans-Red River trade, really roared when her cargo of powder blew up. The *Express Mail* belching smoke and cinders, must have taken a kidding from the river dandies. Her master's name was John *Smoker*. There was a *Frank Morgan* long before the movie star was a twinkle in his great-grandpa's eye, and the steamer *Seven Up* went *down* — near Shreveport. The *Sun* burned, and the *Sunrise* actually had one, an electrical device between her chimneys which simulated a sunrise for the delight of dockside spectators.

Were the boats named *Champion* really champs? Not the *Champions Nos. 3, 5, 9*. They all sank. How about the *Eras*? Now they were something. There were *Eras* from No. 1 to No. 13, and here's how they made out: *Era No. 1*, sank (1858); *No. 2* sank (1864); *No. 3* cleared $8000 profit for her owners in three weeks (1858); *No. 4* died a natural death, it seems, without distinction; *No. 5* was captured by the Federals in 1863; *No. 6* burned in 1860; *No. 7* apparently had no troubles; *No. 8* likewise.

But No. 9! She collided with and sank the *Era No. 10* at the mouth of the Red river in 1868. That's not all. Two years later she hit and sank the *Texas!* As for the *No. 10*, she was raised but finally was destroyed by fire in 1892.

No. 11 deserves a place in the steamboat hall of fame. Besides carrying 4500 bales of cotton, 700 head of cattle, four classes of passengers, she also published a daily newspaper on board.

No. 12 was dismantled in 1875 and her machinery used in the steamer *Dawn*. Finally came *No. 13*. Was she unlucky? Not according to the records. She lived a useful life on the Red river in the '70s. So much for the numerical *Eras*.

That name, "Era," was very popular, as you can see. There was also a *Grand Era*, which burned at New Orleans in 1871; two *New Eras*, and a *Pioneer Era*.

Swapping machinery from an old steamer to a new hull was common practice. Propulsion machinery was expensive. An owner couldn't walk into the nearest hardware store and buy it. So, when a boat was worn out its machinery went into a new construction, as steamboat engines lasted for years.

The *Key West No. 2* gave her machinery in 1864 to the *Admiral Farragut*, and when the *Admiral Farragut* was dismantled in 1871, the same machinery went into the *Mary E. Poe*. Take a look at the good boat *Jesse K. Bell*, built in 1856. Her machinery went into the *Bart Able*

Era 10. Sank, and was raised. Finally burned, 1892.

launched four years later. The *Bart Able* was rebuilt twice, in 1872 and 1878; but when she was dismantled in 1879, her machinery was put back into the new *Jesse K. Bell!*

The *Samuel J. Hale* gave her works to the *G. W. Sentell*, which in turn passed them on to the *Col. T. G. Sparks*. The *Sparks*, incidentally, was a prison steamboat. Her cabins were enclosed with iron bars, and her owner, who was "lessee of the Louisiana Penitentiary" in the 1890's, used the boat to transport prisoners and their products. All the crew except the licensed officers were convicts:

The *Nashville* gave her engines to the *Julia A. Randolph* in 1869, and the *Julia*, when she burned two years later, willed them to the *Fannie Tatum*. The *Assumption* of 1875 assumed the go-rods of the *Lucy Hopkins*.

Naturally, these pioneers of valley civilization

chalked up many a "first." A few of the lesser known steamers, with "firsts" to their credit, are: The *Ashland*, the *Henry Frank,* and the *Maria Louise,* which brought the first locomotives for the Texas and Pacifiic at Alexandria in 1881. The *Cherokee* hauled the first rails. Besides the already-mentioned floating newspaper on the *Era No. 11,* steamboats were veritable news couriers. The *Levant* rushed from Natchez to New Orleans carrying a copy of the *Red River Herald* with first news of the fall of the Alamo in 1836, and the *Beeswing* flew from the upper Red to the Crescent City with news of Alexandria's flooded plight and plague in 1844.

The *Charleston* is said to have brought the first white woman to Shreveport in 1835, the *John T. Moore* was the first steamer with an iron hull, and the *Peninah* had the first wildcat whistle (siren) on the rivers.

The titles of "fastest," "largest," "largest number of bales carried," "shallowest draft," "most expensive," "most palatial" were claimed by various contenders — and such claims will be finally adjudicated only in that happy place to which all good steamboats go. It is fairly safe to say that the famous "Hoppin' Bob," the *Rob't E. Lee,* with perhaps the exception of the *J. M. White,* was the fastest, and that the *J. M. White* slightly surpassed the *Grand Republic* as the most luxurious of the "floating palaces." The *Thompson Dean,* at $400,000 was surely the most expensive (three firms and numerous wealthy owners went broke trying to make her profitable). But the other titles will have to remain unsettled in this world, or at least until the last old-timer or steamboat fan is at the point of no return.

The *City of Camden* claimed to hold the fastest record between New Orleans and Camden, Ark., in 1906. The *General Quitman* in 1860 boasted the record run between New Orleans and Donaldsonville of five hours, six minutes, although four years earlier, the *Princess* was credited with that honor, with a run of four hours and fifty-one minutes.

The *Julia Randolph* was the fastest thing between New Orleans and Jefferson, Tex., she claimed, having made nine successive round trips (1650 miles each trip) in nine weeks, back in 1873. Old river men said she was the fastest sternwheeler ever to leave New Orleans.

The *R. W. McRea* beat the run of the *St. Charles* from Shreveport to the Crescent City, making two days, twelve hours the record mark.

But both boats were owned by the same man, so it didn't really matter.

The steamers served many purposes besides transportation. The *Rob't E. Lee*, like many others, was also a floating bank, carrying up to $25,000 to cash checks and advance funds to planters along the river. Some served as stores supplying dry goods and other merchandise.

The *Banjo* was a showboat, forerunner of the *Cotton Blossom* and many more. The *Black Hawk*, carrying $75,000 in specie, blew up in 1837 on the way to Natchitoches, but her money was saved. Whereas the *Creole*, en route from Natchez to New Orleans in 1841 with $100,000 in specie, cotton, and 100 passengers, sank in the channel, losing specie, thirty-four passengers, and everything aboard!

The *Daniel O'Connell* was reported to have made news in the early days by arriving at New Orleans from Campti, La., with an alligator seventeen feet long. The *Lizzie Hamilton* carried watermelons to buoy her up in case she got caught in low water. Speaking of draught, the *L.*

Dillard in 1865 could be operated in twelve inches of water and it was said she "needed only a little dampness" to run in. But the *Silver Bow* beat that. She claimed she could move in only ten inches — when loaded light.

The *Sam Howell* created a big stink on the river in 1860. She caught fire with 30,000 hides aboard. The *Electra*, on the other hand, was, in the 90's, a fancy steamer. Her staterooms were named for flowers.

And, speaking of "staterooms," does the lay reader know how that name originated? One steamer had a cabin named for every state in the Union. Hence, "staterooms." But one state was left over after all the cabins had been named, and that state was Texas. So that name was given to the cabin on the top, or hurricane, deck. It's been called the "texas" ever since.

Many of the steamboats had almost as many lives as a cat. Take the *Belle of Alton*. She burned twice. The *H. M. Carter* sank at Alexandria in 1905; was rebuilt and blew up that same year;

The Jesse K. Bell. Burned at New Orleans in late 1880's.

was repaired again and caught fire in 1908. She broke in two and was a total wreck. The *Coosa* sank in 1865; was rebuilt and sank again two years later; was raised and burned in 1869, this time beyond recall.

The *Argosy* really had the adventures of an argosy of old. Built in 1863, she burned that same year; was rebuilt the next; taken over by the U. S. Navy in 1864, made into a "tinclad gunboat" by Admiral Porter. She captured the Confederate boat *Ben Franklin*. Returning to trade after the war, she sank in 1875, was raised and rebuilt, and saw her last days quietly on the Ohio. Such a history was typical of many boats caught in the War Between the States.

While violent death seemed to be the fate of a majority of the steamboats, numerous famous boats lived until the railroads replaced them. These old-timers of the river were gradually dismantled and sold for timber; others were made into ferryboats or barges. But the river-bottoms are still strewn with the wreckage of this once-fabulous merchant fleet.

However, some of the boats came to their doom under really unique circumstances, although they escaped the normal hazards of river navigation. The *Celeste* was sunk by ice. The *City of Monroe* was wrecked by the 1915 storm at New Orleans, and the *Mollie Able* was sunk by a cyclone at St. Louis. The *E. F. Dix* ran onto a sunken boat, and the *Red River* sank because she was overloaded. The *Eagle* turned turtle, and the *Concordia* sank in the middle of a cane field! (She was doing rescue work at a crevasse.)

But the steamer *Imperial* will be memorable in history for having the most ignominious end of all time. While standing calmly at a berth at Algiers, no steam in her boilers, nobody on board, she suddenly gave a lurch and settled silently on the muddy bottom.

The mystery occupied newspaper space for weeks. Then the riddle was solved. The oakum in her seams had been eaten out by — river shrimp!

The Concordia. Sank in a cane field while doing rescue work at a Crevasse.

The Ohio. Built 1824. A dramatic portrait of a very
early type of river steamboat.

The Thompson Dean. Built 1872. A striking contrast
to the 1824 *Ohio.* From painting by W. Winter.
When dismantled, her machinery went into the
Will S. Hayes, 1882.

"ENGINE ON A RAFT WITH $11,000

WORTH OF JIG-SAW WORK AROUND IT"

Printed by E. Johns & Co. 87 Chartres St. N. Orleans.

"MAGIC PRESS," 89 Magazine street.

Printed by David Felt & Co., 24 Chartres-st.

HIS is no six-horse stern wheel boat," wrote Col. S. G. French, U.S.A., while a passenger aboard the famous *Eclipse* in 1853. "She is three hundred and sixty-five feet in length, forty feet beam with two engines with thirty-six inch cylinders and eleven foot stroke with sixteen boilers, two doctors, two freight engines and [paddle] wheels forty-two feet in diameter — burns one hundred cords of wood per day, carries 1800 tons and I hope won't burst her "bilers" on 120 pounds of steam to the square inch or under any other circumstances. She is beautifully finished, perfect in her accommodations, being about twice as comfortable as Willard's Hotel — her staterooms are about twice as large as his, and much better furnished, and then the table! why, it would be a good tonic to you and give you a most excellent appetite to read the 'bill of fare' — indeed I would send you one only I fear you would become discontented with your present sumptuous fare [by seeing this] spread out *all at once* before you. But all joking aside, there is more comfort and convenience on this boat than in most Hotels, as you can judge when I state that she

cost $135,000.00 — a great deal for a western style boat. Just imagine our beautiful cabin 110 yards long."

The *Eclipse* was the culmination of forty years of steamboat building, the finest boat to be produced on Western waters prior to the Civil War. She was indeed a far cry from the strange looking *New Orleans* of 1811 which carried masts and sails beside her paddle wheels and looked more like an ocean-going ship with her deep, rounded hull. A great many of the early steamboats sported bowsprits and figureheads and quite a few of them were driven by vertical "steeple" engines, an arrangement more picturesque than practical. An early French traveler, Fleury Generelly, voyaged from New Orleans to St. Louis in 1820 on such a steamboat, the *Maid of Orleans*. Generelly did a water color sketch of this quaint vessel which had been built in Philadelphia in 1818 and sailed to New Orleans where she was placed in service on the Mississippi.

The generation building and running the new boats was not concerned in picturing them and not until the first European-trained artist-travelers arrived to sketch them (from about 1828 on), were many pictures of them made. There weren't many boats, either, only 269 having been built on Western waters from 1811 to 1830. It is no small wonder that less than two dozen pictures of these pioneer vessels survive at all.

The steamboats built in the 1820's were short boats, seldom more than 120 feet in length. Hulls were somewhat shallower than the earliest boats and boilers and engines were now *on* the main deck instead of below it, but the bowsprit (with the addition of a jackstaff fixed to it) still persisted. Chimneys rose in front of the box-like superstructure which housed the passenger cabins with their open, curtained berths and that delightful feature, the awning-covered roof of the boiler deck, always shown crowded with happy passengers enjoying the scenery, was a characteristic of nearly every steamer. Most of the boats had comparatively small paddle wheels and bob-tailed sterns.

The 1830's witnessed a great increase in the number of steamboats built and their improvement in design and construction. (729 were built between 1831 and 1840). The 1840's saw further refinements — the old open berths gave way to staterooms and the "texas," that little series of staterooms on top of the main cabin below the pilot house, made its appearance. Also, builders had found out that long, comparatively narrow boats were faster than short ones, so that they were making them much longer than the early ones. (average 250 feet). Oddly enough, the jig-saw gingerbread decorations which were to earn the steamboat the derisive definition of "engine on a raft with $11,000 worth of jig-saw work around it" didn't develop until after 1850.

Another oddity — for nearly 50 years steamboats were built by craftsmen using rule-of-thumb methods. If any exact plans were used in building the early boats, none have survived, and it was only because the English engineer, Thomas Tredgold, carefully measured, drew and published plans of the *Buckeye State*, a 260-foot steamer built in 1850, that we have a first-hand knowledge of their construction details. In later years, plans were used; but such famous boats as the *Rob't E. Lee* and *Natchez* were built without them.

Pittsburgh, Cincinnati and Louisville became centers for construction of the craft, with the celebrated Howard Yards at Jeffersonville, Indiana perhaps the most prolific. From 1840 to 1880 more than 4,800 boats were turned out before the railroads began to make them obsolete. Specialization soon entered into steamboat con-

struction. Some firms built hulls, other engines, still others cabins. The cabin builders were chiefly responsible for bringing to full flower the "floating palace" tradition, the "elegance which bordered on magnificence," as one of the passengers described the interior of his boat. On the larger boats, the cabin, two hundred or so feet long, was by its very size, impressive, a "long resplendent tunnel" separating staterooms and serving as the social hall and dining room for the passengers. Elaborately carved brackets supported ceiling often covered with a riot of near-Gothic ornament. Light from stained glass clerestory windows fell on vari-colored Brussels carpets; imported chandeliers, paintings, often quite well done, rich draperies, plush-covered furniture, and that ultimate of Victorian elegance, the grand piano, were reflected in the towering, gleaming mirror at the end of the ladies' cabin. This was travel in style!

A humorist once said that: "Steamboats are built of wood, tin, shingles, canvas and twine and look like the Bride of Babylon." Comparatively flimsily built, many of them came to grief through fire, explosion, snagging or collision.

There were many weird superstitions connected with the river boats.

Capt. Frederick Way, Jr., one of the leading authorities on steamboats today, likes to tell about the "Hoodoo of the 'M' Boats."

"Mississippi River steamboats christened with names commencing with 'M' once were doomed from the day they left the shipyard," he states. To substantiate this, he quotes Capt. John N. Bofinger, a popular and successful steamboatman of the 1860's and later president of the Anchor Line:

"I do assert that, with barely an exception, all the steamboats built and run on the Mississippi and its tributaries, whose names commenced with the letter 'M' were either burnt, sunk, exploded, or unsuccessful as an investment to their owners. You can look over the long list of *Missouri, Mississippi, Mary, Michigan, Maria, Monarch, Mediator,* etc. and you will discover that each one met the fate of one as indicated."

Capt. Bofinger told of efforts he made to have his good friends refrain from using "M" names, only to be ridiculed for his silly superstition. Thus it was with the *Metamora* and the *Midas.* The former sank in her prime; the latter did likewise.

The Captain once signed up as master on a new boat, only to learn with horror that the

Cabin of the *Thompson Dean.* Cabin was 246 feet long and last word in Steamboat Gothic.

(Above) Cabin of the *Georgia Lee.* Being Refiitted.

(Below) The cabin of the *City of Providence,* set for dinner.

Menu of the *M. S. Mepham*, 1864.

(*Below*) Menu of the *Rob't E. Lee.* Two days later the *Lee* burned.

(*Below*) Card advertising the *Reuben R. Springer,* one of the first river boats to use an electric searchlight.

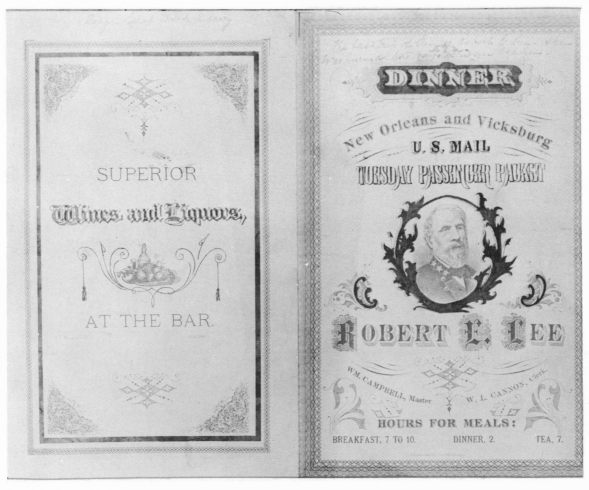

boat had originally been christened the *Magnolia.* He refused the job, and "she burned on her sixth trip to New Orleans."

Capt. Way examined the records of 723 steamboats whose name began with "M" built in the hundred years after 1811, which operated on the Mississippi, and 218 of these met violent ends.

The letter "M" hoodo also extended to the use of the letter in any part of the name of a steamboat, not just the initial letter. Every *City of Memphis,* of which there were several, came to grief, Capt. Ways says.

It was uncanny. A successful excursion boat operator on the Mississippi, Capt. D. W. Wisherd, bought the *Keystone State,* renamed her the *Majestic* and she was promptly wrecked thirteen days later! Capt. Wisherd then bought the *Rees Lee* and gave her the same name. She burned almost immediately. He changed the name of his *G. W. Hill* to *Island Maid.* Fire again — and again. The last fire destroyed the boat completely.

One time the "M" *inside* the name *Americus* was enough to start the old chain reaction. Proceeding along happily, she was hailed by a man on a white horse. The pilot was nervous, telling the captain that if "that man turns out to be a preacher, this boat will burn before morning."

He was, and it did, before daylight.

But the prize story in Capt. Way's collection of "M"-hoodoos is the one about C. A. Hull's trip from Louisville to Pittsburgh. He was hardly aboard the steamer *Mammoth,* when the cry of "fire" rang out and the boat burned to cinders. Hull engaged a nearby farmer to drive him back to Louisville, and a wheel came off the carriage. Next, aboard a train, a cyclone lifted the cars off the track. At Cincinnati, he went to the river to embark for Pittsburgh. The only boat available? *Magnolia.*

Hull allowed himself to be "sold" on the *Magnolia's* fine record of safety. The *Magnolia* blew her boilers, and Hull narrowly escaped with his life, but thirty-five others were killed.

Hoodoo was bad enough, but another "M" boat really went out of her way to make herself a hex. The *Charles Morgan,* built in 1874, was in the Cincinnati-New Orleans trade. She had a spooky peculiarity of running away from her rudders and sheering into a boat coming upstream. She had ten collisions during her career, but strangely, she never sheered when approaching a bridge.

In the early days of steamboating when wood was used for fuel, most boats carried but a half-day's supply and it became necessary to stop frequently at woodyards for "wooding up," a chore which gave rise to many a tale in steamboat lore. As steamboat traffic increased, the sale of wood to the boats became an excellent cash crop for farmers and many riverside wood yards sprang up. In 1844 a newspaper reported that a steamboat crew stole all the wood from the owner of a woodyard and beat him up when he protested. That was an isolated instance. Usually, the shoe was on the other foot. It was the yard owner who generally came out best on the deal.

T. B. Thorpe, in his *Remembrances of the Mississippi* (Harper's 1855) wrote that he had seen 20,000 cords of wood in one pile, with a value of $70,000. This, he added, was an exceptional yard, most of them being more modest enterprises. But the yard owners could be ornery. He tells of a steamboat captain hailing such a character and getting a strictly uncooperative set of replies to his questions:

" 'What kind of wood is that?'

" 'The reply comes back, 'Cord wood.'

"The captain, still in pursuit of information under difficulties, and desirous of learning if the fuel was dry and fit for his purpose, bawls out,

" 'How long has it been cut?'

" 'Four feet' is the prompt response.

"The captain, exceedingly vexed, next inquiries,

" 'What do you sell it for?'

" 'Cash' returns the chopper, replacing the corn-cob pipe in his mouth and smiling benignly on his pile.

The wood yards offered bored travelers an interlude for stretching their legs upon land. Thorpe found the woodyards almost invariably infested with swarms of mosquitoes, which he was told, "a little way down the river are awful — thar they torment alligators to death and sting mules right through their hoofs."

Sol Smith, the ancient thespian of the wilderness, spun a yarn about a woodyard episode which happened to the *Caravan,* a boat that was so slow the crew could eke out a month's wages on the trip from New Orleans to Vicksburg and back.

The captain of the *Caravan* was so fond of playing a card game called "brag," that he appears to have left the boat entirely in the hands of the pilots, who really ran the boats anyway. As it happened, the pilots were *also* devoted brag-players. One night, said Sol, the pilot "above" called down to the captain that the boat's wood was down to half a cord. In spite of holding a promising hand, the captain excused himself and went out on deck to take stock of his location. He discovered from the landmarks that he was about a half-mile from a woodyard, which, he said, "was right around yonder point."

"But," muttered the captain, "I don't much like to take wood of the yellow-faced old scoundrel who owns it; he always charges a quarter of a dollar more than anyone else; however, there's no other chance."

The last stick of wood was under the *Caravan's* boilers when she was finally secured at the bank, among the trees, alongside the wood pile.

"Halloo, Colonel! How much do you sell your wood THIS time?"

"Why, capting, we must charge you three and a quarter THIS time," grunted the old geezer, casting a knowing glance at the empty wood bin of the *Caravan*.

"The devil! What's the odd quarter for, I should like to know. You only charged me three when I went down."

"Why, capting, wood's riz since you went down two weeks ago; besides you are awar' that you very seldom stop going down; when you'r going up you're sometimes obleeged to give me a call because the current's against you, and there's no other woodyard for nine miles ahead; and if you happen to be nearly out of fooel, why. . ."

"Well, well, we'll take a few cords under the circumstances," said the captain and hurried back to his game. In about a half hour, the *Caravan* got under way again. Dinner was served, Sol Smith retired, but the captain kept the game going, remarking to the other pilot who was going on duty that they'd better keep a lookout for the next woodyard and take on some more. He wasn't pleased with the quality of the product just taken aboard.

At 11 o'clock, it was reported that a yard was in sight. The captain ordered the vessel to shore and instructed the pilot to take on six cords "if it's good." He was too occupied with the game to go on deck himself. Soon the boat was under way again and the captain was annoyed when told that the price was again three and a quarter.

By two o'clock, the captain relaxed enough to ask how the boat was getting along. He was told that a fog was keeping the boat in midstream. The wood was low, but the last batch was better than that of "old yellow-face." A light had been sighted ahead, and the captain told the pilot on watch to hail and ask the price of wood.

The calls could be clearly heard in the cabin.

When a youthful voice from the wood yard said: "Three and a quarter," the captain raged and wondered if they would ever get upriver to cheaper wood. He told them to buy 6 cords, that this would carry them until morning when they would be in the country of better and cheaper wood.

When day dawned, the brag game broke up and Sol arose, dressed and joined the captain to "enjoy a view of the bluffs." The fog limited vision to only sixty yards, and the boat was pushing toward the still invisible banks in search of wood again.

"There it is!" exclaimed the captain, "Stop her," amidst the ringing of bells.

"Halloo! The woodyard!" He yelled.

"Halloo yourself!" answered a squeaking female voice.

"What's the price of wood?"

"I think that you ought to know the price by this time. It's three and a quarter, and you know it."

"Three and the devil! have you raised on your wood, too? I'll give you three and not a cent more."

"Well, here comes the old man. He'll talk to you."

It was the same old "yellow-face" of the night before.

"Why, darn it all, capting, there is but three or four cords left, and since it's you, I don't care if I do let you have it for three- as you're a good customer!"

They had been wooding all night at the same woodyard!

The boss of the boat, legally, was of course, the captain. Sometimes he owned it or was a part owner. He was the general manger, the man who oversaw everything. It was he who cultivated the big shippers. He it was who inspired confidence, who arranged for the comfort and safety of the passengers and who spread charm among the ladies, but — and one doesn't need Mark Twain to appreciate this —the real responsibility of getting the boat there and back was the pilot's.

In his lofty aerie atop the texas, encased in glass with a view commanding the river up and down; with bell-pulls at his finger tips and a shiny brass speaking tube to give orders through to the engine room — he was indeed a lord. He also had to know his business and attend to it, strictly. A Mississippi River steamboat pilot was a combination navigator and steersman, and he

Wood-Cutters' Cabin. From Mrs. Trollope's "Domestic Manners of the Americans." "He supplies steamboats with fuel — with the assurance of early death in exchange for dollars and whiskey."

The Wood-Cutter.

Scene at the Landing.

was a regular full-time officer aboard the boat. Pilots "learned" the river by serving as apprentices or "cubs" for 3 years before taking the government examination for a license.

Down below on the main desk was the mate with the common folk —— the deck passengers and the rousters — and with the freight. His was probably the most demanding job on the boat — and the worst paid, for an officer. He had to be tough to get work out of his roustabouts.

His temper and his choice vocabulary were legendary. He had to know the "trades" in which he operated and he had to know how to stow cargo to keep his boat in trim (and where to find it when the boat came to where the freight was to be delivered). He was everywhere at once, especially when the stages were swinging in and out at a landing. Above all, he had to know how to handle Negroes, for roustabouts respected and would work well for a mate who understood them even though he might be stern or take a stick of wood to them on occasion.

The clerk was the business manager of the boat. He was its freight and passenger agent. He purchased the supplies and fuel; made out the payroll and the waybills and hired and fired the ordinary crew members. On some boats the clerk was a mild form of despot for the cabin passengers. He was the man who assigned the staterooms, and his air of superiority is perhaps matched today only by the room clerk of a busy hotel. Said one traveler:

"He assigns us a room with a tone of outraged dignity in his voice, and we wither gradually out of his sight and deposit our valises on our bed and lock them in lest that awful fellow should take it into his head to throw them overboard."

The "mud clerk" was the clerk's assistant — the name came from the muddy feet that the helper would get at landings looking after cargo.

The engineer had the hot and sweaty job of keeping the engines going, often for days at a time with little opportunity to make minor but necessary repairs. Like the airplane pilot of today, the steamboat engineer was almost certain to pay with his life if he made a serious error of judgment with his engine. Generally, the engineer was taken for granted; nobody thought much about him except in case of disaster when he was the first to be blamed, that is, if he was still around. The assistant of the engineer was called a "striker."

With all the service, there came a time on a steamboat trip when passengers had to "turn to" and lend a hand, not in the sense of Mark Twain, who, returning to the Mississippi after twenty-one years, itched so to get his hands on the wheel to steer that he "cast a longing glance at the pilot house" and finally got his wish. No, this "tale" has to do with an earlier day, when officers of steamboats had no assistants. When one important cog in the wheel was incapacitated, somebody had to fill in.

One summer in 1840, our ubiquitous actor, Sol Smith, as he traveled downriver aboard the *Vandalia*, was called on to serve both as the boat's doctor and pilot, doctor not meaning the familiar part of the vessel's machinery, but an emergency amateur physician.

There was a minor epidemic aboard. The trouper being a jack-of-all-trades — or, as he described himself by quoting the Bard, "One man in his time plays many parts" — Sol turned doctor and administered "calomel, jalap and ipecacuanah from the medicine chest. . ."

One evening, while proceeding cautiously due to the river being low, Capt. Small interrupted Smith's sleep to report that "'our first pilot's in a bad way; nothing will stay on his stomach."

The captain was told by Smith that he had already tried "everything in the medicine chest" on the pilot, but there was no hope of his being able to take the wheel for the rest of the trip.

"This is very unlucky," replied Capt. Small, "because I wanted to run nights, and the second pilot can't stand double watches. What's to be done?"

"Doctor" Smith told him he didn't know and expected the captain to depart. But the latter just stood there, "gave two or three 'ahems,' spat violently through the stateroom door and over the guards, changed his position several times, and at length continued the conversation:

"Mr. Sol, I understand that during your life, you've turned your hand to 'most everything. I have heard of your merchandising, your preaching, your acting and your doctoring; did you ever try your hand at piloting?"

Sol allowed as how he'd never piloted and the captain was disappointed.

"I want a pilot," he said, searchingly. "We can't run nights without one. I . . . I thought if you . . . if you could stand a watch as pilot?"

Sol sat up in bed. He asked the captain what would the insurance companies have to say in case of an accident if the regular pilot were not at the wheel.

"That's the point," answered Capt. Small. "I

want you to take Jim's place at the wheel and assume his character at the same time. If you will do this, we shall save at least forty-eight hours between here and New Orleans."

Game as ever, Smith agreed. They planned a careful ruse, announcing to the passengers that Pilot Jim had been cured. Smith donned Jim's clothes and assumed his watches at the wheel, but "it was observable that, when passing over 'bad places,' Capt. Small was always in the pilot house which was somewhat strange, as Jim was known to be one of the most careful and competent pilots on the Mississippi; but this was accounted for from the fact that the captain was young at the business and wanted to learn the river."

They made it to New Orleans, all right, and Sol immediately upon landing dispatched poor Jim to Dr. Stone's hospital for a month, "being much worse from his constant attention to his duties at the wheel."

Jim eventually recovered and resumed his place at the wheel on the next trip of the *Vandalia*. But whenever he saw Smith thereafter, he greeted him with:

"Sol, who's at the wheel?"

At the tender age of 87 years, Henry J. Davis

of Clarksdale, Miss., can still tell with glee about the time he jumped off the *City of St. Louis* to make an unscheduled landing.

"About sixty-five years ago," says Henry, sitting in his little office where he conducts a feed business, putting in eight hours daily, "I had to make a quick trip to Fitler's Landing, Miss., to sell I. Lucas, a local merchant and planter, a boiler for his gin, and get back home.

"Now, son, that's a long time before your day, and I must tell you how I had to plan that round trip which covered several days. I can make that same trip today in my old car on any rainy afternoon." [And he often does, still.]

"Well, sir, I would grab the L. N. O. & T.'s sleeping cars down to Vicksburg, wait at the hotel for one of the Anchor Line's upriver steamers that usually ran on regular advertised schedules, but didn't stop at Fitler's Landing; so I'd have to get off at Lake Providence, eat my breakfast and double back on the local packet, the *Belle of the Bends,* for Fitler's Landing.

"You can imagine my chagrin, son, with such split-second timing ahead of me, to wake up in my stateroom aboard the Anchor Liner *City of St. Louis* and find the steamboat in the willows at Eagle Lake, only a short distance out of Vicks-

St. Louis c. 1843. From engraving by J. C. Wild.
The *Alex Scott* is in the foreground.
Ad of the *Alex. Scott.*

burg, with her starboard wheel out of commission. Already several hours late, we started limping along on the port wheel and soon we meet the *Belle*, which had already left Lake Providence.

"This sad state of affairs, son, meant that I'd be obliged to hang around Lake Providence for several days until the *Belle of the Bends* came on her next trip down — unless I could persuade the irate captain of the *City of St. Louis* to stop when the steamer passed Fitler's Landing and allow me to disembark.

"Well, sir, that fellow had lost all reason, it seemed, in those willows at Eagle Lake before he again headed his crippled craft upstream. In fact, he accused me of being the jinx that caused all his trouble and said I would be treated accordingly.

"But I fooled him, like I'm about to tell you. You see, son, in getting his unwieldly craft back into the river, he had neglected to hoist the starboard stage plank to the usual running position. This neglect upon his part worked directly in my favor. Ha!

"A sand bar had formed against the Mississippi side, and the willow trees had grown there so tall that the lowered stage was dragging their tops into a graceful curve. All of a sudden I saw on the bank a store with the name 'I. LUCAS' on it.

"Thinking fast, I shouted to the captain and asked him if that wasn't Fitler's Landing, and if so, to please stop and let me off. He shouted back positively and emphatically, 'NO.'

"At that point, the river current was running so strong against the willow-covered sand-bar, that the already tired pilot had to maneuver with all his strength to get his crippled steamboat into easier water. For me, it was now or never.

"I raced to my stateroom, grabbed my light bags, ran out onto the dragging stage and leapt into the willows. I landed in what felt like a giant bed-spring and was eased into an upright position as the trees righted themselves after the stage passed on. I crept up the river bank and was soon selling the boiler to I. Lucas — even though the *City of St. Louis* didn't stop at Fitler's Landing."

(Left) Capt. John Klinefelter. He commanded the *Hibernia II* and *Messenger II*.

(Below Left) Capt. Chas. Stone. He owned the *Monongahela* and *Keystone State*.

(Below Right) Capt. Ben Berry of the Anchor Line.

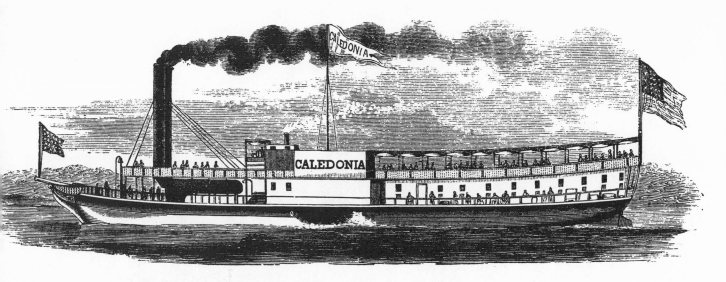

The Caledonia. A steamboat of the early 1820's.

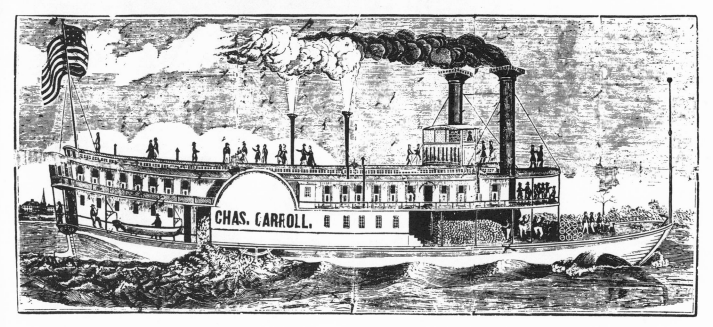

The Chas. Carroll. This vessel was snagged in 1850 at Eddyville, Ky.

The Philadelphia. She struck a rock and sank, in 1856, but was raised and put in the St. Louis-New Orleans trade.

Monkey Wrench Corner, Canal and Royal Streets,
New Orleans 1884.

Captain, Mate and Clerk of the *Alvin*.
Sketch by Kemble.

MONKEY WRENCH CORNER

The Second Steward. Sketch by Alfred R. Waud.

THE intersection of Canal and Royal Streets is one of New Orleans' busiest corners, but it has a distinctive claim to fame other than its strategic location, the place where the old city meets the new. Only a few old-timers still speak of that intersection in endearing terms, like a favorite old chair by the fire, a place that means home, hospitality, and security.

These old-timers know it as Monkey Wrench Corner, and tip your hat when you round the banquettes there, sir! It is hallowed ground. For many decades, until shortly after the turn of the century, it was the sidewalk clubhouse of the riverboat and seagoing fraternity.

Come here, all ye broke and downtrodden, and ye shall find a handout or a loan. Pass by, all ye lonesome, and meet a friend. But most important, tarry and hear a story.

If the sidewalk at Royal and Canal could talk, its words would be worth a fortune. Monkey Wrench Corner was synonymous with Blarney Castle.

All the seasoned veterans needed was a gathering of young, fuzzy-cheeked "cubs." Let the young men stand about with wide-eyed, open-headed expressions, and the veterans would go to town.

Naturally, the discussions often revolved around which was the fastest, largest, biggest-capacity steamboat on the river. Each candidate had its champions. But another favorite topic was: Which was the slowest boat on the river? This topic was duck soup for the yarn-spinners.

It seems that two steamboats vied for this honor, and long and loud were the arguments for giving this distinction to one or the other of them, and preposterous were the stories told about them. They were the *J. M. B. Keeler,* and the *John F. Roe.*

"Yaas, the old *J. M. B. Keeler*," said one of the old pilots, putting his thumbs in his suspenders as the audience gathered for a typical Monkey Wrench Corner session. "Now she was a real, slow boat; there's no doubt she was the slowest on the river.

"Why, I distinc'erly remember when she was operating in the Memphis-lower-bends trade. A passenger, one of the few she ever had, you can be sure, once preferred to get off her and walk because he could make better time!

"She arrived in Memphis one fall with sugar and molasses from New Orleans, and cotton. It took eight whole days to unload her, and her cargo blocked the wharves and burnt out every rouster in Memphis!

"Y'see, she had no lower deck. They just put the freight down in a fifteen-foot hold.

"Race? Shucks, man, the only race the *Keeler* ever won was with some fixed point on the bank. Yeah, once she nearly lost a race with an island. Don't laugh. You heard me, she nearly lost a race with an island.

"How? I'll tell you if you'll listen. While she was roundin' a bend, the river made a cut-off.

"Oh, she was the slowest boat you ever saw! She could run all day in the shade of a big tree and tie up at its foot for the night. Now that's really slow, ain't it?"

The crowd usually admitted that the *J. M. B. Keeler* was pretty slow, or else the narrator was pretty fast. Then somebody'd bring up the *John F. Roe*. Inevitably the name of Mark Twain would be dragged in as witness to the *Roe's* prowess, and that, sir, was no name to bandy about in a spirit of skepticism.

"Waaal, the *John F. Roe* was slow, too, and you can bet on that. Ol' Mark Twain said that while he was a pilot on her once, they changed watches three times in Fort Adams reach, a distance of only about five miles."

That's not all Mark Twain said about the *Roe's* claim to fame. In one of his best passages in *Life on the Mississippi*, Sam Clemens was matching the best Monkey Wrench Corner had to offer as he waxed rhapsodic about the *Roe:*

"We used to forget what year it was we left port. Ferryboats used to lose valuable trips because their passengers grew old and died waiting for us to get by . . . the *John F. Roe* was so slow that, when she finally sunk in Madrid Bend, it was five years before the owners heard of it. . ." He added that he once had the documents to prove all this, but through carelessness they had been mislaid.

Then somebody would undoubtedly chime in with the story about the *Keeler* losing a race to a man on foot because he cut across the bend.

"Speaking of cutting across bends," said a seasoned steamboatman named Capt. Jefferds, "it reminds me of the time Nick Jockerst and I were on the *Belle of Memphis*. He was third clerk and

The Cosmopolitan Hotel on Royal St. Favorite hostelry of rivermen.

(Above) The Old Custom House
on Canal Street.

(Right) The Grand Opera House
on Canal St. Steamboat men's
haunt.

(Left) The Fat Boy. Sketch by
Alfred R. Waud.

I was second mate. We was anxious to get to St. Louis in time for the Veiled Prophet's parade, and the captain was crowdin' her hard. We weren't about to make many stops, but when we was abreast of Slough Landing, we was hailed.

" 'What ya got?" I sang out.

" 'A passenger,' was the reply. So I got the stage ready, and when we came alongside, a boy hopped on. Jockerst met him on the fo'castle. He was madder 'n' heck.

" 'Where to?' he asked.

" 'Cairo, suh,' answered the passenger.

" 'All right, one dollar,' said Jockerst, holding out his hand.

" 'I got a ticket, boss.'

" 'Where in tarnation did you get it?' said Jockerst, mad clear through now for the delay.

" 'You sol' it to me, you'self. I got on back there below the bend, got off again, and went to see my gal whilst you was a-roundin' the bend.'

"Sure enough. The lad only had two miles to walk across the neck of the bend, and we had thirty-five miles of river to get around the bend."

This seemed to be getting into the realm of the probable, so someone would bring up the *Belle Air,* and her notable exploit of nearly wrecking the whole town of Chester, Ill.

"Back in 1844 — that was a leetle before your time, son," would be the conventional opening gambit, "the whole Mississippi valley was under ten, twelve foot of water. The *Belle Air* was a'comin' downriver with a full head o' steam. She was 'feelin' her oats' when she neared Chester, and before the pilot knowed he was off the river,

Gentlemen Talking with the
Captain of the *Teche.*

The "lazy bench" in the pilothouse was a favorite haunt of off-duty rivermen.

she pitched head-foremost into a three-story edifice in one of Chester's principal streets! She knocked off the upper story.

"Not satisfied with that, she demolished a four-story stone mill while trying to turn around and head for the river proper. In so doing, she knocked over several brick buildings including the city jail!

"But the *Belle Air* wasn't even scratched. She finally got back into the river, all right. But you think her work was done? No, sir-ee! When she got down to New Orleans she ran into a ferryboat and almost sunk it! You can look it up, if you care to."

Before this extraordinary session would break up, the steamboat *Nebraska* would be cited as being famous for the amount of wood she used up. Once her captain put her into a bank to take on a hundred cords of cottonwood.

"Thar was nothin' to make 'er fast to, you unnerstan," said another storyteller on Monkey Wrench Corner, "and whilst she was bein' loaded, her captain kept her agin' the bank with his outside wheel.

"When the woodpile was cleared away, it was found that in holdin' er' agin' the bank, all the wood was used up!"

Meeting adjourned!

French quarter.

(*Above*) Royal Street, French Quarter, New Orleans.

(*Left*) Trying to avoid a Bore.

(*Below*) Unloading by Flags. Since the roustabouts could not read, each spot for unloading freight was marked by a special flag. Coffee from South America is still unloaded in this way on the New Orleans docks.

Unloading by flags

Sharp Character.

Steamboat Captain.

Roustabouts. Sketch by W. T. Smedley.

"One from the Steerage."

The *Natchez*. Capt. Blanche Douglass Leathers and
her husband, Bowling Leathers, worked this
steamboat.

"YES, I AM A STEAMBOAT MAN"

Business Card (enlarged) of Capt. Blanche.

APT. James J. Butler, grizzled Inspector of Hulls, looked at his coworker, equally grizzled Capt. William Applegate, Inspector of Boilers, and gave him a private wink which the determined woman standing before them didn't catch.

"But madam," said the hull inspector, "how can we 'captain' a lady?"

The not-to-be-denied little lady standing before them, asking to make application for a master of steamboats license was Mrs. Mary Miller, wife of Capt. George "Old Natural" Miller, owner of the steamboat *Saline*. She was to get that license, after much buck-passing among government offices between New Orleans and Washington. On February 18, 1884, the coveted, gold-seal scroll was officially issued to her, and she went down in history claiming to be the first licensed woman captain "authorized to assume command of steam vessels," with permision to navigate the waters of the Mississippi, Red, Ouachita and other western rivers.

Capt. Mary Miller's claim to this "first" was challenged in later years by the writers who have told the stories of three other contenders.

Who *were* these other gals of the golden era of steamboating? One of them was also named Mary — Capt. Mary Becker Greene. Two others were Capt. Callie Leach French and Capt. Blanche Douglass Leathers.

In half a dozen stories, each is described as "the first woman to command a steamboat," with varying degrees of qualification, and sometimes none at all. Hairs were split over such details as "of a Mail Line trade boat;" "of a passenger steamboat;" or ". . . of a steamboat on the Mississippi."

Actually, in all fairness to Capt. French, she always said that she was "the first woman *pilot*, and the second woman captain." She gave credit to Mary Miller's preëminence, but Capt. Miller didn't return the compliment. She said she knew of only one other *pilot*, a Mrs. Mary Hulett on the Illinois River.

Curiously, each of these four "first" women of the river had one thing definitely in common.

Capt. Mary M. Miller of the *Saline*.

Capt. Mary B. Greene. The flag of the Greene Line still flies proudly on western rivers.

Each became a licensed captain for one and the same reason — economy. Each one specifically stated that she got her license to save money, so that a captain wouldn't have to be hired each time her husband stayed ashore.

Capt. Callie French, or "Aunt Callie" as she was known to thousands of patrons of Capt. French's *New Sensation* showboats along the waterways (see Showboats), got her pilot's license in 1888, her captain's ticket in 1895, but didn't assume her first actual command until ten years later. Then she specialized in showboats. Her husband, the fabulous Capt. Augustus Byron French, ran one *New Sensation* unit, while Aunt Callie captained another unit, double-dipping, as it were.

There is no doubt that Aunt Callie was the genuine article, a real captain of the river's navee, and a darn good captain too, a bell-ringing, horn-tootin', wheel-turnin' captain! There are plenty of people still around who will vouch for that.

When she came up for her pilot's license, the examiners, ol' Capt. Peter J. O'Reilly and Capt. Wilson Youngblood, sized her up, as their prede-

cessors had sized up Mary Miller four years before.

"Waaaal," said Capt. O'Reilly gruffly, "I reckon I don't see anything in the regulations says a woman can't be a river pilot."

"Harumph!", harumphed Capt. Youngblood, "I don't know your name, young lady, but I do know those seven men who endorsed you. They're good enough to pass anybody." They were seven of the most distinguished pilots on the river.

Capt. Callie not only piloted and captained boats on the rivers from 1888 to 1907, but she cooked, mended, nursed, acted, wrote gags, and never lost a boat or had an accident — or dropped a cue. She handled boats, crew, actors, audiences, storms, floods, feasts and famines with equal ease. Through it all, her strongest words were, "Well, I'll be dawg-goned!"

The beloved "Ma" Greene obtained her pilot's license in 1896 and her captain's license in 1897. Her first command was the *H. K. Bedford*, the dream boat envisioned when she and her former flatboatman, Gordon C. Greene, were married in 1890. Capt. Greene had become a pilot and captain, and finally he and his bride bought the *Bedford*. It wasn't long before the eager young wife, after spending hours at her husband's side in the wheel house, began to pick up the knack of the trade. Soon he was teaching her the tricks, too, and finally she knew enough to try for her license and to pass with flying colors.

Hers was no trophy license, either. Expanding business put her to work quickly. In 1897 she was taking the *Bedford* between Cincinnati and Louisville during low water, and the "lady captain's boat" became extremely popular for its dependability and for its air of refinement. Capt. Mary Greene's biggest moment perhaps came when she took the Greene Line's newest marvel, the sidewheeler *Greenland* from Pittsburgh to the St. Louis World's Fair in 1904. The crowds went wild over her.

"Ma" Greene has a unique distinction, not shared by the other members of the female river-going quartette. The flag of the Greene Line, the flag which she and her husband first flew at the masthead of the Bedford, still proudly flies on the rivers today from the masthead of the famous *Delta Queen*, passenger boat, all air conditioned, which keeps a popular schedule out of Cincin-

(*Above*) Capt. Blanche Leathers as a Young Women.

(*Left*) Capt. "Callie" French, of showboat fame.

nati. Most of its cruises are sellouts, a tribute to this stout family of river folk and to the captain known as "Ma."

Which leaves Capt. Blanche Leathers on deck. Blanche Douglass Leathers, daughter of a proud and wealthy Tensas Parish cotton planter, James S. Douglass, grew up along the river and married a river man, Bowling Leathers, son of Capt. Thomas P. Leathers (see Race Course of the Nation).

They were wed in 1880. Capt. Bowling Leathers was already a seasoned river man under his stern father's tutelage. Blanche loved the river, she loved her man, and she wanted to be with him. So aboard the *Natchez* she moved. This boat was the seventh of the mighty steamboats owned and operated by the red-bearded giant, her father-in-law. This was the *Natchez* which followed the celebrated racer of that name.

The old man and Blanche's father were close friends, old friends. For years Leathers had hauled Douglass' cotton to New Orleans. The story is told by Allan Douglass, Blanche's surviving brother, that one year, his father decided to squeeze 800 pounds of cotton into the bales, instead of the usual 500. This made them larger and, of course, heavier. Without any word, he stacked them at the landing for the *Natchez*.

It didn't take many "totes" of those bales to tell Leathers that something was amiss. He weighed the bales.

"Jim," he shouted to Douglass, summoned to the landing. "I have to tell you those bales are too heavy, I'll have to charge you for two."

"Then I'll never ship another pound on your boat," countered the irate planter.

"And, sir, that won't stop the boat from running!" Leathers bellowed.

"They just went and had a few drinks together to cool off," adds Allan Douglass.

It appears that a rift eventually occurred between old Leathers and his son, Bowling, as a result, it is hinted, of the latter's handling of the *Natchez* in 1888.

It was New Year's Eve. Bowling was in command of his father's pride, the greatest *Natchez* ever built, the fastest, most comfortable floating palace of the day — when, however, the railroads had already sounded the death knell of the steamboat. A steamer had to be sumptuous, to hold its passengers, and be fast, to hold its freight. This *Natchez* was both.

Bowling was pushing the big boat. He was trying to reach New Orleans for the year-end festivities. In the darkness, near Lake Providence, the great steamboat suddenly rumbled to a slithering halt. Women screamed. Stacks crashed into staterooms. Furniture slid around dizzily.

In the pilot house, Bowling shouted orders, rang bells, and finally succeeded in pulling her off a newly developed sand bar. But her seams had been opened. Water rushed in as she floated free.

Capt. Leathers ran to his wife's cabin. "We are sinking; get your valuables quickly." Blanche was in bed. She grabbed what she could and with most of the passengers, including her sister, got off into life boats with part of the crew.

Capt. Leathers then raced the sinking boat three miles to a safe beaching place. Most of the cargo and loose property was salvaged next day, but the hull was left, sunk in the river.

Wrote Jefferson Davis to his friends, Capt. and Mrs. Bowling Leathers: "The sailor who in unavoidable wreck protects his passengers and crew before providing for his own safety is the type of true manhood."

A comforting thought, no doubt. But evidently not to old man Leathers. It was the last *Natchez* boat he ever built. It was his last association, business or family, with Bowling and Blanche.

They struck out on their own. They went up to Jeffersonville, Ind., to the traditional Howard Yard, and had built there a stern-wheeler of more than passing beauty and proportions. They named it *Natchez*.

Allan Douglass says old Capt. Leathers bore them no ill will for using the name he put into song and story. Allan says they actually named it for the city, whereas the old man always carefully explained his boats were named for an Indian tribe, the tribe of Pushmataha. Leathers was consequently known as "Old Push."

Be that as it may, the old man never set foot on their sternwheel *Natchez*.

Now to the question: How much of a pilot and captain was Blanche? Listen to Blanche, talking to a reporter:

"He [Capt. Bowling Leathers] was a much better pilot than I was. He taught me everything I know. I would stand beside him at the wheel and repeat to him each snag, each bank, each plantation, each landing place.

"He taught me to steer at night when it was so dark you couldn't actually see your hand before your face . . . you must know every inch of the river so accurately that you will not be deceived by fogs which magnify objects, or moonlight that throws deceptive shadows, or darkness that makes the bank of the river ten feet higher. You must be able to take the watch, take a look at a misty rock or bluff, and know exactly where you are. . . .

"I can tell you that the worry and anxiety used to keep me awake often when I first started in, for it's human life at stake. . . I was constantly having my turn at the wheel, learning to take soundings, learning the signals, in fact all the intricate details that form part of a river captain's training. At times my husband was being called away, and breaking in a new man was always a troublesome process. So it was decided that I should apply for a captain's license!"

Blanche had a flair for publicity, to put it mildly. Until her death in 1940, she was still giving out with river tales. The question is, how much of it was the real thing? Here she goes again:

"I've seen many a cutoff in my time. Often the

The *Natchez VIII*, The Blanche and Bowling Leathers' sternwheel boat. Old Leathers never set foot on it.

channel shifted to opposite sides during the interval of a few days between trips. . . I have done everything [on a steamboat] but marry people. We were so near shore it wasn't necessary, or I'd have done that too. . . You see, the captain has full authority on board over everyone, from the first mate to the cat. It is perhaps the only job in existence where there is no one to answer to. And if you own your own boat, you are answerable only to God."

According to newspapers of the day, Blanche must have actually been at the helm in November, 1894, and the "little captain," as she was billed, took the new *Natchez* as her first command, out of New Orleans, to accompanying shouts from the crowded wharves.

One reporter, evidently aboard the boat, wrote: "With her hand on the wheel, let Capt. Blanche Leathers, the most distinguished among Louisiana's women, be described.

"A slight figure, five feet, five inches in height, with the contour of charming womanhood, small, white, well-kept and perfectly molded hands ornamented with two handsome diamond rings; a face, grand, true, and ennobling to look upon, a fair skin glowing with the pink hue of health, perfect teeth, and a full red-lipped mouth that tells the story of a woman born to love, to feel, and to act kindly toward all humanity . . . her hair a soft brown tinged with gold, is worn pompadour style with innumerable wind-kissed tendrils resting on brow and cheek. Captain Blanche is the angel of the Mississippi. . . ."

As Aunt Callie would say, "Well, I'll be dawggoned!"

Anyway, records do prove that Capt. Blanche "Boss" Leathers really had her pilot and captain licenses, renewed them regularly, even in retirement. But even her brother Allan admits she was never a bell-ringin', whistle-tootin', wheel-turnin' captain.

The Greenland. Capt. Mary B. Greene's *Greenland.* Built 1903, lost in ice jam on the Ohio, 1918.

"Aw, she never did all that stuff," he states, "the actual running o' th' boat. Sure, she had licenses all right. But she let Bowling and the men do that. She tended to the buying and the service; she watched the bills and the cash. Maybe you call that running the boat after all."

In 1901 Blanche and Bowling left the river for keeps, but Blanche kept spinning yarns and renewing her licenses until she died, January 25, 1940.

"Ma" Greene, however, survived her, still on the river as a pilot and captain, until 1949.

All controversies as to "firsts" aside, each of this female quartette could, in Blanche's words, say:

"Yes, I am a steamboat man."

Capt. Blanche Douglass Leathers. After Retirement, with her Captain's License.

Mrs. Cooley and her Three Sons in the Cabin of the *America*. She was matriarch of a famous steamboat family.

(Above) The America Unloading at New Orleans. Owned by Capt. Cooley.

(To Right) The Ouachita. A Cooley steamboat. "Loaded to the Guards."

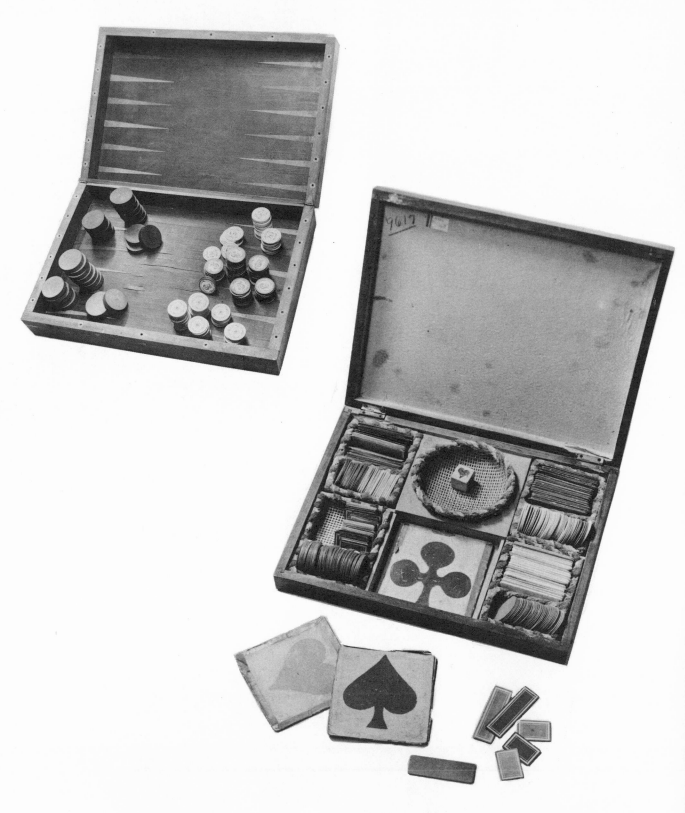

Gambling Paraphernalia used aboard one of the
Natchez steamboats.

THE SLICKEST RASCAL

ON THE MISSISSIPPI

T WAS quite a boast, but then nobody ever accused George H. Devol of concealing his talents under a bushel — or in a deck of cards either. Here is what he claimed in the title page of his amazing book, *Forty Years a Gambler on the Mississippi:*

"A cabin boy in 1839; could steal cards and cheat the boys at eleven; stack a deck at fourteen; bested soldiers on the Rio Grande during the Mexican War; won hundreds of thousands from paymasters, cotton thieves; fought more rough-and-tumble fights than any man in America, and was the most daring gambler in the world."

It is hard to believe that any one man could do all the things George Devol said he did in his memoirs published in 1887. Nevertheless, out of these pages George Devol emerges as a ranking chronicler of the great Mississippi River days of the 1850's and '60's.

He came of pioneer stock. His grandfather, Jonathon Devol, was an illustrious Revolutionary officer, famous in early Ohio frontier history. The love of navigating the western waterways was a part of George's heritage. His grandsire and father were early boatbuilders.

George was born in Aug., 1829, at Marietta, O., and it was not long before he figured in the community as Problem Child No. 1. He admits frankly to having been "the worst boy of my age west of the Allegheny Mountains that was born of good Christian parents . . .", and adds that the townfolks gave him twenty years before he'd wind up on the gallows.

At exactly half that age, George's wanderlust began. He shipped out as cabin boy on the first of a long and illustrious line of steamboats on which he was to become a familiar figure. Its name was *Wacousta.* For nearly six years thereafter, the young boy learned how handle himself and the playing cards, the hard way.

While on the Rio Grande, George learned how to "stack a deck."

"I soon got tired of the Rio Grande," he said, "and after cheating all the soldiers that I could

195

at cards (there was no one else to rob), I took a vessel and came back to New Orleans . . . I was very comfortably fixed. . . ."

He was all of sixteen years old. He had $2700. So he decided to go home, "and see if they will forgive me." He got a job on a northbound steamboat, cleaned out the passengers, bought $400 worth of presents and supplies at Pittsburgh, dressed himself to kill, and surprised his mother and father.

He stayed at home a year, "had a fight nearly every week," and got a job with his brother caulking steamboat hulls.

Meanwhile, he was learning how to play faro, and "it kept me a slave." Then one day, as he and his brother were working on a float behind the wheel of a large steamboat, he suddenly kicked all his tools into the muddy water.

"That's the last lick of work I'll ever do," he said to his startled brother, "and I will make money rain."

You name it, George mastered it — roulette, euchre, rondo, keno, rouge et noir, faro, poker, seven-up, monte — he knew how to make them work for him. In all fairness to this river rogue who had few scruples, it should be explained that he looked upon his strange calling as a finely developed skill, an artistic craftsmanship in which he took great pride. His was no pedestrian, coarse interest in gambling. It was a workmanlike battle of wits and manual dexterity, and he chose to make himself the great master of the craft.

Here is an example of the George Devol finesse:

"I was playing monte one night on the *Rob't E. Lee* when a fellow stepped up to the table and bet me $800 . . . When he had lost his money and spent a few moments studying, he whipped out a Colt's navy [pistol] and said, 'See here, friend, that is all the money I have got, and I am going to have it back.'

"I coolly said, 'Did you think I was going to keep the money?'

"He replied, 'I knew very well you would not keep it. If you had, I would have filled you full of lead. I am from Texas, sir,' and the man straightened himself up. Pulling out a roll of money, I said, 'I want to whisper to you.' He put his head down, and I said, 'I didn't want to give you the money before all those people because then they would all want their money back, too; but you offer to bet me again, and I will bet you $800 against your pistol.'"

The Texan was pleased, and money and pistol

George H. Devol, the Great Mississippi Steamboat Gambler. From his "Forty Years a Gambler on the Mississippi".

were placed with a stakeholder. Devol tossed the three cards, and the Texan turned over the wrong one, naturally. Devol grabbed the pistol and pointed it at his opponent, saying:

"Now, you've acted the wet dog about this and I will not give you a cent of your money, and if you cut any more capers, I will break your nose."

This is perhaps not too typical an example of the Devol technique, as only rarely did this master of monte have to resort to threats to silence a "kicker." Most of them were so ashamed at having been such suckers, they remained bashfully quiet.

What is monte? It was very simple, such a simple way to lose money that, as one reads episode after episode of George Devol's, one wonders how in the world the suckers continued to bite.

He operated three-card monte. The three cards sometimes referred to as "tickets," were usually imprinted respectively with the pictures of a man, a woman, and a baby. Or the king, queen, jack would be used. They were placed face down on table, bar, counter, or suitcase, and "mixed up." Then George would bet the victim that he could not turn up a specified card.

Of course, the gimmick was that George's hand was quicker than the sucker's eye, and if the bet was on turning the lady, the hapless one invariably turned the wrong card — unless it was part of the play for George to let him win a couple of bets. There were endless variations, many employing the services of a "capper," or accomplice, unbeknownst to the victim.

The most common "capper" stunt involved the turning up of a corner of one of the cards, or putting a mark on it, done in view of the victim, but supposedly without George's knowledge. The suckers seeing this maneuver would flock to the game, slitting their clothes to get their savings out of the linings.

It was a sure thing. They saw a chance to cheat George, and he showed them no mercy. When the victim grabbed the marked card and turned it, it was still the wrong one. That little switch, the capper's gambit, worked wonders, made George several fortunes, and seemingly never stopped finding fresh takers. It was uncanny.

Here's a variation of the capper's ruse which worked well:

"We were passengers with Capt. J. M. White on board the steamer *Katie*, bound for New Orleans one night," Devol begins, telling how he engaged in conversation with a "fine-looking gentleman."

Now observe the master: "While we were talking and drinking, I asked the barkeeper if he had any of the tickets that the gentleman played the new game with before supper. He said he had, and gave me some of them." (Devol always kept a good supply of monte cards, stacked decks, and similar "iced" objects with the well-tipped barkeepers.)

"We bet the drinks, cigars, and drinks again. I lost most of the time." George was careful to let the gentleman see an obvious pencil mark on the "baby" card. Enter the capper.

"My capper lost a bet of $500, when the gentleman whispered to him, 'My gracious, man! Where are your eyes? Can't you see the baby card has a spot on it?'

"My partner said he had not noticed the spot,

The Katie. One of Devol's favorite steamboats.

so the man pointed it out to him. Then he made another bet and won." The gentleman was being "worked up," and soon he was quite eager, but George gave him the stand-off treatment:

"Perhaps you had better not bet, for it you lost it might distress you; but if I lose I will not mind it much, as my father has five plantations."

"I can afford to bet you $2000, win or lose," replied the sucker, hurt at the suggestion of poverty. George got him up to five grand easily. "He knew he would win," the gambler commented, "but he was no hog, and he did not want me to ask my old dad for money."

The capper took the cue and offered to put up half the five grand. "No, one at a time, gentlemen," said George.

"I thank you," said the gentleman to the capper, "but I am able to take it myself."

Famous last words. George later bought him a drink, "for I was always very liberal about treating a man who had little, if any money."

Working his "old monte," along with stacked decks in poker, accounted for so much operating capital that George rarely resorted to out-and-out crooked contraptions to bilk the ordinary run of the unwary. But when he tackled a brace of river sharpers like himself, it took all his cunning and ingenuity to outfox them. Let him tell about such an episode:

"Before the War [Between the States] they had an old steamer fitted up as a wharf boat and lodging house at Baton Rouge. This boat was headquarters for the gamblers that ran the river. When thoroughbred gamblers meet around the table at a game of cards, then comes the tug of war. My partner proposed that we fix up some plan to down the gamblers, so we finally hit upon a scheme. . ."

Briefly, they rigged up a long wire from a position behind the wall near the card table. His partner could perch behind the wall and look through a tiny hole into a player's hand. The wire was so rigged that by giving it a tug, it would raise a tiny nail up through the floor boards under the foot of George Devol, as he sat across the table.

If the man in the chair under the peep hole held two pairs, the signal to George would be two nudges into the sole of his shoe. If he had threes, three yanks of the wire, etc. To make sure nobody else got to George's chair when he was traveling the river "for my health," he hired a couple of trusted boys to sit in the game there all the time.

This worked fine, and apparently none of the smart boys caught on. But one night, he had a close call:

"I was playing a friend at our table, and he was seated in his chair. I got the signals all right for some time, and then the 'under-current' seemed to be broken. I waited for the signals until I could not wait any longer, for I was a little behind. I picked up a spittoon and let it fly at the wall, smashing it."

Awakened, George's partner was back on the job.

"That restored communications, and I received the signals all right. My friends wanted to know what I had thrown the spittoon for. I told him the cards were running so bad that I got mad, and that an old Negro had told me once it was a good sign to kick over a spittoon when playing cards.

"He replied, 'I notice your luck changed just after you threw it, and I will try it the next time I play in bad luck.'"

There is perhaps no man still living who can boast that he knew George Devol personally, if boast is the proper word. But such a man was none other than the dean emeritus of Newcomb

The Late Pierce Butler. When only a youngster he met the great gambler.

college, the late Dr. Pierce Butler. Dr. Butler was living the life of a Delta planter on his place, Laurel Hill, near Natchez, and passed on recently.

In his book, *The Unhurried Years,* Dr. Butler tells this incident:

". . . To the grown-ups, the barber-shop might be a very interesting place, for there, on some boats, Devol set up his roulette wheel or set a table for keno. . . On one trip, when I was much younger, Papa took me to get the customary haircut and we found the well-known Devol. Business was nil, he said bitterly, idly twirling his wheel. My big round eyes were fascinated.

" 'Try a whirl, Sonny.'

" 'I have no money.'

" 'Lend you a stake,' as the slim, swift fingers raked a pile of perhaps ten silver dollars toward me. Knowing nothing, of course, I just thought the fierce-looking bird a good bet. Devol spun his wheel. Clickety, click, click, click — and the ball stopped.

" 'First blood on the Eagle Bird,' he sang out, sweeping what looked like a hatful of dollars at me. I was all for taking them, too. But Papa made me thank Devol and give the whole pile back. I confess to regrets that linger yet."

George had another accomplishment besides his gambling technique. For years he used his head not only in three-card monte and other games of manual dexterity, but also, in a more literal sense, in "butting" contests. He was literally "head man" on the river.

Here's how he explained his unique feats of prowess in this field:

"In most all of the many fights I have been engaged in, I made use of what I have called 'that old head of mine.' I don't know (and I guess I never will while I'm alive) just how thick my old skull is; but I do know it must be pretty thick, or it would have been cracked many years ago, for I have been struck some terrible blows on my head with iron dray pins, pokers, clubs, which would have split any man's skull wide open unless it was pretty thick. Doctors have often told me that my skull was nearly an inch in thickness over my forehead. They were only guessing at it then, of course, but if my dear old mother-in-law don't guard my grave, they will know after I'm dead, sure enough, for I have heard them say so. . . ."

As a young man, Devol was pitted against all comers by gamblers, and none could be found to best him, head against head. In later years,

his reputation was a drawback, for it was always getting him into scrapes, and betting bouts. At sixty, he wore his hair long "as the lines of my old scalp look about like the railroad map of the state in which I was born [Ohio]."

He claimed that at sixty, he could still batter down an ordinary door, or smash in a liquor barrel with "that old head of mine," and that matching his age, he could still out-butt any man alive.

Naturally, when a circus billing "The Man with the Thick Skull, or the Great Butter," came along, his friends were always ready to test the side-show skull against that of Devol.

William Carroll was the skull in question, one bright day in the 1860's. He was an attraction of the John Robinson circus playing New Orleans.

It didn't take long before a couple of the Robinson boys had Carroll in tow, making the rounds of the saloons, looking for the local wonder boy — and a few side bets. Quick to take them up was a popular sporting man of the day, one Dutch Jake.

The Gentle Sport of Butting.

"I'll bet a thousand or ten thousand I can find a man to whip him," said Dutch Jake. At the other end of the bar stood our hero, silently sipping his frappé.

"I knew what was up," commented Devol later, "and as we were all friends, I did not want to change the social to a butting match, so I said:

'Don't bet, boys, and Mr. Carroll and I will come together just once for fun.'"

Sizing up Carroll, George knew a fifty-pound advantage would go to himself. He considered giving him only a slanting blow, then realized that Carroll "traveled on his head," so decided to give him "a pretty good one."

The men measured off, ran together. When Carroll picked himself up from the sawdust, he came over and placed his hand on Devol's head.

"Gentlemen," he said, "I have found my papa at last."

George Devol's extravagant claims at gambling have been seriously challenged, but nobody has raised a voice to discount "that old head of mine." The august *Cincinnati Enquirer* once reported, according to Devol, that in a fight with a stevedore, the stevedore's friends stood over George with drawn pistols, threatening to kill him if he did any butting. They wanted the fight "fair." George won anyway.

Once George was on the steamer *John Walsh*, several days up from New Orleans. A fireman began creating a ruckus by butting some of the roustabouts insensible. He was notorious for his head work, having killed several men that way. George rose to the occasion:

"Send him up. I'll butt him 'til he's sick of butting."

Immediately the bets began to fly. Some, knowing the roustabout's fame, tried to argue George out of his folly. That made him mad, and he put up $500 of his own money, a price on his own head, as it were.

The fireman came topside, a string was placed between two uprights, and the men squared off on opposite sides.

"The word was given," George said, "and at the string we both rushed like frenzied bulls. I gave him a glancing blow that skinned his head for about three inches. The next time there was a crash that jarred the boat and drew a shriek of terror from the passengers as the roustabout fell with a dull thud to the deck. . ."

Those who had felt it never ceased paying tribute to George's skull. One man, Bill Legrets, who encountered the cranium at a fair at Cynthiana, Ky., was asked why he didn't shoot George.

"Shoot, h . . l! The first lick he hit me, I thought my neck was disjointed, and when he ran that head into me, I thought it was a cannon-ball!"

George knew he had a dangerous weapon. He could use his fists with amazing power and dexterity; he always carried "Betsy Jane," a fine pistol for when the going was tough, and he was an expert rough-and-tumble wrestler. So he used his head sparingly.

Describing a fracas in the cabin of the steamboat *Niagara*, he tells how he sparred and wrestled his vicious opponent who was bent on doing him in. "I did not want to use my head unless it was necessary . . . It was hard work to keep the old head from taking a hand . . ." George admitted, but he persevered, and bested the man by other means.

Then there was Anderson at Memphis. "I reached down and caught him by the collar, raised him up and struck him with that good old faithful head of mine, and the fight was all over . . ."

There were times when recourse to the head was the only avenue of safety. A poor loser in a game objected to the way George had cheated him, called him a liar, and made the fatal mistake of grabbing George by the collar. "I thought I would get the old head ready for business once more, so I argued with him until I saw an opening, and then let him have it just between the eyes. He dropped all in a heap, and it was some time before they could get him to sit up. . ."

One night in the Jewel Saloon, opposite New Orleans' St. Charles hotel, some previous "head" victims ganged up on him. One John Mortice of Natchez was selected to work over George. He was a powerfully built man, with weight and reach on George.

"Well, to tell you the truth, it was a pretty hard fight; but I got one good lick with my head, and that won the battle for me. It took all the fight out of him. . ."

There was another way George used his head to win bouts besides *hitting* people with it. He let them *hit* his head. Once the toughest river rough of Pittsburgh rashly said to George, "I can lick you in a minute."

"It was a good fight," George recalled, "but I kept dodging my head, so he would hit that, and he soon had his right hand as big as any man's head. . ."

The same treatment worked on one Barlow, a massive longshoreman at New Orleans, who was put up by gamblers to take on George. "I gave him my head for a mark, which he hit clearly, and his fist looked like a boxing glove two minutes afterward... In the squabble I got one solid crack at him between the eyes with my head, which ended the fight."

A man on the steamboat *Duke of Orleans* "struck at me with one of those old-fashioned Dutch-winders. I ducked my head, and he hit that. I knew it hurt him for he did not use that duke any more."

George Devol, the slickest rascal on the river, the man with the iron head, died broke. Said he, shortly before he shot a crap for the last time:

"My old head is hard and thick, and maybe that is the reason I never had enough sense to save my money."

How, when and where he died is something of a mystery. One legend from the upper river says he was finally pushed off a steamboat and drowned. Anyway, his fame still lives along the waterfront of river towns.

A Thrilling Moment.

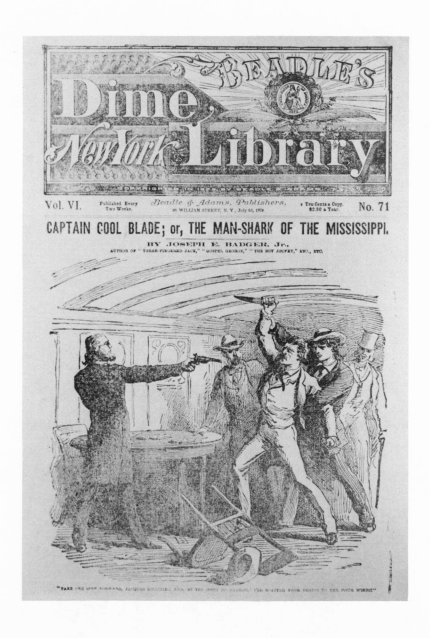

(Above) Devol Swimming for his life.

(Left) "We don't rectify no mistakes in poker mister".
From "Forty Years a Gambler".

"He got out his wallet and put up $1,700".
From "Forty Years a Gambler".

Foiling the Frisco Sharp.

VIEW OF THE FLOATING PALACE IN THE GULF OF MEXICO,
IN HER PASSAGE FROM MOBILE TO THE BALISE

The Floating Palace in a Storm on the Gulf (1853).

(*On Facing Page*) One of French's Ads. On its reverse side the ad reads: "Listen for the toot of the calliope and make a break for the river".

Your Wife and Mother-in-Law.

—WILL VISIT—
FRENCH'S NEW SENSATION
At The River To-Night
TICKETS 25 cts.   RESERVED 35 cts.
The Fashion Plate of River Shows.
First Class in Every Detail. A. B. French, Prop

WHEN BROADWAY

CAME TO THE LEVEE

HATEVER may be said about show-boats, they were clean. From Eugene Robinson's *Floating Palaces, Museum, Menagerie, Aquarium,* and *Opera House* of the '90's, all the way down to Al and Flo Cooper's *Dixie Queen* of 1940, you could safely take your prissy Aunt Agatha to a showboat performance.

That was showboat doctrine. The show folk led a clean life physically and morally, it was said, and the customers along the rivers and tributaries who relied on the floating troupes for entertainment expected the entertainment to be wholesome.

When Capt. Augustus Byron French's *New Sensation* (*Nos. 1* through *5*) hove into sight around the bend, calliope braying, there was a mad rush for the levee. Business came to a standstill as the gaily uniformed band, actors doubling in brass, paraded down the street in a shower of handbills. The townsfolk put on their best clothes, and the kids their best deportment. Cap'n French's *New Sensation* was in town.

The *New Sensation* floated on the rivers from 1878 to 1900, old-timers recall, and in all those years never a word of ill repute was said about this patriarchal river showman.

That's why, at one river town, the captain almost blew his top.

The typical river hamlet was crouched under the protection of the levee, except for the wooden tongue which reached up and over to touch the life-giving steamboats. On this occasion it got the usual *New Sensation* treatment, with flags, calliope, bands, parade and handbills. But that night, Capt. French gazed with incredulity as the crowd started to stream down the gangway into his auditorium.

They were all men! Slowly it dawned on the doughty captain what was going on, what kind of show the men expected.

Capt. French sidled over to the ticket window, whispered something to the man behind the wicket, and then marched into the near-filled theater. Climbing up to the stage, the captain walked to the center behind the footlights as ripples of applause began. The river impressario raised his big hands for silence.

"Men, I have been watching you," he began, making the most of his dramatic heritage. "I know what is in your hearts. There is not a lady among you, not a mother, wife, sweetheart, or sister."

You could have heard a gold toothpick drop. The captain took off his cap, and held it tenderly. "You think, though, that I do not know your reasoning out of which such thoughts are born; that you are going to see the kind of show that is the equivalent of the kinds of stories some men tell among themselves."

His voice dropped to almost a whisper. "You were never more mistaken in your lives." Then . . . "NOW EVERY LAST ONE OF YOU GIT UP AN' GIT OUT!" he bellowed, his voice echoing up and down the river bank in the still night air.

"You will find a man at the ticket office prepared to give you your money back. If you are men, go home and get your womenfolks.

"I shall hold this show until ten tonight. If you return with your womenfolk, my troupe and I are prepared to give you the kind of entertainment we have always given up and down these rivers, and always will as long as I live. But if you are the kind of animals in pants that calls yourself men and ain't, then you'll git up and git. Git your money back, and don't ever show your faces on French's *New Sensation* again!"

Sheepishly, they all rose and weaseled out of the place — and not one of them asked for a refund. In about two hours, they were all back — with the womenfolks. Capt. French returned to stage center.

"Gentlemen, I'm glad we understand one another." Heavy applause — from both sexes.

The captain's wife, Callie, incidentally, followed in his footsteps after he passed on, becoming a licensed pilot.

Further research may yet reveal who actually gave the first performance on a river boat. Philip Graham, in his definitive book on the subject, *Showboats* (University of Texas Press),* agrees that two early American thespians, Noah M. Ludlow and Sol Smith, should have the honor, even though neither, in their colorful reminiscences, mentions having given a "show" of any kind while aboard their river craft.

Ludlow's troupe bought a keel-boat and in

Showboats. The History of An American Institution. University of Texas Press. 1951.

Capt. Augustus Byron French, River Showman.

October, 1817, started drifting down to New Orleans. In the 1820's, Sol Smith was active throughout the region of the Mississippi and its tributaries.

Both do mention, however, having run across the showboat of the William Chapman family in the 1830's. Its name was the *Floating Theater,* and it certainly deserves the credit as the first showboat. Chapman was an Englishman, with a good reputation behind him at Covent Garden where he acted with Mrs. Siddons. He launched his *Floating Theater* at Pittsburgh, according to Graham, in the summer of 1831, with the nine members of the family looking on. By July, the family plus "a riverman and an unnamed extra actor" headed the *Floating Theater* down the Ohio and into the Mississippi for the first venture of its type in theatrical history.

Ludlow, running across it at Cincinnati, described it thus:

"I beheld a large flatboat, with a rude kind of house built upon it having a ridge-roof, above which projected a staff with a flag attached, upon which was plainly visible the word 'Theater.' This singular object attracted my attention as it was tied up at the landing at Cincinnati, and on

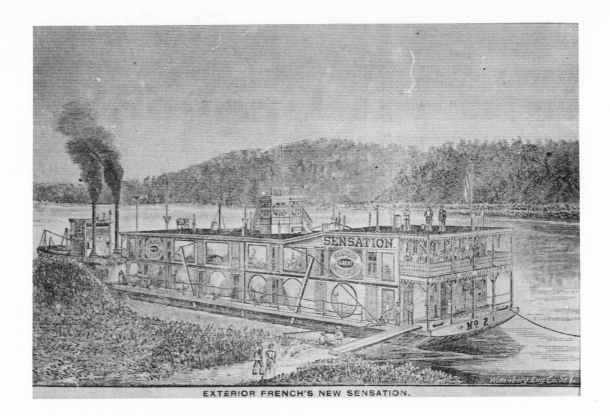

EXTERIOR FRENCH'S NEW SENSATION.

French's *New Sensation*. He had five boats of this
name.

Interior of the *New Sensation*.

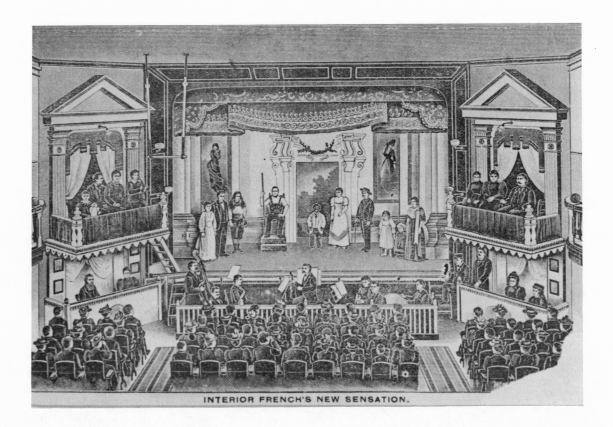

INTERIOR FRENCH'S NEW SENSATION.

The Floating Palace. Old advertisement.

Contemporary Snapshot of French's *New Sensation.*

my making inquiries in regard to it, I learned that it was used for a theatrical company, under the management of a Mr. Chapman. . . They were on their winding way to New Orleans, and, as I heard afterwards, stopped at every town or village on the banks of the river, where they supposed they could get together a sufficient audience."

The famous Tyrone Power had been anxious to see Chapman's showboat, and wrote in 1835:

"This floating theater, about which I make constant inquiry and which I yet hope to fill in with, is not the least original or singular speculation ventured on these waters. It was projected and is carried on by the Elder Chapman, well known for many years as a Covent Garden actor; his practice is to have a building erected upon some point high up the Mississippi, or one of its tributaries. Whence he takes his departure early in the fall, with scenery, dresses and decorations, all prepared for representation. . . When the Mississippi theater reaches New Orleans, it is abandoned and sold for firewood; the manager and troup [sic] returning in a steamer to build a new one, with such improvements as increased experience may have suggested. This course Mr. Chapman has pursued for three or four seasons back, and, as I am told by many who have encountered this aquatic company, very profitably. . ."

Sol Smith related an anecdote entitled, *A Floating Theater,* concerning the Chapmans:

"The 'Chapman family' consisting of old Mr. Chapman, William Chapman, George Chapman, Caroline Chapman, and Harry and Therese Chapman (children), came to the West this summer [presumably around 1830], opened a theater in Louisville, and afterward established and carried into operation that singlar affair, the *Floating Theater,* concerning which so many anectodes are told.

"The 'family' were all extremely fond of fishing, and during the 'waits' the actors amused themselves by 'dropping a line' over the stern of the ark. On one occasion, while playing the 'Stranger' (Act IV, Scene I) there was a long wait for Francis, the servant of the misanthropic Count Walbourgh.

"'Francis! Francis!' called the Stranger. No reply.

"'Francis! Francis!' (a pause) 'Francis!' rather angrily called the Stranger again.

"A very distant voice — 'Coming, Sir!' (a considerable pause, during which the Stranger walks up and down; à la Macready, in a great rage.)

"'Francis!'

"Francis (entering) — 'Here I am, Sir!'

"Stranger — 'Why did you not come when I called?'

"Francis — 'Why, Sir, I was just hauling in one of the d—dest big catfish you ever saw!'

"It was some minutes before the laughter of the audience could be restrained sufficiently to allow the play to proceed.

"It is said of the *Floating Theater* that it was cast loose during a performance at one of the river towns in Indiana by some mischievous boys, and could not be landed for half a dozen miles, the large audience being compelled to walk back to their village."

What Sol Smith does not say in any of his memoirs is that, according to Graham, after Chapman died, his widow sold the *Floating Theater* to Sol Smith in 1847, who lost it completely in a collision with a steamboat on his first trip out.

Having proved the showboat a sound business venture, and a cultural success as well, Chapman's idea quickly spread to the eastern streams taking various departures to suit various tastes. Meanwhile, on the Mississippi, imitation bred an unfortunate twist. The charlatans, seeing a tailor-made vehicle and ready audience, moved in with their medicine shows, followed by a raft of gamblers, crooks, and fakes. The War Between the States ended steamboating for the duration and fortunately put an end to this excrescence.

It was inevitable that two special branches of show business should also take root in showboats: vaudeville and the circus. Both evolved from Chapman's brain child. Vaudeville was actually the minstrel show, in its early stages on the river; whereas, Gilbert R. Spaulding and his partner, Charles J. Rogers, really had a circus, with all the trimmings, aboard their ship *Floating Palace,* which operated from 1851 until the vessel and its attendant craft were taken over at New Orleans and used as the Confederate hospital. A steam calliope appeared on their boat in 1858.

Spaulding and Rogers didn't have the field entirely to themselves. The fabulous Dan Rice also floated a circus of lesser grandeur, and a great rivalry was just reaching legal pitch when the war intervened. Following the war, Dan Rice's circus became famous, but it only traveled by water. Its performances were given ashore.

The first, big, post-war showboat man, the giant of the trade, although he was actually a short, dapper little person, was the aforemen-

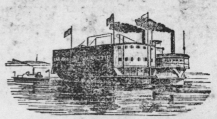
Ads for Van Amburgh's Show, on the *Floating Palace*, at Natchez.

tioned Capt. French (née Dolen). He dominated showboating from 1878 to 1902, and his partners the McNairs and his wife, "Aunt Callie" French, continued his traditions until 1907. He ran a series of five French's *New Sensation* showboats with enormous success, adding colorful chapters to the lore of river theatrics.

E. A. Price of the *Water Queen* which was already giving the French enterprise competition, bought out Callie French, and his boats took over as the star attractions along the levee. Capt. Price had on board his *Water Queen* in 1900 a family of actors named Bryant, and the Bryants would one day carry on where Price left off, as operators of *The Princess* and Bryant's *Showboat* up until the recent date of 1942.

Thus, showboat enterprises had a sort of continuity, even though one name might merge into another; and though the original identity might be lost, a kind of spiritual line of succession was maintained.

Dozens of other famous names could be mentioned here, of impresarios, their boats, and their famous actors, and the sparkle each contributed:

Breidenbaugh's *Theatorium*, Robinson's *Floating Palace*, Markle's *New Grand Floating Palace*, the Eisenbarth-Henderson *Floating Theater* (*The Temple of Amusement*), the McNairs' *New Era*, Emerson's, and later Hitner's *Cotton Blossom*, the Menkes' *Hollywood*, and finally, Al Cooper's *Dixie Queen*.

This last-named showboat was the last one to play New Orleans. She tied up in the New Basin Canal in January, 1940. Seating 540 people, she was advertised as a "new boat," which she was, having been built in 1939.

Today there are but two showboats left on the river (if we except the *Sprague* which is really a retired towboat converted into a floating theatre, at Vicksburg). Capt. T. J. Reynolds' *Majestic* plays the Monongahela and Ohio Rivers each summer with a troupe of college students from Hiram College as players. Capt. J. W. Menke's *Golden Rod* has been playing at St. Louis since 1937. On the *Golden Rod*, it is still possible to see the entertainment of the past interpreted to present-day audiences —a feat that has kept packing them in for eighteen years at one stand.

The Steam Calliope.

GOING FROM DE COTTON FIELDS.

KANSAS

Copyright, 1879, by W. F. Shaw

Thos Hunter, Lith. Phila

SONG AND CHORUS.

Chorus of this Song Ran: "I'm goin' from de cotton fields, An' Oh! It make me sigh, For when de sun goes down tonight, I'm goin' to say goodbye."

And in the summer of 1951, the *Cotton Blossom*, M-G-M's showboat, sailed again. Metro-Goldwyn-Mayer's remake of *Show Boat* came to the technicolored screen and crowded pre-TV moviehouses. This showboat might have gladdened the hearts of all the old river showmen, if it had not also given them an awful jolt.

The Ferber story and the Kern music were all there. The showboat, however, was more of a "dream boat" since it embodied, according to M-G-M's toutings, the features of some fifty river craft which the studio designers studied.

It was decided to build it from scratch on the studio's Lot. No. III, rather than try to find an old boat and refurbish it on the Sacramento River. It wound up a dazzling thing, 171 feet overall, thirty-four foot beam, stacks fifty-seven feet high. It had nineteen-foot paddlewheels, and — shades of Captain French — it was powered by two 225-horsepower AIRCRAFT ENGINES!

Of course, this Hollywood version of a showboat was self-propelled, a far cry from the real thing which had a towboat along for propulsion.

Some scenes were actually shot on location, Natchez being one of the selected spots. The whole city turned out for the event. Many citizens got into the act. One hot day, a doctor was called for, and in three seconds, four of the

extras, all M.D.'s, volunteered. They had all shut up shop for the day!

The entertainment given by showboats ran the gamut, from serious drama to comic stunts; from skilled professionel presentations to rank hokum. But somewhere in between, all the accepted theatrical techniques were employed. Likewise, the managerial and exploitation practices associated with Broadway had their counterparts on the rivers.

One such institution was the advance man. Captain French employed a series of these necessary, but, along the river, unfortunately too fallible adjuncts. The temptations were too strong. They were supposed to scoot down the river ahead of the showboat, post bills, distribute broadsides and give out passes to editors and others who could help swell the crowds for the soon-to-arrive floating theater.

The advance man was, by virtue of his job, rather impressive. He could put his thumb in his suspenders, push his derby down on his forehead, and tell the yokels about life in the big town. Besides, he knew stellar performers by their first names, he had a bag-full of free tickets, and best of all, the boss was miles away up the river!

So, with the sinful attractions that lazy flesh is apt to fall for, it wasn't a surprise to Capt. French

Price's *New Floating Opera*. Built 1891.

Eisenbarth-Henderson *Floating Theater*. Built 1901.

to arrive at a landing, ready for a big audience, only to find his coming unheralded, his bills unposted, and his advance man unconscious.

One day, after operating without an advance man for some time, an eager fellow named Max Stribling applied for the job. Sizing him up as a likely and sober prospect, the Captain gave him some money, a bundle of posters, handbills and tickets, and filled the put-put in the big skiff with gas. Max shoved off down the river in a cloud of exhaust.

At the next several stops, Captain French thought he'd struck solid gold. Crowds waiting on the levee. Excitement high. Then, further downriver, the weather got cold, the river got foggy, and Max got to drinking. One night in a thick pea-souper, French's *New Sensation* quietly drifted past a landing where Max and the put-put were resting, while the advance man slept one off. Sobering up in the morning, Max started

down the river again, but soon found out the showboat was several jumps ahead of him.

Each time he went ashore with his bills, the townsfolk gave him the same news:

"Gosh, Capt. French was here two nights ago, and he sure did put on a fine show. It was a sellout!"

Finally, days later, Max glided alongside the *New Sensation,* and sheepishly bearded the little lion in his office den.

"Stribling, you're fired, of course," snapped the diminutive river Ziegfield.

"But Capt. French, everywhere I went they told me you were wonderful. The show was sold out at each stop. What more could I have done?"

"Waaal," relented Capt. French, "at least you're different. You're rehired, son, and let me tell you something. You're the first advance man I ever heard of who could also give a report on the house."

Markle's *New Sunny South*.
Built 1905.

(Above) Lightner's Floating Palace Showboat. Operated on Lower Mississippi and bayous. Built 1900.

(Left) Menke's Showboat *Gold-enrod,* St. Louis, 1955. Sign on the steamer advertises the play "Convict's Daughter".

Robinson's *Floating Palace* built 1893.

(*Above*) Reynolds' Showboat, *Majestic*. Used for dramatic courses by Hiram College students.

(*Right*) Byrant's *New Showboat*. There were three boats of this name from 1918 to World War II.

(On Facing Page Above) Eva La Reane Playing the
Calliope. Danced on the *Cotton Blossom*, 1930.

(On Facing Page Below) The Showboat
Cotton Blossom, 1930.

(Above) The *Cotton Blossom* 1951. This was Hollywood's 1951 stupendous version of *The Cotton Blossom*,
for third, technicolor film of Edna Ferber's
"Showboat". Built at Hollywood, it had stacks
57 feet high and was self-propelled,
while real showboats were always towed.

Confluence of Old, Red and Atchafalaya Rivers
In Lower Left: Mississippi in upper right.

OLD MAN MISSISSIPPI'S

NEW BAG OF TRICKS

HE first known commercial cargo to be floated down the Mississippi was a load of 15,000 bear and deer hides from around the Wabash. That was the year 1705.

The French *coureurs de bois* brought it down as far as Bayou Manchac, just below present Baton Rouge, La. This bayou was once connected with the river, flowing eventually into Lake Pontchartrain. From the lake, they poled the cargo out into the Mississippi Sound to the French capital of those early days at Biloxi. From there it was shipped to France.

An auspicious start, 15,000 hides, shipped from the Wabash to the Seine, proving that DeSoto, La Salle, Father Marquette, d'Iberville and others had rightly evaluated the commercial possibilties of the Mississippi Valley, although they could not have forseen that this first cargo would lead, eventually to such great "tows" as that single tow in 1931, of 28,200 bales of cotton; tons of gasoline in a single integrated tow today; hundreds of automobiles mounted in three tiers on barges; millions of tons of sulphur, wheat, chem-

icals, and other products, coursing up and down the mighty stream every year.

For the river today is a vital, living thing, doing all its earliest enthusiasts said it would — and more. It has passed through transitions. It has cast off old channels and shortened itself. It has discarded modes of transportation. It has weathered the era of the railroad which threatened to make it useless for anything but fishing.

In the early 19th century, keelboats and flatboats carried the commerce of the Mississippi — and flatboats were still being operated well into the era of the steamboats which gradually supplanted them. In the middle of the 19th century the steamboat was king. Then the railroads ran the packets off the river at the end of that same century. From the turn of 1900 to the early '20's, the Mississippi was commercially dead.

Whereupon history came up with its proverbial irony. Powerful and efficient towboats were developed which could push enough barges of pay cargo, slowly but surely, to make river transportation once more economically interesting to shippers. River terminals were built. The towboats had none of the glamor of the old floating palaces, to be sure. They carried no passengers, provided no nine course meals with all the trimmings, no charming ladies nor suave gamblers.

But neither did they explode or snag, and they carried many times more freight — and they got there just the same. They were the spiritual successors to the packets, minus the passengers, and in this role they took on the packets' old adversary, the railroad. The pendulum had swung back.

The towboat has rebuilt river commerce. By 1925 there were several transportation companies operating fleets of towboats and barges. Towboats, incidentally, don't tow. They push. Today there are about 100 companies operating on the river, with an average annual tonnage of 59,000,-000. You can't keep a good river down.

Yes, the Mississippi has come back strong. Besides the powerful towboats themselves, another factor has been the development of the widespread inland waterway system connecting the Gulf of Mexico with the Missouri, Upper Mississippi, the Ohio, the Illinois, the Cumberland, and the Monongahela, the Muskingum and the Tennessee, linking the Great Lakes to the Seven Seas. Eastward from New Orleans, this system extends to Apalachee Bay, Florida, joining the Lower Mississippi with the seaports of Gulfport, Biloxi, and Pascagoula in Mississippi; Mobile, Ala.; and Pensacola, Fla.; and then it goes on up to Birmingport, near Birmingham, through the Tombigbee-Black-Warrior river system.

From New Orleans westward, the towboats nudge their valuable hauls all the way to the Mexican border at Brownsville, Texas, with stops at such important points as Lake Charles, La., Beaumont, Port Arthur, Houston, Galveston, Freeport, and Corpus Christi, Texas.

This "Ditch that Spans Dixie" alone accounted for 41,727,000 tons in the year 1953.

Thus, Father Mississippi has in effect spread himself out, while keeping within his levees — a neat trick. But in so doing, in building himself back into the position of a national economic asset, he is still costing the government a pretty penny.

The jetty system the government bet Capt. Eads couldn't build in 1875 is still a headache. (See Chapter 6). Eads' "no cure, no pay" arrangement, by means of which he opened the mouth of the river, was an immediate relief. His maintenance contract expired in 1901. Since then,

the passes have presented recurring problems, with vast appropriations spent in upkeep and attempted improvement. The total cost from 1901 to the present, including the opening of Southwest Pass in 1908, has been in excess of $63,000,000.

Was it worth it, then, to accept Eads' plan in the first place? Back in 1874, as we have seen, a strong lobby wanted to build a canal to the Gulf instead. The battle of jetties vs. canal is far from a dead issue. Right now, the Alexander Seaway, an ambitious $90,000,000 project, linking a new inner-navigation harbor at New Orleans directly to the Gulf, a seventy-mile tidewater route, has an excellent chance of realization in this generation. It has already passed many of the Congressional hurdles.

Ships, 10,079 of them carrying 25,802,000 tons of cargo and 22,965 passengers, used the Passes in 1953. If the seaway is built, this ocean-going trade will go by the canal and the Passes will be abandoned or restricted in use.

Some of those who have kept a watchful eye over the river's well-being have fears that the St. Lawrence Seaway will hurt the Father of Waters. It will divert, they claim, much river trade upstream through the Great Lakes to the new seaports. That remains to be seen, but the Old Man doesn't appear worried.

In fact, he has some radical ideas of his own, one in particular, which, if not checked, or at least controlled, might put him in the position of doing two of his best friends a fantastically mean turn.

There is a good chance, the experts say with some alarm, that the Mississippi may within a decade desert its present channel at Old River Junction, 217 river miles above New Orleans, and find a shorter route to the Gulf, thus bypassing Baton Rouge and New Orleans entirely.

There is evidence that this diversion has already begun. Old River is a six-mile section of a former bend in the Mississippi. It leads westward to connect with the Atchafalaya and Red Rivers, which run North and South. By capturing more and more of the Mississippi's flow, Old River will slowly divert the main stream into the Atchafalaya, and southward into the Gulf, a 140-mile jaunt as compared to 313 miles in the present bed. When it reaches the point where it captures forty per cent of the Mississippi, the latter will start silting up below Old River Junction. "That does it," say the engineers. The situation would then be "uncontrollable."

Besides leaving Baton Rouge and New Orleans

with shallow water, it will deprive New Orleans of its chief water supply and sewerage outlet. Yes, sewerage is pumped into the bottom of the river below the city, whence it is carried out into the Gulf.

Fortunately, the Corps of Engineers is aware of the situation. Planning for the control of Old River, and, therefore, Old Man River, has progressed. Arousing public opinion and loosening Congressional purse strings comes next — before it's too late.

What's more, should the Old Man sneak past his mortal enemy, the Corps of Engineers, and take off down the Atchafalaya, he would completely wreck another project which has already cost millions — the Atchafalaya Floodway. This flood prevention project is now nearly complete after many years of anxiety.

Maybe Old Man River "don't say nothin'", but it's a good bet he's chuckling up his chutes.

Crevasse of More Recent Date. Mulatto levee break, March, 1949.

(On Facing Page Above) Modern Levee Construction.

(On Facing Page Below) Another View of Mulatto Levee Break.

(Above) Aerial View of Bonnet Carré Spillway in Operation. Lake Pontchatrain to left.

(Above) Paving Levee Slope
with Concrete.

(On Facing Page Above) Bonnet
Carré Spillway in Operation
(1950).

(On Facing Page Below) Morganza Flood Control Structure,
Atchafalya River, La.

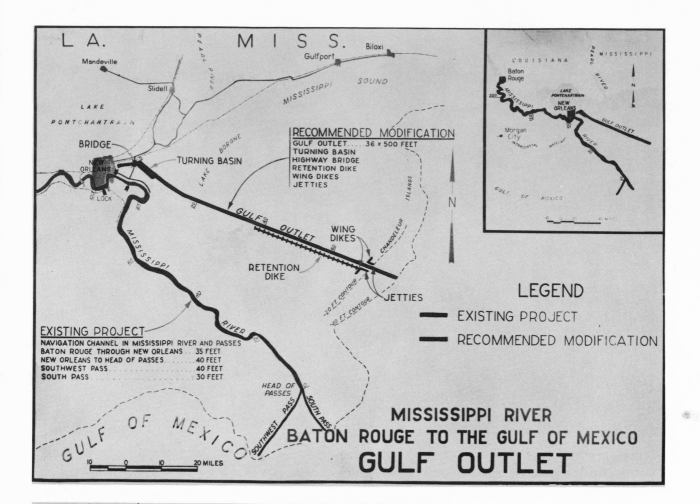

MISSISSIPPI RIVER
BATON ROUGE TO THE GULF OF MEXICO
GULF OUTLET

RECOMMENDED MODIFICATION
GULF OUTLET.....36 × 500 FEET
TURNING BASIN
HIGHWAY BRIDGE
RETENTION DIKE
WING DIKES
JETTIES

EXISTING PROJECT
NAVIGATION CHANNEL IN MISSISSIPPI RIVER AND PASSES
BATON ROUGE THROUGH NEW ORLEANS ... 35 FEET
NEW ORLEANS TO HEAD OF PASSES ...... 40 FEET
SOUTHWEST PASS .... 40 FEET
SOUTH PASS .... 30 FEET

LEGEND
EXISTING PROJECT
RECOMMENDED MODIFICATION

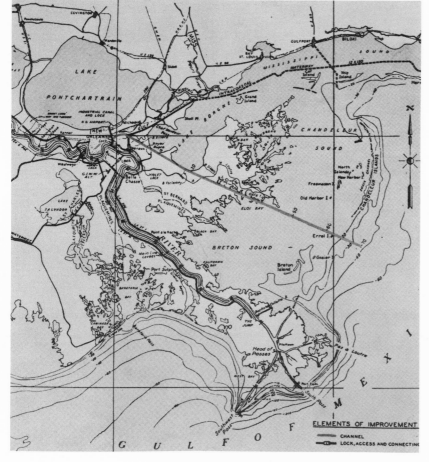

(Above and Left) Proposed Canal From New Orleans to the Gulf.

(On Facing Page)
This Map Shows Old Man River Trying to Take a Short Cut to the Atchafalaya at Old River, and How the Army Engineers are Stopping him.

(Below) Another Map Showing the Old River Break-through.

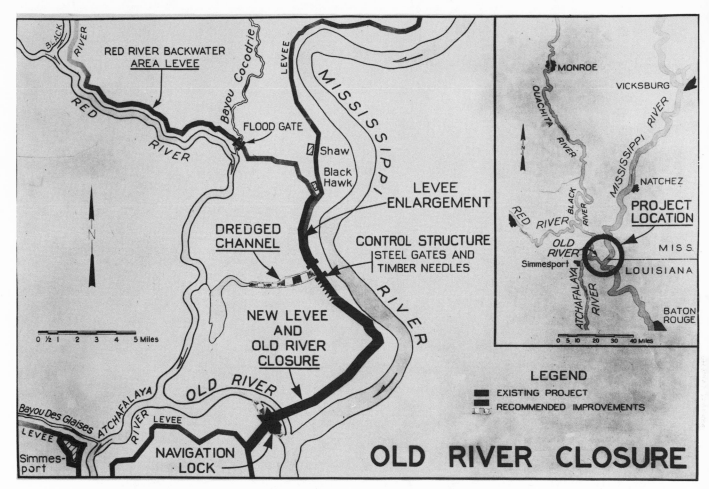

OLD RIVER CLOSURE

RED RIVER BACKWATER AREA LEVEE

FLOOD GATE

Shaw

Black Hawk

LEVEE ENLARGEMENT

DREDGED CHANNEL

CONTROL STRUCTURE
STEEL GATES AND TIMBER NEEDLES

NEW LEVEE AND OLD RIVER CLOSURE

NAVIGATION LOCK

Bayou Des Glaises

Simmesport

LEVEE

0 ½ 1 2 3 4 5 Miles

MONROE

VICKSBURG

NATCHEZ

PROJECT LOCATION

Simmesport

OLD RIVER

MISS.

LOUISIANA

BATON ROUGE

0 5 10 20 30 40 Miles

LEGEND
EXISTING PROJECT
RECOMMENDED IMPROVEMENTS

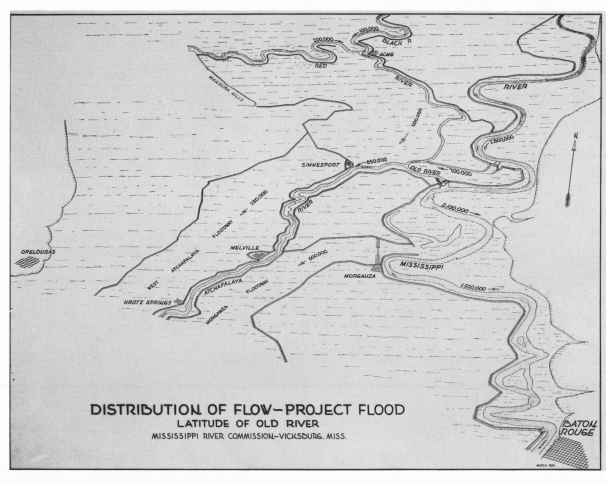

DISTRIBUTION OF FLOW—PROJECT FLOOD
LATITUDE OF OLD RIVER
MISSISSIPPI RIVER COMMISSION—VICKSBURG, MISS.

MARCH 1953

(Above) Mississippi Towboat. (Built 1929).

(On Facing Page Above) Towboat *Harry Truman*
and Tow Travelling Up-river.

(On Facing Page Below) Typical Barge Line Tow on
the Intracoastal Waterway.

CREDITS AND REFERENCES

PAGE	POSITION	
152	bottom	*Illustrated News,* Jan. 8, 1853
153		*Harper's Weekly,* Sept. 15, 1888
154	top	*Illustrated News,* 1853
155	top	Courtesy of Capt. Fred Way, Jr., Sewickley, Pa.
156	top	Photograph by J. Mack Moore
156	bottom	Courtesy of Capt. Fred Way, Jr., Sewickley, Pa.
157	top	Print from photograph by Louis E. Cormier
164	top	Courtesy of the Mariners' Museum, Newport News, Va.
164	bottom	Courtesy of the Louisiana State Museum.
167	top	Courtesy of Capt. Fred Way, Jr., Sewickley, Pa.
167	bottom	Idem.
168	top	From Chromo-Litho. P. S. Duval.
171	bottom	*Harper's New Monthly Magazine,* Dec. 1855
173		Courtesy of the Mariners' Museum, Newport News, Va.
174	top	Courtesy of Capt. Fred Way, Jr., Sewickly, Pa.
174	bottom (R)	Idem.
174	bottom (L)	Idem.
175	top	Library of Congress
175	center	Courtesy of the Historical and Philosophical Society of Ohio.
175	bottom	*Harper's New Monthly Magazine,* 1859
176	top	Photograph by G. F. Mugnier
176	bottom	*Century Magazine,* 1887
177		*Every Saturday,* Aug. 26, 1871
179	top	Photograph by G. F. Mugnier
179	center	Idem.
179	bottom (L)	*Every Saturday,* Aug. 26, 1871
180		*Harper's New Monthly Magazine,* Nov., 1893
182	top	*Harper's,* 1867
182	center	Sketch by J. Wills Smedley, *Harper's New Monthly Magazine,* Jan., 1893
182	bottom	*Harper's,* 1867
183	top (R)	Sketch by J. Wills Smedley in *Harper's New Monthly Magazine,* Jan., 1893
183	top (L)	Sketch by J. Wills Smedley in *Scribner's Monthly,* Sept., 1874
183	center	*Century Magazine,* Jan., 1883
183	bottom	*Harper's New Monthly Magazine,* Jan., 1893
184		Courtesy of Allan Douglass, brother of Blanche Leathers
186	top (L)	*Harper's Weekly,* March 8, 1884
187	top (R)	Courtesy of Allan Douglass, brother of Blanche Leathers
187	bottom (L)	Courtesy of Mrs. Clarkie McNair
189		Courtesy of Mariners' Museum, Newport News, Va.

PAGE	POSITION	
194		Both pictures courtesy of the Louisiana State Museum.
196		From Devol's *Forty Years a Gambler on the Mississippi.*
197		Courtesy of the Louisiana State Museum.
198		Courtesy of the late Dr. Pierce Butler.
199		Sketch by "Skitt" in *Fischer's Review,* 1859
202		Pictures on this page are from Devol's *Forty Years a Gambler on the Mississippi.*
203	top	Idem.
204		From a lithograph of Sarony and Major, N. Y. Courtesy of Mr. Albert L. Lieutaud.
206		Courtesy of Mrs. W. P. McNair.
207		Both illustrations: Courtesy of Mrs. W. P. McNair.
208		Photographs of *The New Sensation,* Courtesy of Capt. Fred Way, Jr., Sewickley, Pa.
210	(L)	*Natchez Free Trader,* Dec. 7, 1853
210	top (R)	*Natchez Free Trade,* May 20, 1856
210	bottom (R)	Idem., March 6, 1861
211		Idem., Nov. 29, 1853
212		*Harper's Weekly,* May 12, 1866
214		Courtesy of Mrs. W. P. McNair.
215		Courtesy of Capt. Fred Way, Jr., Sewickley, Pa.
216	All	Idem.
217		Robinson's *Floating Palace,* Courtesy of the Howard-Tilton Memorial Library, Tulane University. The other two pictures are by the courtesy of Capt. Fred Way, Jr., Sewickley, Pa.
218		Pictures on this page are by the courtesy of *The Times-Picayune.*
219		Courtesy of Metro - Goldwyn - Mayer.
220		Photographs by the Corps of Engineers, U. S. Army, New Orleans District.
223		Idem.
224		Idem.
225		Idem.
226		Idem.
227		Idem.
228		Idem.
229		Idem.
230	top	Photograph by Charles L. Franck.
231	top	Courtesy of the Corps of Engineers, U. S. Army, New Orleans District.
231	bottom	Idem.
232		Idem.

ABBOTT, JOHN S. C., *Ferdinand de Soto.* Dodd, Mead & Co., New York, 1873.

BALDWIN, LELAND D., *The Keelboat Age on Western Waters.* University of Pittsburgh Press, Pittsburgh, 1941.

BARKAU, CAPT. ROY, *The Great Steamboat Race.* The Picture Marine Publishing Co., Cincinnati, 1952.

BERRY, REV. CHESTER D., *Loss of the Sultana and Reminiscences of Survivors.* Darius D. Thorp, Lansing, Mich., 1892.

BLAIR WALTER, and MEINE, FRANKLIN J., *Mike Fink, King of Mississippi Keelboatmen.* Henry Holt & Co., New York, 1933.

BOATWRIGHT, MODY C., *Folk Laughter on the American Frontier.* McMillan Co., New York, 1949.

BRYANT, BILLY, *Children of Ol' Man River; the Life and Times of a Show-boat Trouper.* Lee Furman, Inc., New York, 1936.

BUTLER, PIERCE, *The Unhurried Years.* Louisiana State University Press, Baton Rouge, 1948.

BRADLEY, JAMES, *The Confederate Mail Carrier or From Missouri to Arkansas.* Mexico, Mo., 1894.

COCHRAN, WM. C., *Perils of River Navigation in the Sixties. Mississippi Valley Historical Association Proceedings, Vol. X, Part II.*

CHASE, JOHN C., *Frenchmen, Desire, Goodchildren and Other Streets of New Orleans.* Robert L. Crager & Co., New Orleans, 1949.

COOLEY, CAPT. LeVERIER, *Letters in Huber Collection.*

COOLEY, STOUGHTON, *The Mississippi Roustabout. New England Magazine, Vol. XI, No. 1* (November 1894).

CORTHELL, ELMER L., *A History of the Jetties at the Mouth of the Mississippi River.* J. Wiley & Sons, New York, 1881.

CLEMENT, WILLIAM E, *Plantation Life on the Mississippi.* Pelican Publishing Co., New Orleans, 1953.

DEVOL, GEORGE H., *Forty Years a Gambler on the Mississippi.* Devol-Haines, Cincinnati, 1887.

DORSEY, FLORENCE L., *Master of the Mississippi, Henry Shreve and the Conquest of the Mississippi.* Houghton Mifflin Co., Boston, 1941.
Road to the Sea: The Story of James B. Eads and Mississippi River. Rinehart & Co., Inc., New York, 1947.

DOUGLAS, CLAUDE L., *James Bowie; the Life of a Bravo.* B. Upshaw & Co., Dallas, 1944.

EADS, JAMES B., *Jetty System Explained. Phenomena of the Mississippi River.* St. Louis, 1874.
Report on the Mississippi Jetties. New Orleans Picayune Job Print, 1876.

FEDERAL WRITERS PROJECT, *New Orleans City Guide.* Houghton-Mifflin Co., Boston, 1938.
Louisiana, A Guide to the State. Hastings House, New York, 1945.

FEDERAL WRITERS PROJECT, *Ship Registers and Enrollments of New Orleans, Louisiana, 1804-1870.* 6 volumes, W.P.A., Baton Rouge, La., 1941-42.
Navigation Casualties, 1866-1900, on Mississippi, Red and Ouachita Rivers. W.P.A., New Orleans, 1937-8.
U. S. Customhouse Wreck Reports, 1873-1924. W.P.A., New Orleans, 1937-38.

FLEXNER, JAMES T., *Steamboats Come True: American Inventors in Action.* The Viking Press, New York, 1944.

FUGINA, CAPT. FRANK J., *Lore and Lure of the Scenic Upper Mississippi River.* Jones & Kroger Co., Winona, Minn., 1945.

GAYARRE, CHARLES, *A Louisiana Sugar Plantation of the Old Regime.* Harper's Monthly, March, 1887.

GOULD, CAPT. EMERSON W., *Fifty Years on the Mississippi; or Gould's History of River Navigation.* Nixon-Jones, St. Louis, 1889.

GRAHAM, PHILIP, *Showboats; The history of an American institution.* University of Texas Press, Austin, 1951.

HINDSON, ARTHUR P., *Humor of the Old Deep South.* McMillan Co., New York, 1949.

HILL, JIM DAN., *The Texas Navy.* The University of Chicago Press, Chicago, 1937.

HUBER, LEONARD V., and WAGNER, C. A., JR., *The Great Mail: A Postal History of New Orleans.* The American Philatelic Society, State College, Pa., 1949.

HUNTER, LOUIS C., *Steamboats on the Western Waters.* Harvard University Press, Cambridge, 1949.

KANE, HARNETT T., *Deep Delta Country.* Duell, Sloan & Pearce, New York, 1944.

KEELER, RALPH and WAUD, ALFRED R., *On the Mississippi. Every Saturday,* Boston, May-Sept., 1871.

KLEIN, EUGENE, *United States Waterway Packetmarks, 1832-1899.* J. W. Stowell Printing Co., Federalsburg, Md., 1940.

LYTLE, WILLIAM L., and HOLDCAMPER, FORREST R., *Merchant Steam Vessels of the United States.* The Steamship Historical Society of America, Mystic, Conn., 1952.

LATROBE, JOHN H. B., *The First Steamboat Voyage on the Western Water.* Maryland Historical Society Fund Publications, Baltimore, 1871.

LLOYD, JAMES T., *Lloyd's Steamboat Dictory and Disasters on the Western Waters.* J. T. Lloyd & Co., Cincinnati, 1856.

LEATHERS, CAPT. THOS. P., *Personal Scrapbook.*

LUDLOW, NOAH M., *Dramatic Life as I Found It.* Jones, St. Louis, 1880.

MARESTIER, JEAN-BAPTISTE, *Memoire sur les Bateaux a Vapeurs des Etats-Unis d'Amerique.* Paris, 1824.

MARTIN, FRANCOIS-XAVIER, *The History of Louisiana from the Earliest Times.* Lyman & Beardsley, New Orleans, 1827-29.

MERRICK, GEORGE B., *Old Times on the Upper Mississippi.* The Arthur H. Clark Co., Cleveland, Ohio, 1909.

MUGRIDGE, D. H. (Ed.), *An Album of American Battle Art, 1775-1918.* The Library of Congress, Washington, 1947.

NORMAN, N. PHILIP, *The Red River of the South. Louisiana Historical Quarterly,* XXV, No. 2, 1942.

OBER, FREDERICK A., *Ferdinand de Soto.* Harper & Bros., New York, 1906.

OLMSTEAD, FREDERICK LAW, *A Journey in The Seaboard Slave States.* Dix & Edwards, New York, 1856.

QUAIFE, M. M., *Absalom Grimes—Confederate Mail Runner.* Yale University Press, New Haven, 1926.

REES, JAMES, & SONS CO., *Catalog of James Rees & Sons Co., Steamboat Builders,* Pittsburgh, 1913.

ROWLAND, DUNBAR, *Symposium on the Place of Discovery of the Mississippi River by Hernando deSoto. Mississippi Historical Society,* Jackson, 1927.

SMITH, BUCKINGHAM, *Narratives of the Career of Hernando deSoto; As Told by a Knight of Elvas (Translation).* New York, 1866.

SMITH, SOLOMON F., *Theatrical Management in the West and South for Thirty Years.* Harper & Bros., New York, 1868.

SOMDAL, DEWEY A., *A Century of Steamboating on Red River to Shreveport. Louisiana Historical Quarterly,* XVIII, 1935
Captain Leathers and His Famous Mississippi Packet Natchez. Stamps Magazine, New York, Sept. 12, 1942.

TROLLOPE, MRS. FRANCES, *Domestic Manners of the Americans.* Whittaker, Treacher, London, 1832.

THORPE, THOMAS BANGS, *Remembrance of the Mississippi.* Boston, 1855.
The Hive of the Bee Hunter. D. Appleton & Co., New York, 1854.

TWAIN, MARK (Samuel L. Clemens), *Life on the Mississippi.* James R. Osgood & Co., Boston, 1883.

U. S. CORPS OF ENGINEERS, *Flood Control and Navigation Maps of the Mississippi River.*

U. S. DeSOTO EXPEDITION COMMISSION, *Final Report (House Document 71, 76th Congress, 1st Session, Serial Set #10328).* Washington, 1939.

VARNER, JOHN & JEANETTE, *The Florida of the Inca, by Garcilasco de la Vega, (Translation).* University of Texas Press, Austin, 1951.

WAY, CAPT. FREDERICK, JR., *The Log of the Betsy Ann.* Robert M. McBride & Co., New York, 1933.
Pilotin' Comes Natural. Farrar and Rinehart, Inc., New York, 1943.
Way's Directory of Western River Packets, 1950 Edition. Privately printed, Sewickley, Pa., 1950.
The Saga of the Delta Queen. Picture Marine Publishing Co., Cincinnati, 1951.
She Takes the Horns. Young & Klein, Inc., Cincinnati, 1953.

WARMOTH, HENRY CLAY, *War, Politics and Reconstruction.* The McMillan Co., New York, 1930.

WHEELER, MARY, *Steamboatin' Days.* Louisiana State University Press, Baton Rouge, 1944.

WILMER, LAMBERT A., *The Life, Travels, and Adventures of Ferdinand deSoto.* Philadelphia, 1858.
Illustrated Guide and Sketch Book of New Orleans, by Several Leading Writers of the New Orleans Press. Will H. Coleman, New York, 1885.

NEWSPAPERS

New Orleans Daily Delta
New Orleans Bee
New Orleans Times
New Orleans Daily Picayune
Louisville Courier-Journal
Natchez Banner
New Orleans True Delta
New Orleans Crescent
New Orleans Democrat
New Orleans Times-Picayune
Natchez Daily Courier
Mississippi Free Trader (Natchez)

PERIODICALS

Ballauo's Pictorial Drawing Room Companion
Gleason's Pictorial Drawing Room Companion
Harper's Weekly
Frank Leslie's Illustrated Weekly Newspaper
Every Saturday
Harper's New Monthly Magazine
The New England Magazine
The Atlantic Monthly
Scribner's Magazine
The Waterways Journal
Louisiana Historical Quarterly